SUNDAYS

IN THE

SOUTH

ENDORSEMENTS

"Praise God for your gift of writing and articulating these things. It brought me a ton of joy to read through your thoughts and prayers. You and your wife are always welcome with us. Please let us know the next time you'll be in town."

—**STEWART SCOTT**
Veritas Church, Fayetteville, NC

"Thanks for the great write-up, Tom. It's awesome. I really enjoyed reading it. I'm very impressed with your writing and your attention to detail. I was wearing sneakers, yes, lol. Thanks for what you're doing. Visit any time!"

—**MITCH MILLER**
Briggs Memorial Baptist Church, Greenville, SC

"Brother, I wish I could express how much I grinned reading this. You brought it to life, and Mr. Smith's story is a compelling one indeed. All those years at Greenville High are sort of now chronicled in this recap of your Sunday there, and I'm grateful for it."

—**CORY TRUAX**
Beechwood Church, Greenville, SC

"It was very exciting to read your take of Living Water. Overall, I sat and cried because your take is exactly what I've always wanted for our church."

—**Tony Birkhead**
Living Water, Hendersonville, NC

SUNDAYS

IN THE

SOUTH

TOM KUPEC

AMBASSADOR INTERNATIONAL
GREENVILLE, SOUTH CAROLINA & BELFAST, NORTHERN IRELAND

www.ambassador-international.com

SUNDAYS IN THE SOUTH

ISBN: 978-1-64960-048-6
eISBN: 978-1-64960-049-3

Cover Design by Hannah Linder Designs
Interior Typesetting by Dentelle Design
Edited by Katie Cruice Smith

AMBASSADOR INTERNATIONAL
Emerald House
411 University Ridge, Suite B14
Greenville, SC 29601, USA
www.ambassador-international.com

AMBASSADOR BOOKS
The Mount
2 Woodstock Link
Belfast, BT6 8DD, Northern Ireland, UK
www.ambassadormedia.co.uk

The colophon is a trademark of Ambassador, a Christian publishing company.

This book is dedicated to the three people
who have taught me what it means to lay down their lives for others:

Williams Kupec, Sr.

Helen Kupec

William Kupec, Jr.

They are not with us today, but their influence continues to touch many lives.

CONTENTS

INTRODUCTION

Many people long to visit faraway lands or cities with endless activities that will create a break from the mundane and memories to share with others for years to come. My family has always been a little different, however, even when it comes to vacations.

In the summer of 2018, my wife and I awoke one Sunday morning and decided to take a day trip to Moravian Falls, North Carolina, a two-and-a-half-hour trek from our home in Greenville, South Carolina. In my fifty-five years on this Earth, I have never heard of anyone expressing a desire to visit this tiny town in the obscure hills of North Carolina.

There is a story behind this unusual quest, of course. It all started with our watching a video on the life of Jon Huss, one of the precursors to Martin Luther and the world-altering Reformation of the sixteenth century. A century earlier, the Word of God was being held back from the common people by the religious and governmental leaders who desired to maintain their control over the people. Huss knew, however, that the Word of God contained the redemptive account of Jesus' atoning sacrifice for the sin of mankind. If people were able to read the Word of God for themselves in their own language, they could find not only salvation but also the abundant life that Jesus promised to all who align their lives with His.

Huss boldly proclaimed the life-changing message of the Gospel, in spite of heavy opposition. Despite ongoing death threats, Huss continued to share the Gospel that would set people free, not only from tyrannical authorities but also, more importantly, from their own sin that enslaved them and kept them separated from the living God. Eventually, Huss paid the ultimate price for his convictions, burning at the stake at the age of forty-six. He died while singing the Psalms.

Touched by this unwavering commitment to God and to His Word and wondering what had happened to Huss' followers, we learned that over the course of many years, many of them eventually migrated to Pennsylvania and, ultimately, to their final settlement, Moravian Falls, North Carolina. We would end up visiting Moravian Falls that seemingly uneventful Sunday. What exactly we were looking for, I am not really sure. From our standpoint, we were hungering and thirsting more after God. But God always has a bigger picture in mind for His children. The same Spirit Who raised Jesus from the dead and Who had revealed the living God to John Huss was working in the hearts of two of His followers many years later. Just as Huss had read in the Word of God over six hundred years earlier, we would discover that God "is able to do far more abundantly beyond all that we ask or think, according to the power that works within us" (Eph. 3:20). We would also discover that we were being called by God to take more than just this one jaunt to the mountains of North Carolina.

This is where our journey began, leading us to a fifty-four-week-long adventure to discover what God is doing in the lives of believers today.

WEEK 1

IN SEARCH OF JOHN HUSS

WILKESBORO, NORTH CAROLINA

My deep inhale and slow exhale gave indication that it was one of those "good to be alive days." The sky was clear blue; the temperature was seventy-five; the roads were empty; and once we left Interstate 85 North behind just outside of Charlotte, North Carolina, the views for the next hour and a half drew more "oohs" and "ahs" from my wife and me than most Fourth of July fireworks shows could ever ignite.

It was good for Linda and me to get away. Our marriage and family life for the past twenty-five years had not been the prettiest. My wife has a real heart for God and a love of His Word. She is one of the loveliest persons you will ever meet—when she is doing well. Her severely injured back led to a dependency on prescriptive opiate drugs, which led to a lot of chaos—a truth that anyone from any addictive background will attest. She also had many unresolved issues from her childhood that she brought into our marriage. She triggers easily and forcefully.

I am not innocent, either. I, too, have a heart for God and a love of His Word. I, too, have an addiction problem—not to any alcohol or drug, but to any and all things edible. Do not leave a chocolate bar unguarded when I am around. Your twenty-dollar bill is safe, but your Snickers bar is highly at risk.

I am also very independent. That is another way of saying self-directed and self-willed. When John the Baptist made the proclamation that he needed to decrease and Jesus needed to increase (John 3:30), he should have repeated that many times just for me.

The combination of a troubled wife and a self-directed husband does not make two become one very smoothly. Despite our many warts and our inconsistent marriage, God has remained very faithful to us. One of my favorite Scriptures is found in 2 Timothy 2:13: "If we are faithless, He remains faithful, for He cannot deny Himself." Another is Hebrews 12:6: "FOR THOSE WHOM THE LORD LOVES HE DISCIPLINES, AND HE SCOURGES EVERY SON WHOM HE RECEIVES." He must love us a lot!

Linda and I are recipients of the grace and discipline of a very merciful God. That grace eventually led us to Gene Wagstaff and the Word of God Counseling Center in Greenville, South Carolina. Through much counsel in dealing with our pasts and his constant exhortations to forgive everyone for everything right away every day, my wife and I are now on a path where we are truly experiencing the blessings that God has ordained for any marriage that is united with Him.

Despite our infatuation with the sights of the surrounding countryside and our enjoyment of each other, the GPS delivered our first bad news of the trip. It insisted that the trees in front of us were The Gathering Church in Moravian Falls. We looked around but saw nothing but tree trunks and hanging limbs. There was no mistaking it—we were in the middle of a forest. A quick jaunt further up the gravelly mountain road and back proved fruitless. Something was wrong. Either the church was meeting in the woods, or we had the wrong address.

Dejectedly, we meandered down the mountain and back onto the picturesque highway, neither of us saying a word. Not wanting to miss a Sunday with the saints, or "called apart ones," we looked for a Bible-believing church in the area with an 11:00 a.m. service. Within a couple of minutes,

Linda spotted the sign for Cub Creek Baptist Church in Wilkesboro, a stone's throw from Moravian Falls.

Working in a rural setting in the Upstate of South Carolina for the past fourteen years has made me very familiar with churches in rural areas. Everyone seems to know everyone. The pastor is the jack of all trades—preacher, counselor, and miracle worker (at least, that is the expectations of the congregants). He always seems to have a heart for his people. Brian Sampson was no exception to this stereotype. He made the announcements, preached the sermon, and reminded everyone of the upcoming July fourth barbecue and family gathering the following week. This down-to-earth and slightly overweight preacher gave his message in a simple but authoritative way. Though we had never met before, I felt like I knew him, like he was a cousin I hadn't seen in years. It seemed like the man knew Jesus personally. That the same Spirit Who raised Christ Jesus from the dead was evident in this humble pastor.

He spoke of positional sanctification and practical sanctification. Positional sanctification, he explained, is the position that each person holds who has put his trust in the finished and atoning work of Jesus on the cross and who has received Jesus as Lord and Savior. In God's economy, we are declared innocent. The great exchange has occurred. We have given Christ our sinfulness, and He has given us His righteousness. We have made peace with God. We are in right standing with Him according to His statutes, not ours. We have "the right to become children of God" (John 1:12).

Practical sanctification involves the process of surrendering more and more of our will to God's. It is a process where we become more like Jesus—not by our efforts but by the working of the Holy Spirit in us as we align our lives with His commandments. The more I surrender to Him in this process through life's trials and tribulations, the more freedom I experience, the more peace I have, the more purpose I discover. "Give, and it will be given to you. They will pour into your lap a good measure—pressed down, shaken together, *and* running over" (Luke 6:38). When I surrender to God, He gives me back more than I could ever have imagined.

When the service ended and we headed past the stained glass windows to the exit in the rear of the church, Pastor Sampson was quick to greet us and inquire about where we lived. A handshake and some niceties later, my wife and I exited the church. Touched by God in a profound way, it seemed almost sinful to leave in a hurry and move on to the next event.

Sensing our sentiment, a park-like bench overlooking the church's cemetery and the beautiful mountains in the distance invited us to sit and ponder the things of God. As we were soaking in the reverent atmosphere, we heard the voice of Tina Borrows, who was being pushed in her wheelchair by her husband, John. Her balding hair and very pail head made it obvious that she had been through some type of traumatic ordeal.

"Isn't that a beautiful view?" she questioned us very cheerfully.

After a few pleasantries, my wife, not one for too much surface conversation, lovingly asked Janet, "How long have you had cancer?"

Tina told us her story. Of all the things that Tina stated in our short encounter, two things touched my heart about this gentle woman: how grateful she was to God for the life He had given her and how much she appreciated her husband taking care of her during their life-altering ordeal. Their smiles defied their circumstances. Whining or complaining would have been understandable. But there was no blaming when questions must have been raging. No self-pity about her plight in life. What a blessed couple. How rich they are. They found out that real love is sacrifice. They found out the most important things in life are connected to the eternal. They found out that Moravian Falls is a lovely place, but it is not their permanent home. Their true home awaits them. It will last forever. Their Heavenly Father eagerly anticipates their homecoming.

We had one last thing to do before we headed back to Greenville, South Carolina. The ancestors of John Huss—the Moravians—have impacted

Europe and the United States in ways we will never realize on this side of Heaven. In 1752, in the backwoods of North Carolina, the Moravians purchased a tract of almost one hundred thousand acres. They continued a legacy of twenty-four-hour prayer and worship centers that were started in Eastern Europe by their ancestors. Their prayer and missionary spirit still have effects in the foothills of North Carolina, where today, many ministries have established their home bases.[1]

Since we had come this far, we decided we might as well see the body of water from which Moravian Falls derives its name. We were told that to get there, we needed to take a left at the first stop sign and a right at the second. To our amazement, however, we saw something much more exciting than any waterfall. It stopped us in our tracks. The wood sign was big and clear: "The Gathering Church, Moravian Falls, North Carolina." The GPS had failed us, but God had not. His timing is perfect.

We would be back in a few weeks after the church reconvened from its summer sabbatical. We could sense that we were to continue with our adventures; for how long, we were not sure. That was up to the Holy Spirit. For the next week, however, Rocky Top was calling loudly.

---

1   "Moravian Falls: A Brief History of the Moravians," MoravianFalls.org, http://www.moravianfalls.org/aboutmoravianfalls.html (accessed June 24, 2018).

COUNTRY ROADS

KINGSPORT, TENNESSEE

The famous singer John Denver was partially correct. His number one hit song proclaimed, "Country roads, take me home / to the place I belong / West Virginia . . . "[2] However, on this particular Sunday, those country roads took us "home" to East Tennessee—Kingsport in Sullivan County, to be exact.

At least, that's how the people of Kingsport Community Church made us feel—at home. When my wife and I stepped into the sanctuary for the 10:45 a.m. worship service, we were greeted by some of the most loving and gracious people we had ever met. We were treated as if we were really special. Like we were famous athletes or politicians who hold power over others. I immediately thought of Paul's admonition to believers in Philippians 2:3: "Do nothing from selfishness or empty conceit, but with humility of mind regard one another as more important than yourselves."

Brenda, the dignified woman who sat in front of us, treated us like we were her long-lost siblings, but she also tried to sign us up for the choir! After all, a couple of choir members were needed. I think my elementary school music teacher, Mr. Kemp, might have raised both eyebrows at that request. Besides her, we were welcomed by retired air force chaplain Colonel Bob Rothman.

---

2   John Denver, "Take Me Home Country Roads," The Essential John Denver, 3, Sony Legacy, 2007, Compact Disc.

The leadership team was especially warm as well. Twin brothers and associate pastors Brian and Chris Ricketts immediately hugged us when my wife and I welled up in describing our reason for the adventure we were on. They brought such great comfort to us! And the minister of music, Mark Stayton, and his wife, Jenny, encouraged us in our worship of the Lord. Plus, we had the blessing of being there for the last Sunday of Pastor Ron Lowe, who was retiring after thirty-seven years of faithful service.

It was fitting that we were showed great value that day. We felt great love from our brothers and sisters in Christ in eastern Tennessee. God has been emphasizing that kind of love to me over the last couple of years. Our pastor, and counselor, has taught us a lot about love these past twenty-four months.

Take my marriage, for example. Pastor Gene showed me that it is not enough for me to think that I show my love for my wife but that *she* has to feel loved by me. There's a big difference. When I think that I love her, I am evaluating my love for her though my lenses only. After all, I do laundry, empty the dishes, and help with many chores around the house. What woman wouldn't want that? Yet there was a gap between what I thought and how my wife felt. From Linda's perspective, she feels most loved by me when I spend time with her and listen attentively. She feels loved by me when I show genuine interest in her. She feels loved by me when I speak kindly and show concern for her. She feels loved by me when I put my arm around her in church. Now, that has been a hard one for me. While I did grow up in a loving home, we weren't exactly the most affectionate family—in private or in public. While Linda can appreciate that how I serve her is how I express my love, she *feels* most loved by me when I spend time with her.

Gene also taught us that the real definition of love is sacrifice. It means that you are willing to do what you don't want to do when you don't want to do it with the right attitude (as long as it is not causing you to sin). When my wife wants me to watch a Hallmark movie with her, my answer needs to be yes or a negotiated yes. "Linda, I can't watch tonight because of work, but could we watch tomorrow night when I'm off?" In the past, I would have said, "A movie? Really? I'm not really a movie guy."

I know this may sound strange to most people, but I actually hate movies. I consider it torture to sit for two hours when I could be doing something more productive. You can blame my earthly father for that influence. He once said that he wasn't interested in anything unless he could keep score. Dad, I agree with you wholeheartedly! But Linda doesn't, unfortunately. Love is doing what you don't want to do when you don't want to do it with the right attitude. Do you think my wife feels loved when we sit together, rub arms together, and stare up at the screen? Yes, she does. And you know what? I hate to admit this, but I am actually starting to enjoy some of those time-consuming movies. All except for the Christmas miracle parts. Please don't tell my male friends, though. It could crush my image.

One other person did what He didn't want to do when He didn't want to do it with the right attitude. On the night before His crucifixion, Jesus prayed three times in agony that the Father would take the cup from Him, and three times, He followed that up with "yet not My will, but Yours be done" (Luke 22:42). He showed us His love by His sacrifice for us. It is one thing to proclaim love; it is another to display it. Words are needed, for sure, but actions are even more powerful.

"For God so loved the world, that He gave His only begotten Son" (John 3:16). He showed His love for us by dying on the cross in our place to take our punishment. He took our bullet. We show love for Him by humbling ourselves, admitting that we have sinned and fallen short of His glory, repenting of our sinful and self-willed life, and putting our trust and faith in His finished work that reconciles us to God.

Back to John Denver's vision of almost-home, however. If you have not taken a ride from just above Asheville, North Carolina, to Kingsport, Tennessee, make sure you do if you get a chance. Waking up at 6:00 a.m. that day, my wife and I did not realize the beauty of God's creation that awaited us. Route

26 West through the Blue Ridge Mountains is one of the most scenic rides we have experienced east of the Mississippi River. Commanding mountains, open meadows, and winding roads greeted us throughout the ride. Lush greenery covering the mountains drew us into an awareness of God's glory. Steep declines and sharp inclines tested our car's resiliency and made me hold onto the wheel tightly and with two hands. We sped past many eighteen-wheelers that seemed to be in jeopardy of not making it to the top of the incline, like an out-of-shape jogger trying to complete the course that he wished he never started.

As much as we didn't want to, it was time to bid the mountains farewell. Unlike the Volunteers of Tennessee who had marched south with Andrew Jackson for a stunning victory in the Battle of New Orleans in the War of 1812, we had to stop for a quick bite and head back to everyday life in the Palmetto State.

While Linda was humming God's praises in the bathroom at a local restaurant, the lady in the next stall joyfully asked my wife if she had just come from church. They shared stories. They shared struggles. Marcie confessed to Linda that she had backslidden into drugs and alcohol dependency. She was on her way to a rehab program with Miracle Hill Ministries. Marcie asked my wife where she lived. When Linda told her the town, Marcie was astonished. Her rehab program was in Greenville, South Carolina. They exchanged phone numbers. Marcie was encouraged, like God was confirming with her that she was doing the right thing. We were encouraged that God had used us to encourage a hurting sister in the Lord.

Thank you, Kingsport Community Church. Thank you, Lord. God's people, God's creation, God's plan. Is there any better place to be? I am growing more and more convinced that there isn't.

We would become even more convinced of that truth the following Sunday in Bristol, Virginia.

START YOUR ENGINES

BRISTOL, VIRGINIA (OR TENNESSEE)

I couldn't keep my eyes off of him. The more I tried, the harder it became. While the whole congregation was clapping with the beat of "Your Grace is Enough," the man sitting in the front row in the front right side of the three-sectioned sanctuary was clapping off-beat on the same song. *There is always one in the crowd*, I thought.

It happens in church. It happened in football, too. From the time that I played Spartans midget football in Syosset, New York, until my last year in college, there was always a player who was off in the jumping jacks exercise that was part of every pre-game ritual. While the majority of the team was on "two," the player off-beat was usually on "four." The guilty party was usually numbered somewhere in the seventies, typically an offensive lineman who was playing his first year of organized football or who had little or no chance to see any playing time.

But the man in the black shirt didn't have a number. He was a member of the First Assembly of God Church in Bristol, Virginia, the home of the famous Bristol Motor Speedway.

First Assembly takes worshipping God very seriously. They should. Jesus made a revealing statement about the Heavenly Father when He said, "But an hour is coming, and now is, when the true worshipers will worship the Father in spirit and truth; for such people the Father seeks to be His worshipers" (John 4:23). It was nice to see people being demonstrative in their time of worshipping God at First Assembly.

I thought back again to football. Fans at football games are more than demonstrative. They can be downright fanatical. They yell. They scream. They cheer on their team. They paint their faces the color of their favorite team. They regard the best players as heroes, like generals who return victoriously from battle. I am no stranger to this phenomenon. I remember when my nephew, Andrew, threw a game-winning touchdown pass on the last play of a game, leading Assumption College to a dramatic, nail-biting victory over Millersville College of Pennsylvania. We were so excited about the final play that when we were all jumping up and down celebrating the incredible feat, my older brother of two years (and father of the quarterback) fell down in the stands. I, and the other men around us, looked down momentarily at my brother as he was sprawled out on the stands. We then resumed our celebration, trusting my brother to fend for himself (don't worry, he was not injured).

Something greater than football is here, however. Someone more important than any athlete has made His presence known. Something more exciting and exhilarating than any heroic effort on the gridiron could ever produce. The Creator of the universe took on bodily form, died on the cross for the sins of humankind, and rose from the dead to defeat the power of death. He has done what no one else has ever done. What no man could ever do. He has prepared a place in Heaven for anyone who has put his or her trust in His finished work on the cross. That is exciting news. It is eternal news. It will not fade with aging bones and failing eyes. It is a glory that will be fully realized when we see Him face to face. As a result, we can live life free from the worry of what will happen to us after we die. We can take these seventy-plus years and extend them for eternity.

Furthermore, we have a God Who has made a covenant with us. We have a God Who has promised to never leave us or forsake us (Heb. 13:5). We have a God Who promises "to work together for good to those who love [Him], to those who are called according to *His* purpose" (Rom. 8:28). We have a God Who has put His Spirit in our body, making us temples of His very presence (1 Cor. 6:19). We have a God Who has even entrusted His mission to us (Matt. 28:16-20). He is worthy to be applauded. He is worthy of our lifting our hands to Him in praise as the Word of God exhorts (Psalm 134:2). He is worthy of our proclaiming His glory. He is worthy of our outward expression of love and praise.

Pastor Jeff Carico, the shepherd of First Assembly of God for over sixteen years, made a statement in his sermon that made me think about why God is worthy to be praised. In conversing with a person who was sharing his many problems, the six-foot-three pastor responded to the man, "I am not trying to minimize your problems; I am trying to elevate the God Who is above them."

Jesus is above our problems. It is why Paul and Silas could sing hymns while being treated horribly and unjustly in a jail in Philippi (Acts 16:22-30). It is why we can praise Him while our circumstances are daring us to do the opposite. It is why I can worship God at First Assembly as if I have been worshipping the Lord there for many years. It is why I can feel at home sitting next to John, a joyful eighty-year-old grandfather and former welder and coal miner from West Virginia. It is why I can turn around and greet Rose, whose daughter is a nurse in our hometown of Greenville, South Carolina. We were all worshipping our Father, Who has given us a bond that nothing else can.

We left our new friends from the southernmost point of the Commonwealth of Virginia, stopping to take a picture at the famous entrance to Bristol. A large, steel-gated sign with the abbreviations for Tennessee and Virginia covered the street where these two states share the state line. Driving on further along U.S. 11 West, we stopped to take a picture of the Bristol Motor Speedway. Soon, 162,000 adoring sports fans would fill this magnificent stadium and revel in the excitement of cars speeding loudly to the finish line. They would extol the talents of Kyle Busch, Jeff Gordon, and many others. It is exciting, for sure. But I'd rather be in church with common people praising the King of kings and the Lord of lords—the One Who will never see decay.

I think the good people of North Carolina will agree with my sentiment. We would find out for sure the next Sunday as we returned to Moravian Falls for some unfinished business.

THE FIRST TIME

MORAVIAN FALLS, NORTH CAROLINA

There is nothing like the "first" of anything and the excitement that goes with it. Like when parents marvel at the miracle of their first child and consider the weight of the responsibility that has just been thrust upon them. Or on the first day of school, when students, parents, and teachers are hopeful that this will be the best school year yet. Or the opening day for the sports teams when fans throughout the country are optimistic that this may be the year that their team makes the playoffs—or even win the championship!

I had this "first" feeling as we headed back on the road again to Moravian Falls, North Carolina. Even the soft rain and threatening skies could not dampen my feelings of excitement. Many thoughts went through my mind as we traveled. Thinking about John Huss again. Wondering why his story seems to resonate in my mind. Thinking about all that the Holy Spirit has done in my heart these past few years. Wondering what He would do on Sunday as we met with the brethren at The Gathering Church again.

I remember as a young child, the initial time I had that feeling of expectancy. My father took my brother Andy and me to Yankee Stadium for the first time. We had heard so much about the New York Yankees baseball tradition growing up. "The house that Ruth built." Lou Gehrig's chilling proclamation that he considered himself to be the luckiest man on the face of the Earth, while facing a death sentence with a disease that would later be named for him. Roger Maris' sixty-one homeruns. Mickey Mantle's greatness and what would have been had he not hurt his knees. These men were part of my life. They were a part of me. I was each one of them in my backyard playing whiffle ball. Rounding the bases after each Ruthian shot, you could have put a three, four, seven, or nine on my back. I would have believed it.

Back then, we drove for what seemed like an eternity through Nassau County, Long Island, Queens, and then the Bronx on our way to Yankee Stadium. Looking at the tall apartment houses that encased both sides of the highway, the cab drivers, trucks and hundreds of honking cars seemed to want to keep us from reaching our destination. Suddenly, after what felt like an eternity, we dipped through a kind of tunnel and came out on the other side with the most glorious picture I had ever seen in my short life. My mouth dropped open. I was speechless. There it was—majestic, overpowering, larger than life—Yankee Stadium! The world stopped at that moment. We inched on, no one in the car saying a word. It was as if we had stumbled upon holy ground.

I am not a young boy fantasizing about mortal men any longer. They have faded like the grass as their memory slowly fades with them. My pursuit is the living God, Who will never fade away or be forgotten in any generation. What God was going to do this Sunday, I did not know. But I have learned through the years that when I get that sense of expectancy, something significant is going to happen. It is usually a surprise, however—something that I had never expected. After all, the Word of God says He gives exceedingly more than we could ever ask or imagine (Eph. 3:20). That makes sense because His ways are above our ways and His thoughts above our thoughts (Isa. 55:8-9).

Strangely, we never saw the sign for The Gathering Church that we had stumbled upon the last time we were leaving Moravian Falls four weeks earlier. Somehow, some way, Linda noticed a little street sign on the left that seemed to be calling to her. We got off the main road, driving up a gravelly and winding road that was surrounded by trees on both sides of the road. The sound of the tires on the gravel seemed to magnify our concern that we might not be on the road that would lead us to the church. Driving past two cabins on the right and trying not to drive too quickly on the gravel, we came to a clearing. There it was, nestled in the picturesque mountains, majestic, inviting, and beautiful—The Gathering!

Surrounded by hills, the modern structure took on an almost barn-like feel as it blended in perfectly with its surroundings. The scene outside demanded a picture, one that would be ideal for any postcard. The inside of the sanctuary had the same country feel as the outside. Greeted by an usher and many friendly faces, we took our seat in the back row (Luke 14:10). There was a feeling of excitement in the air. The large cross in the front was made up of two pieces of wood that could have been taken from the surrounding forests. The flags flanking the cross—Israel's to the left and the United States' to the right—gave me a feeling that the leadership at this church understood Christ-followers' deep, eternal roots with Israel. Without the Jewish people, God's chosen people, there are no Gentile believers in the Messiah (Eph. 2:19). God's covenants stand forever.

The members of The Gathering came to worship their God. It was refreshing to see Christ-followers expressing their gratitude to the God Who saved them and, by the sound of their utterances, the God Who was among them. The singing reached a crescendo when the chorus of the song "Sing Hosanna to the King of Kings" came upon the screen. The message was uplifting, too. It is always encouraging to see a young man give the sermon who has a Kingdom of God mindset and an excitement about what God is doing in his life. This young man from South Africa spoke of the fact that we Christians are in the world but not of it (1 John 2:15-17). We have to make a concentrated effort to be separate from the world in terms of its influences but inundated in it in terms of God's purposes. Not surprisingly, however, it was two unscripted encounters with two men that made this trip unique.

Fourteen years ago, our family moved from Long Island, New York, to Greenville, South Carolina, leaving most of our remaining family members behind. We became members of Mount Zion Christian Fellowship under the leadership of Pastor Orie Wenger. My wife and I served as leaders of a small group of about ten people.

The first meeting we held was surprisingly emotional for the both of us. I asked each person present to share his or her life story to the group as a form of introduction. A vibrant, elderly, gray-haired man with a full crop of hair slicked from front to back shared his testimony of how Jesus set him free from a life of alcoholism and womanizing and made him into the man he is today.

As he spoke, Linda and I struggled to hold back the tears. Unbeknownst to this gentleman, Bill Valentine, we were staring at the exact physical replica of Linda's earthly dad, John. He looked like him. His heavy New Jersey accent had the same ring as John's Hoboken and Queens Village accent. But he was joyful, excited about what God was doing in his life, even at the age of eighty. John, on the other hand, had died a few years before we sojourned south.

Linda's relationship with her dad was a tense one. Her parents had married when they discovered they were pregnant with Linda. From the time Linda was born, John was a hardworking man, holding down three jobs while sacrificially providing for his wife, Rosemary, Linda, and her three siblings to come. He was also a drinking man. When he drank, he became even more intimidating than his everyday persona. When Linda was eighteen, her mom sprang the news on her that her dad was about to leave the family with a woman down the street. Full of turmoil and rage, Linda confronted him, pointedly asking if he ever planned to see the family again. Surprisingly, he put his suitcase back in the closet. Four uneasy years later, the family was faced with another crisis. Linda's mother was diagnosed with breast cancer. A painful year later, she succumbed to the disease at the age of forty-six. John was left a hard-working, hard-drinking, defeated man racked with guilt.

When Bill finished his testimony in our inaugural meeting, I asked his forgiveness. By this time, it seemed like the entire group was aware of our emotional turmoil. I explained to him why Linda and I were tearing up as he spoke. It was nothing he had said. He was a living picture of what could have been for Linda's father, for Linda, for all of us.

Just minutes before the service was about to begin, I was talking with Jimmy, a retired air force man who had moved to Moravian Falls from Charlotte, North Carolina. My wife excitedly poked my shoulder to introduce me to another gentleman a row behind us. Like a young girl who wants her parents to watch her perform some task, she asked me who I thought her new friend looked like. In two seconds, I responded, "Your dad!"

He introduced himself. His name was "Jack," an octogenarian with an ear-to-ear smile. Unlike our initial encounter with Bill Valentine, our conversation with Jack elicited a different response. We laughed. We were at peace. Linda has been through a lot of healing in regards to her relationship with her dad since his passing. Through much forgiveness of wrongs done (both real and perceived) to her and much confession of sin regarding the dishonoring of her father (both real and perceived), Linda has come to grips with this most vital earthly relationship. How kind of her Heavenly Father to bring her from Bill to Jack. To a present no longer bound by its past. But God is no respecter of persons (Acts 10:34). What He has done for Linda, He desires to do for everyone who comes to Him with "a broken and contrite heart" (Psalm 51:17). It's Who He Is.

After the time of ministry at the altar finished and we were dismissed by the young South African youth pastor, Linda and I departed past the sound boards and through the exit in the rear without any fanfare. While sauntering to our car and marveling one last time at the beautiful surroundings, we noticed a few chairs on a deck off the side of the church that invited us to sit and take in the postcard scenes in the distance. Out of nowhere, a young man joined us. Normally, I am somewhat standoffish to a "foreigner" who "invades" my space. But God is doing a lot of healing in me, too.

I invited Jeremy to sit with us. The young man with hair parted down the middle and held back by his ears told us his incredible testimony of how he came to know Jesus. Raised in a culturally Christian home in Indiana, he had become very involved in the occult, living a life that was spiraling out of control quickly and dangerously. He finally came to what he felt was the best remedy for the incredible turmoil he found himself in. He would drive to a mountain, pull out a sturdy rope, and hang himself on a tree. Determined to carry out his plan, he set off with rope in hand.

Somewhere, someplace, someone must have been praying for Jeremy, though. As he headed up the mountain, he burst into tears, sensing a love that he had never felt before in his life. The Holy Spirit "came upon him" as he described the experience. He later discovered that many people had been praying for him through the years, not giving up, even though what they were seeing in his life could easily have been a reason for not persevering in prayer. What would have happened to Jeremy had these faithful prayer warriors not stormed the throne room of grace? If they had not yielded their swords in the heavenly realm? I shudder to think.

We prayed for Jeremy, asking the Lord to guide him, protect him, and keep him on the straight and narrow until *God* decides when it is time for Jeremy's life to end. Jeremy then prayed for a young man who is very dear to us, a young man who is opposed to the Gospel and who has involved himself in some things that have bordered, if not directly landed, on the occult. Jeremy prayed against the sin that this young man is involved in. He then prayed for our friend's salvation.

There are some things in life that only God can do. He brought a traveling, single young man from Indiana and intersected him with a traveling married couple from Greenville, South Carolina, in the hills of Moravian Falls, North Carolina. We attended the same service but didn't meet until we bumped into each other as we stopped to take in the beauty of God's creation on the way to our cars. Now, I think I know why I had that feeling of expectancy that morning. There are always "firsts" with the living God—"firsts" that never end. We took a day's pilgrimage to North Carolina that day. Life in union with Christ is a journey that will never become dull or stagnant. It is the most purposeful life a person can experience. Somewhere, with the great crowd of witnesses (Heb. 12:1), John Huss must be smiling.

He would be smiling the next week as well, as we ventured into a conflicting land.

AN OASIS

ASHEVILLE, NORTH CAROLINA

You can feel it.

You can sense it.

For some reason, there is something different about Asheville, North Carolina, and its surrounding areas. Different isn't always better, however—especially in this case. Traveling a stunning five-mile stretch down Highway 24 East (which turns into Highway 40 East) toward Exit 55 for the Billy Graham Training Center at The Cove, we passed one view after another that demanded our admiration. The clean, freshly paved highway blended in beautifully with the lush, green mountains that seemed to coexist effortlessly with them. The exits before our destination, however, reminded us that there is more to Asheville than the beautiful surroundings that make it a popular get-away for many folks.

One exit sign we passed signaled that the University of North Carolina at Asheville was near. Another revealed that Warren Wilson College could be reached in one mile. Two colleges in the beautiful mountains of western North Carolina. Two colleges in the heart of the Bible Belt. Sadly, two colleges that have reputations of promoting many ideas and behaviors that are in total contradiction to the Bible. UNC-Asheville hosts an annual F-Word Film

Festival—"f" for feminist—and biennial Queer Studies Conference.[3] Warren Wilson College's website proudly informs prospective visitors, "When you visit, you'll have the opportunity to select your gender pronoun from our bucket of pins."[4] Huh? Really? What else do they have that's not advertised?

Near to these colleges is the exit for The Cove, a Christian Conference Center and home of the Billy Graham Training Center, bearing the name of the man who was a beacon of light to millions who once lived in darkness. With great disappointment, we discovered that The Cove was closed on Sundays. We were able to enter the grounds before having to turn around at the security checkpoint. In that short time span, we sensed a different presence. Like an oasis in the desert, the feeling of reverence to God for what He had accomplished through a humble man devoted to the Gospel came over us like a fog on an unsuspecting town. The beautiful, stately grounds of the entrance to The Cove and the sensing of God's presence made us commit to a return trip in the near future. Onward to our destination, however—New Life Community Church of Asheville.

When we left the beauty of Highway 40, we entered the terrain of Riverside Drive. Expecting to see the river as we approached the vicinity of the church, we instead traveled down a road that seemed more of a reminder of Asheville's past. Old train tracks near the river's edge gave the impression that the railroad does not stop at this spot any longer. Old box car bins dotted the grounds of old and dilapidating businesses. Every now and then, the river peaked its head to remind us that it was running parallel to the road that we were traveling. We then took a sharp right on a steep incline that led us up to the grounds of New Life.

Sitting on a plateau, the modern structure seemed more like a reception hall than a traditional church building. It was surrounded by beautiful

---

3   "Women, Gender, and Sexuality Studies," UNCA.edu, https://www.unca.edu/programs/women-gender-and-sexuality-studies (accessed July 29, 2018).
4   Warren Wilson College, https://www.warren-wilson.edu/. The comment has since been taken off the website (accessed July 29, 2018).

mountain views in the distance. Part of me wanted to pull out a lawn chair and rest. The scene screamed for me to inhale deeply through my nose and exhale slowly through my mouth. I told Linda that if I lived in the area, I would come here just to "cease *striving* and know that [He is] God (Psalm 46:10). Somehow, the world seemed to slow down in this respite. The worries of this world seemed far beyond our grasp. I knew, however, that I belonged inside with God's people on the Lord's Day.

I was glad I did. The nine-member worship team led us in worship, sounding as peaceful as the surrounding countryside outside its walls. In fact, it was the most tranquil, most melodic sound I have ever heard from a worship band. Like King Saul in the presence of David's harp playing, my soul became even calmer. My heart beat slower. The worship team seemed to have the ability to nudge us forward in our worship of God while never letting themselves get in the way in the process. It was like they were setting up a time for each of us to be alone with our Father, even though we were all in the same room.

Three songs later, Dr. Steve Harris gave an insightful sermon about the difference between legalism and grace. Steve was the founder of the church more than twenty years ago. He now serves as strategy coordinator for the Blue Ridge Strategic Focus Team of the Baptist Convention of North Carolina. Interestingly, he also serves at New Life as an elder. He gave credit to New Life's current lead pastor and former missionary in Southeast Asia, Chris Dillon, for being secure enough to encourage the former founder to play an integral part in the church.

Steve made many interesting points in his message. He stated that everyone worships something or someone. Everyone! It is not a question of whether we worship someone or something or not, but rather, what that object of worship is. It is in this truth that we find current levels of idolatry. Where are we looking to meet our needs other than God? Sensuality, busyness, materialism, self-worship, and people-worship are all cheap substitutes for knowing and being known by the living God. We need people around us who will point us in the right direction. To nudge us back on the right path when we wander off in other directions. Steve also challenged us with the following soul-searching questions:

- What if there were a church so safe that the worst of you could be known, and you would be loved more for the telling of it?
- What if there was a life of total liberty that would give you the greatest freedom anyone can experience—total freedom to grow into the person you were destined to be?

If it is not there already, New Life of Asheville is on its way to being that type of church. Fortunately, I have been connected to churches that have lived up to the lofty goals to which these two questions aspire.

I lived in the subtle world of idolatry before my new life in Christ, before God led me to places of refuge that teach the full counsel of God (Acts 20:27). The world offers cheap substitutes for the true freedom that can only be found in union with Christ. Think about it for a minute. God says you will find freedom when you surrender your life to Him (Mark 8:35). That seeming paradox is based solely on His goodness, grace, and power to give more than we can attain ourselves. The world says you will find freedom when you are in control, when you experience all that this temporal world has to offer, when you get free of the shackles that impede your independence. The world says that you should trust your heart; that you should pursue your dreams; that if it feels right, you should do it. The world says to follow your own path, to self-actualize, to be a good person. Without realizing it, we can make a god of ourselves with this mindset. It is why we will eventually run out of gas, why we sense a purposelessness that gnaws at our insides until we are finally ready to try another path.

God's Word exhorts us to keep our eyes fixed on Jesus, "the author and perfecter of faith" (Heb. 12:2). He will lead us to places unimaginable for the finite, limited human mind. We will find freedom when we live in obedience to His Word, trusting that He is good, that His ways are above our ways, and that He knows what is best for our lives, our families, and our future. He is the Potter, and we are the clay (Isa. 64:8).

Like the contrasting exits off Highway 40 in Asheville, there are ultimately two exits to choose from as we journey through this life. One exit offers the best the humanistic world or man-centered religion has to offer. The other exit offers a lasting peace and purpose that no alternative path can match. To me, Asheville, North Carolina, is a microcosm of the world in which we live. Two paths right in the midst of each other.

One path is temporal. It makes promises that give pleasure for a season. It also delivers trials and tribulations that eventually lead to emptiness, purposelessness, and even bitterness in the end. The other path is eternal. It delivers new life. It, too, comes with trials and tribulations. But it provides a refining process through these challenging times that leaves us deeper, more complete, more purposeful, and more content. I have taken both exits, both paths available to man. I have watched countless others choose between the two as well. "Enter through the narrow gate; for the gate is wide and the way is broad that leads to destruction, and there are many who enter through it. For the gate is small and the way is narrow that leads to life, and there are few who find it" (Matt. 7:13-14).

You can feel it. You can sense it. The stakes are high. The gray is being taken out of our culture more and more. Thank God there is a church in "The Land of the Sky," pointing people down the right path.

There is another church doing the same, this time deeper into the South. They are hunting for lost souls in Bear Country.

BEAR BRYANT COUNTRY

OXFORD, ALABAMA

Hope must be a powerful emotion. When the apostle Paul, under the inspiration of the Holy Spirit, finished penning his transformative treatise on love in 1 Corinthians 13, he concluded his discourse with the following statement: "But now faith, hope, love, abide these three; but the greatest of these is love."

Love was the motivating force behind God's sending His only begotten Son into the world to do for us what we could not do for ourselves because of the predicament our sin had put us in. Faith is the conduit from which that love is received. "For by grace you have been saved through faith; and that not of yourselves, *it is* the gift of God; not as a result of works, so that no one may boast" (Eph. 2:8). Like a plug is to the connection to light, faith in Jesus' finished work on the cross is the connection to the salvation of one's soul.

Where does that leave hope? Hope is in good company. If my hitting a baseball elicits comparisons to Babe Ruth or Mobile, Alabama, native, Hank Aaron, I would be surprised at how highly people consider my baseball prowess. If my singing evokes comparisons to greats like Luciano Pavarotti or Guy Penrod, I would be in lofty company. Hope is touted as one of the big three.

Hope is not dependent on circumstances. It cannot be bothered with the things of this world that cry for our attention but deliver unmet promises. Hope is based on the character and nature of God Himself. Hope is eternal. It is future-minded. The reason that I have hope in my eternal destination is based on Jesus' actions on my behalf, not on my ability to merit anything. I can be at peace when the world around me seems to be in chaos. The world is just doing what the world does best. The Spirit of God within me says I can be of good cheer while those around me are experiencing turmoil (John 16:33). I can be of good cheer while the political party I oppose is in power. While people I love are doing things that I know are not the best for them. When I see people with misdirected passion giving their hearts and souls for causes that have little to no eternal value. Hope nudges me to focus on God's faithfulness to me and His Covenant and not to drown in regret over my lack of faithfulness to Him. Hope gives me the opportunity to look at a Kingdom with no end (Luke 1:33). Hope gives me confidence.

Hope also comes when you see a community of believers in Christ holding to the biblical framework and foundations clearly outlined in Scripture when too many churches today are acquiescing to the flow of a culture that is increasingly in opposition to God's Word.

The Church of the Highlands in Alabama is one of those churches. Birthed in 2001 in the heart of Montgomery, the state capital, it has grown to be a multi-site community with twenty-three campuses dispersed around the state (and one across the state line in Columbus, Georgia). Each campus shares the Sunday messages (via simulcast) and overall leadership of founding pastor Chris Hodges. When Pastor Hodges preaches his sermon live on the campus of Birmingham each Sunday, all the other campuses see and hear the same message. The campus we visited this particular Sunday was in the town of Oxford, Alabama. Situated roughly between Atlanta and Birmingham, Oxford is a picturesque small town. Easily visible from Interstate 20 West on our right, we could see the Oxford Civic Center with the local high school and middle school in its shadow. The hills backing them up only added to the picturesque scene.

The newly built Civic Center is the location where this congregation meets each Sunday and throughout the week for training and small groups. As my former pastor in New York, John Nyhan, used to say, "The church is a people, not a steeple." How insightful he was. Chairs lined up on the Civic Center's gymnasium floor, all pointing toward the stage that doubled as an altar, did not make this meeting place any less of a church. More seats were available to congregants in the highly elevated stands that backed the main floor. Could Chip Hilton be far behind? The lobby area outside of the sanctuary was dotted with many professional-looking signs that gave the impression that this campus was well-managed and well-staffed. How the people interacted and operated only solidified that hunch.

Before the service began, Brian Bagwell—the young, professional-looking campus pastor with short, reddish-blonde hair, glasses, and an engaging personality—walked through the aisles, greeting each of the persons flanking the ends of every row. When it came time to greet me, I stood to shake his hand as a sign of respect for the leader of this congregation. It was fitting that I had a chance to do this in a town whose old downtown area had reminded me of the fictional town of Mayberry, the town that brought Andy Taylor, Barney Fife, Aunt Bee, Floyd the Barber, Helen Crump, Thelma Lou (my first love), and Opie into our New York living room for many years. As a young boy, I took notice that the honorable sheriff stood each time he was introduced to a new person. Forty-five years later, I sensed that the vivacious pastor appreciated my gesture of honor.

If I hadn't been fully awake when the time of worshipping God began the service, I was now. The exuberant, talented musicians played at a decibel that my fifty-five-year-old soul was not accustomed to. Despite this not being my particular favorite style of music, the hearts of the people seemed to be in the right place. The final slower, more melodic worship song seemed to satisfy my individual preference of music as we all sang together, "You set the stars in the heavens/ You set the world into motion/ Oh-oh-ohh, Jesus, You alone/ You breathed Your life in creation/ You walked among Your created/ Oh-oh-ohh, Jesus, You alone."[5]

When the music ended, Pastor Hodges emerged on the big screen on the stage. Just like the personable leader of the local Oxford congregation, the founding pastor of Highland exuded the same excitement and passion for the Church of the Highlands and for the Gospel of Jesus. The fifty-year-old pastor also appeared to be transparent. While exhorting the listeners to bring their level of worshipping God to a higher level, he mixed in revelations of his own personal struggles as they related to prayer and to parenting.

Using the text of Exodus 25:8-9, he explained how each part of the Tabernacle of God in ancient Israel symbolizes a pattern of prayer for us today. Exodus 25:8-9 states the following: "Let them construct a sanctuary for Me, that I may dwell among them. According to all that I am going to show you, *as* the pattern of the tabernacle and the pattern of all its furniture, just so you shall construct it."

While the pastor embellished each point in this message, I will leave you with the following items of the tabernacle and their corresponding points of prayer that he tied together:

The Parts of the Tabernacle	Corresponding Aspects of Prayer
1. The Outer Court	1. Start by giving thanks to God
2. The Brazen Altar	2. Focus on the cross
3. The Laver	3. Offer every part of my life to God
4. The Candlestick	4. Invite the work of the Holy Spirit in my life

---

5   Highlands Worship, Jesus You Alone, 12, March 1, 2019, Compact Disc.

5. The Table of Showbread   5. Claim the promises of the Word of God

6. The altar of incense   6. Worshipping His Name

7. The Ark of the Covenant   7. Interceding for others

The website of the Church of the Highlands states that the church's purpose is based on three commands of Jesus. The first states the following: "'YOU SHALL LOVE THE LORD YOUR GOD WITH ALL YOUR HEART, AND WITH ALL YOUR SOUL, AND WITH ALL YOUR MIND'" (Matt. 22:37). This is the first and greatest commandment. The second is closely connected: "'YOU SHALL LOVE YOUR NEIGHBOR AS YOURSELF'" (Mark 12:31). All the Law and the Prophets hang on these two commandments. The third gives us our marching orders. "'Go therefore and make disciples of all the nations, baptizing them in the name of the Father and the Son and the Holy Spirit, teaching them to observe all that I commanded you; and lo, I am with you always, even to the end of the age'" (Matt. 28:19-20).

Webster's dictionary defines *commission* as "an authorization or command to act in a prescribed manner or to perform prescribed acts."[6] Jesus ended His ministry by giving His disciples the Great Commission. The church (the "called out ones" or the "set apart ones") are now commissioned by Him to carry out the work of the Kingdom of God on Earth. The Body of Christ that makes up the Church of the Highlands in the Yellowhammer State is committed to this mandate. They are committed to loving God with all their heart, soul, and mind. They are determined to love others as Christ loves them. They are strategic in their goals. Today, they have twenty-three campuses and various prison outreaches networked together to bring the Good News of Jesus to their communities, their state, and beyond. I will not be surprised if I return in another seventeen years to find they have started an additional twenty-three campuses in Alabama and beyond. Better yet, I

---

6   *Merriam-Webster, s.v.* "commission," accessed August 5, 2018, https://www.merriam-webster.com/dictionary/commission.

will not be surprised if they are doing exactly whatever it is God has called them to do.

Churches like this give me hope. They give me reason to believe that there will always be a voice calling people to repent and turn to the living God. They give me assurance that there are people who will genuinely love others with the love they have received from God. They give me confidence that there will always be places where people can find salvation and be discipled in the ways of God. Paul was right—the three greatest are faith, hope, and . . . I think I will stop at hope today.

That sense of hope continued throughout the week and into our next visit in the city where the only soft drink is Coke.

ETERNITY

ATLANTA, GEORGIA

Driving without a car radio on Interstate 85 South starting in our hometown in Greenville and ending in the ever-expanding metropolis of Atlanta gives a driver a lot of time to think. The two-and-a-half-hour drive certainly did that for this particular driver. Free from the distractions of everyday life and the many things that can call for my attention, I was free to ponder other things on this warm summer morning. Mainly, the quickly passing thing called life.

"Yet you do not know what your life will be like tomorrow. You are *just* a vapor that appears for a little while and then vanishes away" (James 4:14).

"Man is like a mere breath; His days are like a passing shadow (Psalm 144:4).

Billy Graham was once asked what surprised him most about life. Without hesitation, he responded, "The brevity of it."[7]

I am discovering the same thing. The older I get, the more I realize that my time here on Earth is numbered. The clock is ticking louder. My grandparents are gone. My parents have passed. My oldest brother was taken at an age close to mine. We all share one thing in common—we are all going

---

7   BGEA, "Billy Graham Trivia: What Is Life's Greatest Surprise," Billy Graham Evangelistic Association, https://billygraham.org/story/billy-graham-trivia-lifes-greatest-surprise (accessed August 12, 2018).

to die. American women can expect to be here for 81.2 years. Men can expect to face Judgement Day at age 76.4.[8] Eternity is coming (Heb. 9:27). The Bible is clear about that!

We are going to spend roughly eighty years on this Earth. According to Jesus, we will spend all of eternity in either Heaven or Hell. If we tried to quantify eternity and ascribed a finite number to it such as one thousand years, would it not make sense to focus on the one thousand years rather than the eighty? Would it not be imperative to know where we will be in the one-thousand-year setting than worrying endlessly about the worries of the first eighty years? Of course, we can't limit eternity to even one thousand years.

If you ask the average person if he or she expects to go to Heaven, the answer is most likely to be "I hope so." I hope so? Is that the best we can come up with? Would it not make more sense to dig a little deeper into this most critical topic? Wouldn't it be worth our time to search the sacred texts for ourselves to see if there is a more concrete answer? If we were told that gold was somewhere in our house, would we not take the time to search for it, rather than "hope to find it" someday?

Something much greater than a precious metal is here. Fortunately, the truth of eternity does not require a tremendous amount of excavating. In fact, it is surprisingly simple. The greatest source on the matter is the Word of God.

John the apostle records a powerful conversation between Jesus and Mary a few days after the death of her brother, Lazarus. Jesus said to her, "'I am the resurrection and the life; he who believes in Me will live even if he dies, and everyone who lives and believes in Me will never die'" (John 11:25-26).

John records another conversation Jesus had, this time with a prominent religious leader of his day. "'For God so loved the world, that He gave His only begotten Son, that whoever believes in Him shall not perish, but have eternal life'" (John 3:16). The key word is "whoever." No one is more of an

---

8   Larry Copeland, "Life Expectancy in the U.S. Hits a Record High," USAToday.com, https://www.usatoday.com/story/news/nation/2014/10/08/us-life-expectancy-hits-record-high/16874039 (accessed August 12, 2018).

equal opportunity "Provider" than Jesus. No one has leveled the playing field better than He. He has no favorites (Acts 10:34). The "whoever" of John 3:16 is anyone—the atheist, the agnostic, the Jew, the Christian, the intellectual, the simple, the most egregious sinner, and the most covert one. You, me, anyone. His door is open to all. A person must simply come humbly to God, acknowledge his sinfulness, repent, and accept the free offer of salvation that can only be received by faith in Jesus' atoning work. It is why the apostle Paul wrote, "That if you confess with your mouth Jesus *as* Lord, and believe in your heart that God raised Him from the dead, you will be saved" (Rom. 10:9). Saved from what? The answer is sobering—Hell. There is no getting around it.

There is a sad reality in our modern-day culture that appears to be spreading like a cancer. We are ignorant regarding the laws of God and the truth of His Word. I certainly was for many years. Jesus uttered a revelatory statement: "'And you will know the truth, and the truth will make you free'" (John 8:32). Being illiterate of science does not change the reality of gravity's pull. Being ignorant of the state driving laws does not exempt you from the consequence of driving fifty-five miles per hour in a thirty-five-miles-per-hour zone.

I don't think we have even a hint of understanding of the severity of sin and how it separates us from God and damages others. I am just beginning to see it for myself. The Bible states, "For the wages of sin is death" (Rom. 6:23). In other words, we deserve death. We have earned it. The consequences of sin are monumental. It wreaks havoc in the life of the person who commits it and in the lives of the persons who are the recipients of it. It is something that must be dealt with—not on our terms, but on God's. If we were told we had cancer, most of us would not brush it aside and go on with our lives. We would be shaken by the news. It would be as if we had run into a brick wall. It would propel the reality of our predicament to the forefront of our thinking. We would need to address it, courageously and thoughtfully. We would need to seek out the best help to conquer it and hope to beat it, so we could live the life we want to live. Sin is like a cancer, only worse. Cancer can only claim our lives for our time here on Earth. Sin can claim the entire person—body, soul, mind and spirit—for all of eternity.

Honestly, from a natural standpoint, I am not capable of understanding Hell. I have no frame of reference for it in my finite mind. It makes me uneasy to think about it, let alone talk about it. That doesn't change the reality of it. Yet, once again, the Word of God is our authority. Specifically, Jesus doesn't only reference Hell: He describes it in great detail. He says it is a place of eternal torment (Luke 16:23), of "unquenchable fire" (Mark 9:43), "where THEIR WORM DOES NOT DIE" (Mark 9:48), where people will gnash their teeth in anguish and regret (Matt. 13:42), and from which there is no return—even to warn loved ones (Luke 16:19-31). He calls Hell a place of "outer darkness" (Matt. 25:30) and the place where both body and soul are destroyed by God" (Matt. 10:28). Jesus talks about Hell more than he talks about Heaven and describes it more vividly.[9]

I once had a person close to me say in a mocking tone, "I don't believe anyone goes to Hell." Unfortunately, personal opinions don't hold any weight in this ultimate concern. The defendant can claim his innocence all he wants; but if the Judge decides he's "guilty," then guilty he is. I heard a wiser man comment, "If any man goes to Hell, he has to step over Jesus in order to get there." Well said!

Hell is truly the most unnecessary place for anyone to be. It is a travesty that anyone would choose to be separated from God for all of eternity. Why would someone want to go to a place that was created for Satan and his angels (Matt. 25:41)? God, in His great mercy toward us, sent His only begotten Son into the world with one specific task in mind—to be the perfect sacrifice for sin that would satisfy God's demand for justice.

---

9   Leslie Schmucker, "The Uncomfortable Subject Jesus Addressed More Than Anyone Else," The Gospel Coalition, Inc., https://www.thegospelcoalition.org/article/the-uncomfortable-subject-jesus-addressed-more-than-anyone-else (accessed August 12, 2018).

Inwardly, we all have an innate desire for justice. From our earliest moments on this Earth, we learned the phrase, "It's not fair." We can see the need for justice a mile away. We can look back in history and wonder how some could have treated others so harshly, so cruelly, so unfairly. It is probably a trait in our DNA that was given to us when we were created in the image of God. God is just. His justice is pure, objective, and true. He cannot let sin go unpunished. Would we expect anything less? Yet, He satisfied the need for justice by sending His Son to take upon Himself that punishment for sin that was rightly due you and me. Ironically and paradoxically, it was an unjust act that satisfied the demands of justice. We walk away free, unscathed. Thank God life's not fair!

Grace has been defined as "God's Riches At Christ's Expense." Jesus took the penalty for your sin and mine, was nailed to the cross, and rose from the dead to defeat the power of death, the consequence of our sin. Paul sums it up well: "He made Him who knew no sin *to be* sin on our behalf, so that we might become the righteousness of God in Him" (2 Cor. 5:21). It is why Jesus uttered, "'It is finished'" (John 19:30). It is the reason John the Baptist proclaimed, "'Behold, the Lamb of God who takes away the sin of the world'" (John 1:29). Jesus provided the way for anyone to go to Heaven if he or she so chooses. His sacrifice has made us righteous in God's eyes, in right standing with Him. That is the good news of the Gospel.

Jesus often spoke in parables to explain spiritual truths. This is a modern-day attempt to do the same. There once was a ship that was about to sink. In a great panic, a passenger jumped off the sinking ship in a desperate attempt to save his life. However, the man couldn't swim. Just as the ocean was about to swallow him up, a life preserver from another ship splashed in the water beside him. The desperate man looked up and saw a man on the other end of the rope. Hopeful for the first time, he held on to the preserver for dear life as the man pulled him to safety. The man in the water is you and me. The other man who threw the life preserver is Jesus.

My deep thoughts ended as we glimpsed for the first time at our destination for the day—The Church of the Apostles. Linda and I gasped. Wow, we thought. What a beautiful building. How unique. It was one of the most outstanding church structures we had ever seen. Easily visible form Northside Parkway in Atlanta, Georgia, it has the look of a modern-day monastery or a well-maintained Ivy League college building, maybe even a palace. Because it is located in an urban setting, it has its own five-story parking garage. This imposing, yet classy, neo-Gothic building has ninety stained glass windows in the sanctuary. The large stained glass windows on the west wall are renderings of the apostles. The sanctuary seats twenty-eight hundred—sixteen hundred on the main floor and twelve hundred in the balcony.

Why such an elaborate structure? In its online video that explains the history of the church building, one of the committee members in charge of the building plans remarked, ""How can we do less for God than we would do for ourselves?"[10] Good question! And that they did! This was not the first time such a sentiment was offered. King David had the same mindset when he contemplated the construction of the temple in Jerusalem. His son, King Solomon, carried it through to completion in 930 B.C. It took the Israelites roughly twenty years to build the temple (1 Kings 9:10). It took the builders of The Church of the Apostles about two years.

Perhaps even more magnificent than the Anglican church building and its sanctuary is the story of the church's founding lector. Dr. Michael Youssef experienced the salvation of God as a sixteen-year-old in the country of Egypt.

> Even before he was born, it was evident that God had a vision for Michael Amerhorn Youssef. His mother was in poor health at the time she became pregnant with Michael, and because her life would be jeopardized by his birth, the doctor recommended terminating the pregnancy. An abortion procedure was

---

10 "About Us: Our Facility," The Church of the Apostles, https://apostles.org/about (accessed August 12, 2018).

scheduled. But God intervened, and sent the family pastor to reassure them the night before the procedure was to take place that God was involved in this pregnancy, not to be afraid, and that this child would be "born to serve the Lord." Michael's parents accepted the pastor's word as a message from God and obeyed. His mother gave birth, and lived to see him surrender his life to the Lord in 1964 at age sixteen.[11]

That surrender would lead to incredible feats for decades to come.

Dr. Youssef, whose radio and television programs *Leading the Way* are heard and seen around the world, shared with Linda and me another incredible story when we approached the friendly and engaging pastor following the morning service. Believing that God was calling him out of Egypt, he sought an exit visa at a time when no university student was permitted to hold a passport or leave the country due to civil unrest in the land. God intervened and miraculously provided approval of his application. That was the first miracle needed. On the day that he would leave Egypt for good, the airline officials were preparing to board the passengers for the last flight out of Egypt. For some unexpected reason, Michael was told abruptly that he was not allowed to board the plane. Perplexed, he prayed to God and waited anxiously on the side. A short time later, the airline agent called to him to board the plane. No explanation was given; no apology was offered. He was the last passenger to board the plane that day—or any ones after it. The Six-Day War with Israel followed.

Michael Youssef has seen the hand of God on his life for seventy-one years, beginning with his miraculous birth, his supernatural exodus out of Egypt, and his founding of The Church of the Apostles in a land far from his birth. I suspect if I asked him what has surprised him most about life, he might respond, "The brevity of it." Whether prominent leaders like Billy Graham or Michael Youssef or common people like Linda and me, we all

---

11   "Dr. Michael Youssef: Founding Rector," The Church of the Apostles, https://apostles. org/leadership (accessed August 12, 2018).

share a common fate. This life as we know it will end—sooner than we could have ever imagined. We have little control, if any, of the day and time it will terminate (Heb. 9:27). The one thing we have complete control over is where we will spend eternity. The penalty of sin has been eradicated. The preparations for Heaven and Hell have been made. The two doors are open. Which of the two will you choose?

YOU HAVE AN ENEMY

CENTRAL, SOUTH CAROLINA

The Gospel is good news. I take that back. It is great news. When we turn to Jesus for salvation, we become a new creation in Christ (2 Cor. 5:17). The Creator of the universe makes a covenant with us that He will not break. The Holy Spirit takes up residence in our lives to teach us and bring to our remembrance everything that Jesus said (John 14:26). Our new walk with Him is a process that will bring more and more revelation of Jesus and His Kingdom. Paul stated, *"For I am* confident of this very thing, that He who began a good work in you will perfect it until the day of Christ Jesus" (Phil. 1:6). God accepts us as we are and molds us, over time, into the people He wants us to be. We are "earthen vessels" with a great treasure inside us (2 Cor. 4:7). The Lord even uses us in His work of redemption, commissioning us to bring the message of salvation to all nations (Matt. 28:19-20).

There is a sobering reality that goes with this good news. There is an enemy of humankind who hates God. He hates you. And he hates me. His main goal is "to steal and kill and destroy" (John 10:10). He is opposed to everything that God is. He will do whatever is in his power to keep people from a saving knowledge of the Lord Jesus Christ. If he cannot accomplish that, he looks to neutralize those who have come to a saving knowledge of

Jesus. Jesus provided a chilling description of Satan: "He was a murderer from the beginning, and does not stand in the truth because there is no truth in him. Whenever he speaks a lie, he speaks from his own *nature*, for he is a liar and the father of lies" (John 8:44). His nature is so bad, and his destructive ways are so vast that God has prepared a place for him and his angels (Matt. 25:41).

Satan knows that the best way to neutralize a Christ-follower is to isolate him or her from others. When we are isolated, we cannot benefit from the support of others (Rom. 12:15). Like fruit cut from the vine, a slow death begins. Our thinking tends to get off-course. We become offended easily and carry unforgiveness in our hearts. We begin to believe lies and internalize them as truth without anyone around to challenge our thinking. Slowly, over time, we become bitter, writing others off and determining them unfit to associate with. We become self-focused and self-centered without even realizing it. Satan has us right where he wants us, like a lamb before the slaughter.

Linda and I experienced the reality of Satan's prowess that weekend. Worse yet, we gave him a saddle to make his job much easier. We were at each other's throats, forgetting that the battle is in the heavenly realm, not against each other in this earthly one (Eph. 6:12). We discarded everything we have learned about forgiving and blessing and temporarily made Satan our lord. That is where he wants us—to be critical of each other, to accuse each other, and to find fault with each other. Things got so bad for Linda and me that she threatened to go to a different church alone on Sunday rather than join me to our planned destination, Alive Wesleyan Church in Central, South Carolina. Regaining some semblance of composure, I asked Linda if she thought her decision lined up with the Word of God or if she was being led by her feelings. To her credit, she knew the answer. Through many years of falling prey to Satan's schemes, I have learned—rather, I am learning gradually and slowly— that when I *feel* like canceling any scheduled prayer meeting, Bible study, or gathering due to any turmoil that I am experiencing, I need to go. Period. No ifs, ands, or buts. No rationalizations. No justifications. Through my poor decisions many times before, I now *know* there is a blessing awaiting me *if* I *persevere* through the raw emotions. Onward, Christian soldier.

ALIVE Wesleyan Church in Central, a forty-five-minute ride west of our home, knows these truths all too well. The town got its name from the Atlanta and Richmond Air-Line Railway—today Norfolk Southern—when it served as the halfway point between Atlanta and Charlotte. The church, founded in 1893, has been a beacon of light to the people of Pickens County. Most people know Pickens County as the home of Clemson University, NCAA football champions in 2016 and 2018. Others know it for some of its natural beauty, including Lake Keowee, Lake Jocassee, and Table Rock State Park.

Pickens County (named after American Revolutionary War Brigadier General Andrew Pickens) is also home to ninety-six thousand unchurched people. Shockingly, eighty percent of South Carolina is unchurched. How can that be? South Carolina is in the heart of the Bible Belt!

ALIVE Wesleyan Church is committed to lowering this startling percentage. Located on a forty-five-acre property, the church building is 1.6 miles from Southern Wesleyan University and 6.4 miles from Clemson University. The newly constructed church building is designed with unchurched people in mind. The only Christian symbol sits on a window above the main entrance to the sanctuary. It is a form of the cross that portrays all types of people, young and old, churched and unchurched, coming together at the cross. The entrance of the lobby area of the church continues this theme. Linda noticed four professional-looking coffee urns that invited visitors to have a cup of coffee that could rival Dunkin Donuts' best. The comfortable, cushioned chairs gave the impression that this was a safe place to relax, that it was different than the one visitors might have been exposed to when they were young, when that "old time religion" seemed irrelevant or out of touch.

The one-thousand-seat sanctuary seemed somewhat like a cozy movie theater. Void of all Christian symbolism, four vertical lights hovered over the stage, separating the two screens that flanked them. The two side walls of the church angled in from the back to front, doubling as a place for the church to advertise upcoming events or portray images that support what was unfolding in the sanctuary. Even the pre-service music playing in the background was of a secular nature. The only band I recognized was Needetobreathe, a contemporary band from Possum Kingdom, South Carolina, whose lyrics in some of their songs include some references to Christian themes. The entire setting was designed to make it comfortable for unchurched people to visit and see what the church had to offer. To see how they could possibly fit in and find a place to call home.

Once the service began, everything was Christ-centered. The music, though loud, was worshipful. Four songs into the service, Pastor Tom Harding took the stage. The rugged, country-looking pastor quickly connected with the audience. With a variation of "Name that Tune," he asked the audience to identify the singers from the first few verses of the songs that he played. The answers were obvious, except for the one which featured an impersonator voicing the words of Morgan Freeman. This led to the theme of his talk— learning how to hear God's voice.

The humble and transparent teacher shared how he was struggling lately, yearning to hear God's voice in the midst of his angst. Turning one day to the sixth chapter of the book of Isaiah, God spoke to his situation directly through His Word. Even in the middle of his turmoil, Pastor Tom was assured that God is still on the throne. He was still in control of Tom's life. The revelation was calming. It was transformative. It was exactly what Tom needed to hear, when he needed to hear it.

It is exactly what we all need to hear. Anyone in union with Christ can hear from their Heavenly Father. Jesus said, "My sheep hear My voice, and I know them, and they follow Me; and I give eternal life to them, and they will never perish; and no one will snatch them out of My hand" (John 10:27-28). The writer of Hebrews informs us, "God, after He spoke long ago to the fathers in the prophets in many portions and in many ways, in these last days has spoken to us in His Son, whom He appointed heir of all things, through whom also He made the world (Heb. 1:1-2). Paul tells us that the Word of God is "the mystery which has been hidden from the *past* ages and generations, but has now been manifested to His saints, to whom God willed to make known what is the riches of the glory of this mystery among the Gentiles, which is Christ in you, the hope of glory" (Col. 1:26-27). As a result of these transformative revelations, "We proclaim Him, admonishing every man and teaching every man with all wisdom, so that we may present every man complete in Christ" (v. 28).

God has spoken to us through His Son. We are exposed to truths that men of old longed to hear (Matt. 13:17). The powerful truths of Scripture make us complete in Christ. As we abide in Him, His Word "is a lamp to [our] feet and a light to [our] path" (Psalm 119:105). We hear Him clearly as His Spirit illumines His Word. We hear His Word in the Spirit in which it is intended (1 Cor. 2:13-14). When Satan comes as an angel of light and presents the truths of God's Word taken out of context and/or given in the wrong spirit, we can wield the "sword of the Spirit" (Eph. 6:17) and demolish Satan's distortions with the true "'WORD THAT PROCEEDS OUT OF THE MOUTH OF GOD (Matt. 4:4). It is in His Word and in the timing and Spirit of His Word that we hear God clearly.

Imagine all the people of ALIVE Wesleyan Church hearing from God every day for themselves as they read the Word of God. Picture the ninety-six thousand unchurched people of Pickens County becoming members of Alive or other Bible-believing churches and learning to distinguish God's voice from the world's. What if the eighty percent of unchurched people of South Carolina not only read God's Word but also became doers of that very Word? Don't blame Alive Wesleyan Church if they don't. They can't do it alone. They have an enemy who is doing his best to keep them from reaching their goal. Jesus, the Word Himself, told His disciples, "'The harvest is plentiful, but the workers are few. Therefore, beseech the Lord of the harvest to send out workers into His harvest" (Matt. 9:37-38). Let's pray that some workers join the efforts of ALIVE Church in Central, South Carolina. There is too much at stake.

BIG PICTURE PEOPLE

FORT MILL, SOUTH CAROLINA

I am always amazed at "big picture" people. People who can see something in others that very few others can see. People who can see into the future while what we see at the moment paints an entirely different picture. People who can focus on eternal matters while others are bogged down with the concerns of this Earth. People who can take the carnage from a scandal and turn it into a training ground for the purposes of the Kingdom of God.

In the 1980s, evangelical Christianity had reached heights in the United States that it had never reached before. Celebrities from the music industry, professional sports teams, and television industry were giving testimonies of turning to Jesus as their Lord and Savior. It was the "in" thing to be an evangelical Christian.

And then the scandals hit.

Some prominent "televangelists" fell from grace—some with sexual misconduct, others with financial improprieties. For the first time in many years, evangelical Christianity had a black eye on a national level. It was less popular. People began giving less of their money to charitable organizations, wielding a wide brush that swept across all lines of ministry. It was not "in" to be a born-again Christian.

The most publicized scandal seemed to occur in Fort Mill, South Carolina. Jim Bakker and his wife, Tammy, had built Heritage USA, a twenty-three-hundred-acre Christian theme park and resort that drew nearly six million visitors at its peak in 1986. Everything came tumbling down in 1987, amid accusations of sexual misconduct and financial impropriety. Bakker later served in federal prison for nearly five years for fraud.[12] While many pointed fingers, others were listening to the stirring of God in their hearts.

Rick Joyner was one of those leaders God was prompting. A former pilot turned pastor and author, Joyner moved his MorningStar Ministries to the Charlotte area in 1988, just after Jim Bakker resigned from Praise the Lord (PTL). Through prophetic leadings from the Holy Spirit, much prayer, and three confirmations from respected Christian leaders, he sensed that God would resurrect the fallen ministry of PTL.

Sixteen years later, MorningStar Ministries—an organization that has churches, missions, and schools around the world—bought fifty-two acres of the old PTL property in 2004.[13] Joyner's excellent book *A Prophetic History* tells of much of the details that went into this adventurous process.

Fourteen years after MorningStar's purchase of PTL, Linda and I drove through a residential community of Fort Mill before taking a left onto the church grounds. We passed the high-rise hotel that stood as a reminder to the property's past glory. Since we did not know about the history of PTL at the time and its subsequent purchase by MorningStar, Linda and I drove around the high-rise wondering if it was still being used. With bricks fallen to the ground, windows missing, and a chained link fence around its perimeter, it became obvious that the high-rise was not functional.

---

12   Tim Funk, "Fallen PTL preacher Jim Bakker is back with a new message about the Apocalypse," CharlotteObserver.com, https://www.charlotteobserver.com/living/religion/article200297074.html (accessed August 26, 2018).

13   Tim Funk, "Jim Bakker's theme park was like a Christian Disneyland. Here's what happened to it," CharlotteObserver.com, https://www.charlotteobserver.com/living/religion/article205362719.html (accessed August 26, 2018).

The rest of the complex was clearly in use, however. As we headed to the rear entrance of the MorningStar complex, we were welcomed by greeters who gave us a copy of Joyner's book. Entering into the building, it felt like we were entering a hotel. A short walk down a hotel corridor, we entered into the "sanctuary" area, where the church service would be held. This was definitely unlike any we had seen. Like being in the middle of an older Embassy Suites, we took our seats in the rear middle facing the stage area. The sanctuary was in the midst of the squared-in, four-story conference center/hotel. The side behind the stage, the side to the left of the stage, and the one directly facing it had four stories of hotel rooms overlooking the open sanctuary. Visitors could leave their rooms and walk ten feet to the white rails that overlook the sanctuary. Two glass elevators split the middle of the two side walls of the sanctuary. On each side of the elevator on the right-side wall were large windows that brought in light between the layers of floors. On the ground level, three sections of chairs faced the stage with two large screens flanking each side. Five white columns supported the facing that sat above the stage.

As part of its function in the Body of Christ, MorningStar is committed to having three-day conferences each month to equip believers for acts of service. Speakers of international renown are invited to speak. Linda has always been captivated by what God has done through the passionate and fiery German evangelist, Reinhard Bonke. Unbeknownst to us, the evangelist was to give that day's sermon. However, due to illness, Pastor Tom Hardimann took his place.

Pastor Tom spoke of the Welsh Revival of 1904 and the Azuza Street Revival from 1906-1910. He then made a startling statement: More Muslims have come to Christ since 9-11 (the date of the attacks on American soil) than in the past fourteen centuries combined. He reviewed the previous week's sermon from 1 Chronicles 12, stating that the men of Issachar understood the times they were living in and knew what God wanted them to do.

We, too, need to adjust our thinking to what God wants us to do, to be prepared for what the Spirit of God is preparing to release to the nations. God is looking for a new level of heart devotion to Him. For that day's message, Pastor Tom used Isaiah 54:1-6 as his text. The text has special meaning for Linda and me.

Many years ago, the assistant pastor at our church in New York, Tom Zawacki, prayed over Linda and me before he left for West Virginia to pastor a church. He told us he had a word from God for us. It was from Isaiah 54. He stated, "God wants to 'enlarge the place of your tent.' Stretch your tent curtains wide; do not hold back; 'lengthen your cords and strengthen your [stakes]'" (v. 2). When Pastor Hardimann read that verse from Isaiah, Linda and I looked at each other. We didn't need to say a word. We both thought back to Zawacki's word. Both Toms had spoken the same word to us—one twenty-plus years earlier, the other while we were in the middle of our present-day adventure.

The prophetic words did not end there. MorningStar is committed to encouraging Christ-followers to pursue God with all their heart and to have the Holy Spirit lead them where He wants them to go. As part of this function, the church offers each visiting person a chance to have a man and woman pray for them after the service in a room dedicated for this purpose.

Linda and I accepted that offer with excitement. We came to a circular table that was manned by Jerry and Ethel, two MorningStar Church members who have the spiritual gift of prophecy. Ethel prayed that God would give us the right word to speak into our hearts for this season of our lives and for God's glory. For the next thirteen minutes, they shared with us what the Holy Spirit was speaking to them.

"The Lord is joyful for you guys for the season you are moving into. He is accelerating you guys to where He is taking you. There are a lot of people who need help where you will be. People will look at you and say, 'They can help me.' Tom, rest in Him. Don't be concerned; let God. Enter His rest by faith. Say, 'God use me.' Your greatest joy will be yielding to His Spirit. You are unsure of yourself, but it's not about you—it's about Him. Enjoy. Because it's going to be good. He has trusted you as His vessel. As you rest in Him, let go. Let go of control. The Lord would have you take time to be with Him. Say, 'Okay, God, I am going to sit here.' Make yourself available to Him. You will feel a tangible anointing. Say to Him, 'God, use me.' As you enter His rest and let go, He is going to show you the next step. You will know that it is Him as you experience His peace. He is moving you into a new classroom—from the head to the heart. God is going to show you stuff about men. Once you allow people to be real, they can really change inside more than ever before. You are going to help a lot of men. God is going to help you help them.

"Linda, trust Him. Just trust Him. He knows what's on your heart. He knows what you carry. Do not lean on your own understanding. He's put the desires on your heart. He will bring it forth as you praise and thank Him every day. Rest, trust, praise, and thanksgiving are weapons. Put the past behind you. He's working on your behalf. This is a season when you will be more connected together. It is going to be different than the season you are coming out of. This is going to be very exciting. There are a lot of needs out there. You will be examples for other couples. Everybody needs different stuff. The Lord is going to speak to you regarding their needs. At times, you will just need to listen to them. They are going to say, 'I like talking to Tom and Linda. They listen.' They are not going to be afraid to say anything to you because they know you went through the same things. The Lord's going to use you with married couples. You are going to take from your own lives to help them with theirs. You are going to help other couples come through, since you've been there. Look with expectancy. Don't look to the past. I hear the word *influence*. He is going to equip you to help them. Nothing with God is wasted. He is going to bring abundant fruit in your lives to help others."

Ethel and Jerry then prayed a blessing over us. We thanked them and walked slowly and quietly to the back door of the room, contemplating what had just happened to us. God had just used two of His humble servants to speak into a husband and wife team who have had a desire for God to use them for His glory and for His purposes. God heard that cry and spoke a vision into us individually and as a couple.

We left MorningStar grateful that God had taken a fallen ministry and replaced it with another one that would meet the needs of His people and spur them on to work in His Kingdom. He continues to rebuild the walls of Jericho far beyond the land of Israel. He continues to pour new wine into new wineskins. Nothing is wasted in God's economy. Nothing is unredeemable. He is a God Who is always moving forward, always looking for humble hearts that He can pour His grace into.

That grace has been manifest in a worldwide ministry in Fort Mill, South Carolina. We would see another manifestation of that grace the next week, this time in a remote part of the Palmetto State.

IN SEARCH FOR SIMPLICITY

TRAVELERS REST, SOUTH CAROLINA

I think I am a lot like many of the older people I interact with. The more we advance in years, the more we long for simplicity. With emerging grins, we reminisce about the days of innocence when we rode our bicycles instead of cars. The days when we whooped with joy when we were granted permission to stay up later than normal. The days when kids used to play with other neighborhood kids until the departure of the sun signaled the day was coming to an end. When the actors in *Bonanza* and *Marcus Welby, M.D.* were regarded as honorable. Perhaps that is why Linda and I felt so enamored with Mountain Ridge Bible Fellowship as soon as we arrived.

We drove thirty-five minutes from our home to this tiny church in a rural part of northern Greenville County. In fact, if we had been driving too fast, we could have easily passed the church without realizing it. Mush Creek Road is a thoroughfare where you can drive without worrying about cars coming in the opposite direction. If it weren't for the GPS shouting at me to turn right into the church parking lot, I would have continued on in my faraway thoughts. Turning into the lot, there were no signs instructing first time visitors to flash their lights. There were no parking lot attendants waving their flashlights for us to proceed further down and park around the bend. In fact, securing a parking spot was effortless.

The short stroll to the sanctuary was even easier. There were no formal greeters to welcome us; but George, an antiques dealer who had lived in the area his whole life (except for one year in Colorado), took it upon himself to acknowledge our presence and welcome us to Mountain Bridge Bible Fellowship. Right before we entered the sanctuary, we bumped into a low-key, personable man, whom I would not have known until I heard his voice. This was the first time I met Pastor Kevin Boling. However, I had heard him speak many times before on Christian radio as I traveled around the Greenville area the past fourteen years. He took a genuine interest in Linda and me, asking us where we lived and what we did for a living. I am always touched by people like him who act as if others are more important than they are. They stand out like men among boys.

Pastor Boling seemed like he was in no rush to end our conversation, in spite of the fact that the start of the 11:00 a.m. service was fast approaching. Having learned well from my thoughtful mother, I told the pastor we would let him go so he could prepare for the service.

When we entered the front of the simple sanctuary, we had to wind our way through a few aisles to get to a couple of open spots in one of the vacated back pews toward the side rear windows. There were ten pews on each side with room enough for five adults to sit. At least, before lunch, anyway. The sides were separated by a center aisle, which led up to the podium in the front of the church. Preparing themselves for the service were four musicians, three with acoustic guitars and one with a keyboard. I quickly noted the absence of drums. Spanning the rectangularly shaped room, it was as if we were in an historic, one-room schoolhouse from the past or on the set of a *Little House of the Prairie* episode. The setting was simple. We felt we could sit back and take a deep breath. I could have sworn I smelled supper slowly cooking on the wood-burning stove.

The teaching, however, was far from simple. It was quite the opposite. While not an imposing physical specimen, Pastor Boling had an authority about him as soon as he began to teach the Bible. The Buffalo transplant who now lives on a twenty-plus-acre parcel (including some sheep) used Peter's first epistle as his text for his sermon. I am a person who takes notes while the pastor delivers his message. Armed with my pen and Linda's paper (I forget paper every week), Kevin Boling made my job difficult. Every sentence he uttered was profound. While I was busy trying to write down one sentence, he was onto another anointed one that needed time to be absorbed. This continued for the next hour. Like a long-distance runner huffing and puffing across the finish line, I dotted my last "i" and crossed my last "t" exhausted. But exhilarated.

He made the Word of God come alive. It is easy to recognize when a person has the spiritual gift of teaching (Rom. 12:6-8, 1 Cor. 12:28, Eph. 4:1-12). Many times, after hearing someone preach from the Word of God, I wonder, "Why didn't I see that?" I felt that way with Pastor Boling. He stated that the goal of his church was to help people understand and apply the Word of God. He quoted J.C. Ryle, the Anglican Bishop of Liverpool from 1880 to 1900, who had been converted to Christ while a student at Oxford University:

> I want people to fill their minds with passages of Scripture while they are well and strong that they may be sure help in the day of need. I want them to be diligent in studying their Bibles and become familiar with their contents in order that the grand old book may stand by them and talk with them when all earthly friends fail.[14]

Pastor Boling then quoted the late R.C. Sproul, whose teaching is still heard on the radio program, *Renewing Your Mind*: "The Word of God was intended by God to be intelligible, and only as we understand it does it get

---

14   J.C. Ryle, quoted in Kevin Boling, "1st Peter," Sermon, Mountain Bridge Bible Fellowship, Travelers Rest, SC (September 2, 2018).

into our blood streams and into our hearts and show up in changed lives."[15] From the head to the heart to the hand!

Pastor Boling then laid out an outline for the first epistle written by the apostle Peter. The Christian life needs to proceed from doctrine to deeds. A call to do the deeds without the correct doctrine is lacking the proper foundation and thus a misguided motivation. Pastor Boling separated Peter's first epistle into two parts. The first segment began at 1 Peter 1 and ended with 1 Peter 2:10. This is the foundational doctrine of the Christian faith—the doctrine of salvation.

The second part began with 1 Peter 2:11 and ended at 1 Peter 5:14. This lays out the foundational duties for those who have been called to follow Christ. Here we find that submission to the will of God is the proper biblical response of the redeemed. First Peter 5:6-7 reveals a powerful truth: "Therefore humble yourselves under the mighty hand of God, that He may exalt you at the proper time, casting all your anxiety on Him, because He cares for you."

Just as Timothy received the apostle Paul's admonishment centuries earlier to "be diligent to present yourself approved to God as a workman who does not need to be ashamed, accurately handling the word of truth" (2 Tim. 2:15), Pastor Boling seemed to be doing the same.

Feeling like we had eaten a three-course spiritual meal, we conversed with George one final time before departing the simple church with the powerful message.

The GPS told us that our next destination, North Greenville University, was five minutes from Mountain Ridge Bible Fellowship. It instructed us to head east on Mush Creek Road. Guessing that east was to our right, we turned in that direction. I was wrong; the GPS rebounded to tell us to take our next right. We turned onto a seldom-traveled road that could barely contain two cars coming in the opposite direction of each other. I quickly slowed the car to take in what we were seeing.

15 Ibid.

This was the most picturesque country road we had witnessed in our travels. The road was blanketed by trees on both sides that reached toward each other as they met over the road. It was as if we were covered by a canopy. Looking up, we could barely see the blue sky between the converged trees. Linda quickly told me to stop the car so she could take a picture of what we were beholding. Even I took one with my phone; it was too picturesque a scene to pass up. We marveled again how God *always* gives us more than we ever ask or imagine. He knows how much we love these simple scenes. He didn't have to give that to us that Sunday, but He chose to. He is a God of blessings.

We continued on to our lunchtime destination, the North Greenville University campus. This is my favorite college in South Carolina. Any college with the motto "Where Christ Makes the Difference" is going to be high on my list. Their words are not hollow.

North Greenville was created in 1892 to make a difference in the "Dark Corner" of northern Greenville County. This section of the county was a place where ignorance abounded, superstition flourished, and quarrels were settled with the knife or the gun.[16] The founders of the Christian school believed educating the young people in the ways of God was the answer to the senseless violence and flowing moonshine. That attitude of concern for young people continues to this day. You can perceive it as you stroll through its pretty campus. You can sense it in the people who work there. It seemed tangible when we joined the undergraduates for lunch in the cafeteria that day.

The people of NGU are not perfect—they will be the first to point that out. But they know the perfect One. They desire to have Him supreme in the education they offer to young lives. They desire to be more like Him. They desire to keep life simple. To love their God with all their heart, mind, and strength and to love others as themselves (Luke 10:27). They love the simplicity

---

16   Jean Martin Flynn, *A History of North Greenville College*, Greer: North Greenville Junior College, 1953.

of the Gospel. That God died to save sinners. That He takes up residence in the very lives of those who call to Him out of a humble heart. That He leads us as we make Him our priority. A simple Sunday. A simple life. A simple Gospel. We all long for it. Many of us, by God's grace, have grabbed hold of it. It's available to anyone who wants it.

We would see the effect of that simple, yet powerful, Gospel the next week in the life of a one-time drug addict.

GOD CHANGES LIVES

HENDERSONVILLE, NORTH CAROLINA

The man I was watching was wearing a number thirteen jersey from the Tampa Bay Buccaneers professional football team—Mike Evans' jersey. But this man had been on an altogether different journey than the real Mike Evans, who graduated from Texas A&M University and went on to be a probowl wide receiver in the National Football League. I didn't know his real name, but he caught my eye. In addition to wearing the football jersey, he had his baseball cap on backwards. He had tattoos on both arms.

When the worship at Living Water Church started, he and a few others sauntered up to the front near the stage at the pastor's invitation. When the music started, "Mike" started jumping up and down. He raised his index finger toward Heaven, making a declaration that he believed God was number one. He looked to the left and smiled at the older man with the ZZ Top beard and the leather motorcycle jacket. He then smiled at the lady to his right with the tattoos all over her arms. They seemed to know each other. It was as if they knew where they had come from and were surprised at where they were presently. I tried to take a guess. I pictured "Mike" as the student in school who was always in trouble. I guessed that he got into a life of drugs with all the carnage that goes with that type of lifestyle. I thought to myself, *I would really like to talk to Mike after the service is over.* I prayed that if it were God's will, He would ordain that meeting.

I looked around at the cavernous sanctuary that looked more like an auditorium than a typical church sanctuary. The two white side walls seemed to reach to the heavens. They had vertical, rectangular beige "panels" designed to give some contrast to the walls that would have seemed otherwise overwhelming. Surprisingly, in spite of the expanse of the building, the seating capacity appeared to be about 850. The seats were arranged in four sections from front to back, followed by circular tables and chairs that connected the formal with the informal. The wall to the front was black with two screens for lyrics to the worship songs and for announcements. The most significant announcement that appeared over and over while we were waiting for the service to begin was the one regarding the upcoming Celebrate Recovery meeting, a kind of Christ-centered twelve-step program designed to free people from their "hurts, habits and hang-ups." The worship team dressed very informally, looking more like a rock band ready to give a concert than a group of musicians preparing to exhort the congregation to worship the King of kings "in spirit and truth" (John 4:24).

As the saying goes, "Don't judge a book by its cover." For twenty-three minutes, the band performed, with four vocalists taking turns in leading the congregation in singing. We ended with the chorus, "The Rock won't move and His word is strong/ The Rock won't move and His love can't be undone."[17] I sensed the Holy Spirit stirring my heart in ways that only He can move.

When Pastor Tony spoke, that stirring continued. The fifty-year-old with the goatee, blue jeans, and untucked shirt revealed a statistic that alarmed me: eighty-five percent of evangelical Christians have never shared their faith with anyone! The Bible informs us that "faith *comes* by hearing, and hearing by the word of Christ" (Rom. 10:17). If no one had shared their faith with me, I would not be saved today. If Andrew had not shared his story of finding Jesus,

---

17 Vertical Church Band, "The Rock Won't Move," Essential Worship, October 25, 2013.

there may have been no Peter. When Phillip encountered the living God, he found Nathaniel and pointed him to Jesus. Pastor Tony continued that when you have been found, you will look for someone and tell them so that they can be found. No one can argue with our story. No one can take our story away from us. God never wastes a story. Our stories are a way that God uses to bring people to Himself. It is God Who does the saving; our part is to share what He has done in our lives.

Pastor Tony then gave two invitations at the end of his message. The first was for anyone who had not received Jesus as his or her personal Savior. He added a challenging, soul-searching addendum to that segment. Perhaps some people in the audience were not looking for people to be found because they themselves had not really been found. A few people responded. The second invitation was for those who have been found, who truly have come to know Jesus as Lord and Savior but, for whatever reasons, were not sharing their stories with others as much as they should be. A few more raised their hands. To Linda's surprise, I was one of them. She knows that I have a heart to see people saved and sanctified in Christ. But only God knows the depths of a man's heart, and He, in His sovereignty, knew that I was allowing other things of this world to compete with my devotion to Him and the concern I had for people's souls.

When the message was over and the pastor finished praying for those who had responded to his two invitations, I was surprised to see "Mike" come to the front stage to lead the congregation in the time of offering. He gave a short, unpolished exhortation for those in the audience to give their tithe to God. He then slipped off the stage and out the front doors while we were all putting our offerings in the plates that were being passed through each aisle.

When we were dismissed, my wife and I headed to the back entrance. She asked me if I would wait for her while she went to the bathroom, a ritual I have been accustomed to in our twenty-six years of marriage. While I waited in the lobby area for her, I spotted Mike. It was obvious he was popular. Everyone seemed to be checking in with him. Finally, I got my chance.

"Mike Evans, what has Jesus done for you?" I asked him. He smiled. "Everything," he answered. He took a deep breath and told me his story. Rejected by his father at birth and his mother a few years later, he developed a deep sense of a fear of abandonment. He could never fit in with any group in any setting. He developed a dependency on alcohol and drugs. He couldn't hold down a job. Three marriages ended in divorce. Hopeless and distraught, he decided ending his life would be better than trying to fix the one that was totally out of control. He had tried unsuccessfully in the past, but this time would be different, he thought. But God intervened.

"Mike" put away the rope. He put the pills back in the bottle. He moved back to Hendersonville. He joined the Celebrate Recovery group at Living Water. Today, he is engaged to be married. Two of his kids from prior marriages joined him at church that Sunday. He has a job that pays enough to support his family. He is joyful. When he hugged me, he couldn't have known that I don't like when guys wear their hat backwards. He most likely wasn't aware that I am embarrassed by male adults who wear the jerseys of professional athletes. He was probably oblivious to the reality that I label people who get tattoos as followers. "Mike" is not the only one God is healing and delivering. "Mike" is jumping up and down because God delivered him from a life of drugs and alcohol, and his issues of abandonment are being addressed. He is accepted by God Himself and by other sojourners who are supporting Him in His walk with God.

I, too, am jumping up and down. My sins are just as destructive as Mike's. God is delivering me from a critical spirit, from being hard on others when I, myself, have received grace upon grace. From stifling the Spirit of God within me, grieving Him with my poor attitude toward the people for whom His Son shed His blood. "Mike" Evans. Tom Kupec. Different outsides, similar insides. Brothers in Christ. Joined together by a God Who loves them both, a God

Whose mercies are new every morning (Lam. 3:23), a God Who came "to seek and to save that which was lost" (Luke 19:10).

Two lost men now found. Two men discovering the ongoing work of the Holy Spirit in their lives. I am happy for me. I am really happy for "Mike"!

WEEK 12

HURRICANE SEASON

GREENVILLE, SOUTH CAROLINA

We are not as strong as we think we are. Hurricane Florence reminded us of that truth as she ravaged the coasts of North and South Carolina. With each approaching day, the meteorologists warned us of her coming fury. I became concerned when we were informed Florence could leave her destruction on the coastal areas and creep northwest toward our home in Greenville, South Carolina. In spite of all the advances in technology and all the collective intelligence and prowess of humankind, there was nothing we could do. We were powerless. We just had to wait and prepare. We were at the mercy of God.

That is a daunting feeling, a truly humbling one. It's also a good place to be. Imagine if we lived our lives with a healthy understanding of what we can control and what we can't. How much more stable our lives would be if we lived out this balanced approach!

The twelve-step programs are in tune with this ideal. Every meeting is ended with the serenity prayer, "God, grant me the serenity to accept the things I cannot change, courage to change the things I can, and wisdom to know the difference."[18] I am nothing if not observant. For years, I have watched people lose their peace, trying to control things they were incapable of controlling. I

---

18   Reinhold Niebuhr, "Prayer for Serenity," CelebrateRecovery.com, https://www. celebraterecovery.com/resources/cr-tools/serenityprayer (accessed September 16, 2018).

was the chief among them. The truth is that we have the potential to do some remarkable things in this life we are given. The minute we try to control things out of fear and desperation, that potential is compromised at best and negated at worst. We become frustrated. We become irrational. Our thinking becomes eschewed. We become difficult to live with. We become oppressive to others. It is only a short time before others say enough is enough. We then wonder what is wrong with them.

Tropical Storm Florence derailed our plans that week. Or did she? Because of responsibilities at home and the uncertainly of where Florence would strike, we decided to take the anemic 1.8-mile trek down Pelham Road to Grace Church. Fortunately for us, Grace has a 5:00 p.m. service on Sunday nights. By that time, we were convinced that Florence was no longer a threat.

What if we let God be God and us be us? The Bible tells us, "There is a way *which seems* right to a man, But its end is the way of death (Prov. 14:12). Conversely, what if we were led by the Spirit of God at all times, seeking to hear His voice and Word before acting impulsively and recklessly? Jesus knows best. His Word will last forever. He can see all things. He is the First and the Last. He is the Bread of Life. His ways are above our ways. But He is as gracious as He is powerful. He allows us in. He encourages us to gain His perspective. He leads us when we seek to follow Him. He is approachable. He will not cast away anyone who humbly comes before Him. "[He] causes all things to work together for good to those who love God, to those who are called according to *His* purpose (Rom. 8:28).

Matt Williams, the teaching pastor at Grace Church, illustrated these truths as they related to the lives of Isaac, Leah, and Rachel. Isaac was the heir to God's promises through Abraham. Leah and Rachel became his wives. Both of them struggled finding their purposes in life in general and also as it related to their relationship with their husband. Matt did a good job exhorting us not to be distracted by the culture of the day, where men sometimes took on multiple wives. After all, he said, how will people look back on us, wondering how we did certain things like owning multiple cars when people were starving in the world?

Both women let fear and control run their lives. Both lost their sense of identity as daughters of God. Competing with each other, they either gave birth to their own children or had their maidservants lie with Jacob to produce even more.

Fear, conflict, and attempts to control reigned. Chaos lurked around the corner. There is no mention in Scripture about Jacob, Leah, or Rachel seeking God about His will for their predicament. Each acted according to his/her own understanding. Each left a footprint that was clear and undeniable. Fortunately, a sovereign God was working above and through them, and the twelve tribes of Israel were formed, all according to God's faithfulness to His covenants.

Pastor Matt ended his sermon with four probing questions for all of us in the audience to ponder. First, what is the dream for which you are tempted to sacrifice anything? Second, is there a wound so large that you have built your identity around it? Third, what is it that you protect at all costs? Finally, what is it that you can't live without? The answer to these questions will lead us to the source of idolatry in our lives.

We are called to put Jesus first in all things. We are called to hear His voice and follow Him. "For we are His workmanship, created in Christ Jesus for good works, which God prepared beforehand so that we would walk in them" (Eph. 2:10). Our call is to walk out the plan that God has for our lives. We don't initiate our works. We don't try to be good people who do good things. Those efforts can help, but they are limited by our own finite vision and power. We can even do "good" things that may gain the applause of men but have nothing to do with the will of God. Jesus gave us that warning in Matthew 7:21-23.

We can even make idols out of good things. Families are extremely important, the mechanism by which we learn how to interact with the world around us. When family comes before God, however, it takes a place that it was never intended to be. Water is necessary for life. Too much water and a flood reeks destruction. We can have idols of our traditions. When traditions do not line up with the Word of God, they become religious expressions that are devoid of power. We can make idols of anything. However, when we abide in Christ, study His Word, and allow His Spirit to lead us, we are moved to a higher level of living that is ordained of God for His glory, for His Name's sake, and for His purposes. "For all who are being led by the Spirit of God, these are sons of God" (Rom. 8:14).

When the preaching and two subsequent powerful songs of worship ended, I glanced at Linda to my left. Her eyes were moist with tears. It was obvious something had touched her. She asked if we could sit while the others departed to the back exits. Linda shared her burden. Three years before, God had set her free from a dependence on opioid pain medications that had been prescribed to her when she first hurt her back twenty-three years earlier. The side effects of those drugs had impacted her thinking and behavior over the years. Even her memory of events was altered by the potent drugs. Slowly but surely, the Lord has been doing a work of healing and restoration in Linda's life.

Mercifully, He continued that work that night. Like the peeling of an onion, the Lord had revealed another layer of pain Linda was feeling from the dysfunction that she had battled with over the years. Her twenty-plus years of parenting came before her mind's eye again. She regretted not enjoying her sons more. She lamented over not being fully engaged in their lives throughout her time as a parent. She felt like she was Satan's rag doll, being tossed back and forth, feeling like her growth was stunted for twenty-one years. Like Rachel and Leah, she had lost a good sense of her identity.

She confided in me that she wanted to be a good mother, but felt stymied by her hurts and hang-ups that prevented her from doing the very thing she wanted to do. She was becoming increasingly concerned, even fearful, of what might happen to her sons as a result of her struggles. She asked me if

I thought this excessive concern for her sons' future and relationship with them bordered on idolatry, fear, and control. I sensed that it did. I also sensed that Linda needed more than me at the moment. I encouraged her to go forward for prayer. She asked if I would go with her. A gracious man prayed with Linda, sharing how he, too, had struggled with fear and control. He was on a journey of learning to trust God in all things. He extended an invitation to us to join others in the church who met weekly over these same issues. It led to Linda's being a part of Grace Church's Tuesday night "Re:generation" ministry, a Christ-centered program of recognition, renewal, restoration, and growth with biblical parallels to AA's twelve-step program.

Life humbles us. It reminds us that we are not as strong as we think we are. It is in our weakness, however, that we experience God's strength and an even greater awareness of His presence. It is in our humility that we learn to share our burdens with others and allow others to share their burdens with us. We experience the true *koinonia* that God desires us to experience with each other. Above all else, God gives us Himself, promising never to abandon us, asking us to control what we can control and surrender to Him what only He is capable of controlling, and asking us to keep our eyes fixed on Him, "the author and perfecter of faith" (Heb. 12:2).

We are not as weak as we think we are.

OVERCOMING OURSELVES

COLUMBIA, SOUTH CAROLINA

If Linda and I had reenacted the Battle of Antietam a few weeks prior, we elevated to the Battle of Gettysburg on this particular morning. I can't even remember what started the fracas. But it took flight like most of our childish squabbles. Most likely, I said something stupid (James 3:9-10). Linda responded with raw emotion. She became more and more emotional and animated with each word she expressed. Like the mature Christian man that I am, I began responding to her in a way that I still cannot find in the Bible to justify my actions. I began to act out what she was saying. One hand on the wheel, the other pointing to the sky when she said "God." One hand on the wheel, the other wiping a pretend tear when she said she was really upset with me. One hand on the wheel, the other pointing back at her when she said that I always do this or that. When she put her finger in her good ear while she talked even louder, I chose the higher road, telling her that she was nuts. Not to be outdone, she motioned back at me, telling me I was number one, only using the wrong finger in the process.

On this particular Sunday, we were heading directly south to the state capital of South Carolina, Columbia. More succinctly, we were heading to the epicenter of the greatest argument our country has ever had. In 1859, the leaders of the state government of South Carolina met at First Baptist Church in the heart of downtown Columbia. Because the state house was not big enough at the time to accommodate the expected large crowd, the decision was made to meet at First Baptist. Gathering for one day, the attendees agreed on the language to be used in the document. Fearing the ramifications of a smallpox outbreak, the men headed to Charleston to follow through with their monumental decision. The verdict was decided. There would be no turning back. The divorce was final.

Today, we would call them irreconcilable differences. The South, with the Palmetto State in the lead, would leave her husband of eighty-three years to form her own country, seeking refuge from the conflicts and struggles that had plagued her and the Union for many years.

Jesus' earthly brother James reveals to us the real reason my wife and I were treating each other as if we were the enemy this Sunday. It even branches out into broader scopes that encompass millions, determining even the fate of nations. "What is the source of quarrels and conflicts among you? Is not the source your pleasures that wage war in your members? You lust and do not have; *so* you fight and quarrel. You do not have because you do not ask" (James 4:1-2). It's pretty simple. Linda wanted something and couldn't get it. I wanted something and couldn't get it. Neither of us was submitted to God. It became a battle of the wills. Jesus was pushed off the throne (at least of our hearts) and told to sit this one out. Subtly and quietly, like a thief in the night, Satan filled the void and took Jesus' place. We gave him that right. He cannot take it on his own.

One hundred and fifty-nine years earlier, it was the same dynamic at work. The South wanted something and couldn't get it. The North wanted something and couldn't get it. The quarrel escalated to a civil war. Solomon reminds us that "there is nothing new under the sun" (Eccl. 1:9). We see the same dynamic playing out today in our American society. Pro-life Americans want a nation where every life is welcome, where God is respected and honored as the Author of life. Pro-abortion Americans want a nation where a woman determines the ultimate fate of the life forming within her.

You would have never known by the time we spent at First Baptist in Columbia that a century-and-a-half ago, Bucky and Vicki would have been Linda's and my enemies. Greeting us with old southern charm that we had not experienced before, the husband and wife greeters made us two New York transplants feel like we were family that they hadn't seen in years. The classy, dignified couple went the extra mile for us, even when it was clear we were visiting town and would most likely never return. Seeing our excitement about the history we were experiencing, they patiently explained the background of the church, how we could get to the original 1859 building that was attached to the current building (built in 1949), and how the church was prospering in the present. No question went unanswered. No question seemed unimportant. After Bucky took our picture by the winding staircase that led to the balcony, we thanked our newfound friends and entered the sanctuary to get to our pew before the service began.

Eighty-seven-year-old Emily, kind and dignified, sat in the pew in front of us. Linda gravitates to older women, who remind her of her relationship with her deceased grandmother and Jessie, an elderly woman Linda had nursed in Queens, New York. Jessie, suffering from Alzheimer's at the end of her life, affectionately called Linda "Ruthie," the name of her long-departed sister. When Jessie was taken from her apartment (where Linda was her live-in nurse) and whisked to a nursing home, Linda was devastated. Her support system was ripped from her like a pocketbook taken by a thief.

To our left sat Patsy, another elderly woman with a pleasant smile. When she heard we were from Greenville, she excitedly informed us that her son is an architect, who works not far from our house. Behind us sat Barbara and Jim, smiling at us as if they had recently won the lottery. Barbara insisted that we visit again if we were ever again in these parts. Scanning from left to right, the sanctuary, with organ pipes stretching to the heavens and the two-storied balcony, seemed to take on the charm and dignity of the people who fill its pews each Sunday. It was a church that you would hope for in a historic, charming, Southern, urban city. The church building made me think of a theater similar to where President Lincoln was shot by John Wilkes Booth. It made me think of *Gone with the Wind* and the images of Miss Scarlett and Mr. Rhett that have stayed with me since my youth.

The worship time, the time of prayer, and the preaching all seemed to emphasize a consistent theme—the importance of being led by the Holy Spirit and being a part of what God is doing in the lives of His people and in the lives of those who have yet to know Him. Pastor Church stated that the book of Acts and all that is recorded there is our heritage. This heritage is even greater than the one I admired as we interacted with the many persons here whose grandparents very likely could have dated back to the Civil War era.

Pastor Church's startling revelation highlighted the importance of our continuing this heritage in the present day. He stated that 3.6 million people in South Carolina are not connected to churches. Again, we heard that startling statistic. In the Bible Belt, of all places. That is sad. What they are missing! How could I ever explain to anyone what I was experiencing this particular Sunday? And not only on this Sabbath day of rest, but the many others as well. I was only there because the Spirit of God had led Linda and me there. He started us on this journey three months before and was pouring on the blessings week after week as we sought Him to direct us to our next destination, our next manifestation of His goodness and presence.

Before leaving, we had to see the original 1859 church building. Weaving our way through the young adults' luncheon (many of whom are University of South Carolina students), Jim, a regal, elderly man, a worker with the young adults group, kindly left his post and escorted us to our desired destination. We slowed our pace. A hush came upon us. We gingerly touched the old bricks. We saw the original table where the secession document was reported to have been signed. There was the door to the stairs leading up to the balcony where the slaves used to sit during Sunday services. We walked up the stairs in honor of them.

Again, Jim's patience with us was noteworthy. He answered all our questions, even though he had nothing to gain from our presence. We were not potential members. He was just doing what a servant of God does—serving others as if he was serving the King Himself.

Jim told us one final story. When General Sherman's Union troops were marching through the South, torching much of what was in their path, they came to the site of First Baptist Church. The Union soldiers were in Columbia with one thing in mind. It was time to annihilate the place where the secession document was formulated, where it all began. Knowing that the Union soldiers were coming, First Baptist went to great lengths to conceal the church's identity. Sherman and his men came upon the site. They asked a slave out front if the church was First Baptist. He shook his head no. He then pointed to the church to the left of First Baptist. The soldiers then burned down the Methodist Church!

Linda and I raised our white flags and called for a ceasefire. We did what we should have done hours earlier. Our hearts, softened by the kindness that we were shown by our elderly brothers and sisters in Christ from Columbia, became tender again toward each other. We confessed our sin to each other. We forgave each other's sins. The Bible promises us, "If we confess our sins, He is faithful and righteous to forgive us our sins and to cleanse us from all unrighteousness" (1 John 1:9). He is faithful to His Covenant. Satan no longer had any right to be on the throne we had unknowingly given him. God's kindness led us to repentance. His mercies are new every morning (Lam. 3:23). They were new to us this day in a tangible way that led us back to life in ways that restored our equilibrium. His ways are steadfast. He makes the broken whole. He makes a family of people who were once separated by distance and conflicting loyalties. He is the Head; we are the Body—whether we were born and bred deep in the South or born and raised in New York and transplanted to Greenville, South Carolina.

The Bible compares the leading of the Holy Spirit to the wind. "The wind blows where it wishes and you hear the sound of it, but do not know where it comes from and where it is going; so is everyone who born of the Spirit" (John 3:8). He had led us to this incredible respite in the heart of the state capital.

Little did we know at the time that the Holy Spirit would be leading this united husband and wife team to another state capital area, this time to meet a former Syracuse University professor who had left her lesbian lifestyle.

SIGNS OF THE TIMES

DURHAM, NORTH CAROLINA

Nothing should surprise us in this world. In fact, I think I get more surprised that I become surprised over some occurrence that has happened than over the occurrence itself. With that being said, no issue in our generation has surprised me more than the push to have homosexuality normalized in our society. Homosexuality, or any sexual sin, was always on the fringe of our society when I was a kid and certainly when my parents were growing up. Of course, sin has always abounded. Adam and Eve can attest to that. What is striking is the strong-armed push and the concentrated effort of a few that have demanded the acceptance of unbiblical behavior into the mainstream without much resistance.

Homosexuality has become the idol of our present day. Many years ago, the Holy Spirit revealed to me an observation that would provide insight into this phenomenon or any like it. He said that a small percentage will always be strongly for or against a particular issue. The eighty percent in between will follow whatever direction the cultural wind is blowing. It would explain why an institution such as slavery could exist. It would explain why sex trafficking could flourish today.

When we traveled three-and-a-half hours to First Reformed Presbyterian Church that morning, we set out not only to visit with a small group of believers in the community of Durham, North Carolina, but also to search for further clarity in regard to the mainstreaming attempts of a well-funded minority to normalize what the Bible clearly defines as sinful.

Why First Reformed Presbyterian? Linda had read a book by Rosaria Butterfield, *The Secret Thoughts of an Unlikely Convert: An English Professor's Journey into Christian Faith*. Rosaria is the wife of FRP's pastor, Kent Butterfield, and the mother of four adopted children. She is a former professor of English at Syracuse University. She is also a person who turned away from a homosexual lifestyle following her conversion to Christ.

I have learned a great deal from listening to Kent and Rosaria on the internet as they discussed her conversion to Christ and her insights into homosexuality. Previously, I had learned the most from LIFE Ministries in New York City, a ministry that works with people to free them from the bondage of this complicated sin. Kent and Rosaria do not make this issue their main focus. They teach that a relationship with Jesus, finding one's identity in Christ, and repenting and turning away from things that God classifies as sin are the foundations from which a person is to live. It is the highest calling of any human being. It is a truth that sets people free—some instantly and others gradually.

Because of Rosaria's past life, the issue many times seems to come to them rather than the other way around. The Christian's response is simple, stated Kent to me. "It's one thing to accept what they (proponents of homosexuality) are saying; it's another to open your home to them." Jesus is the model for Christ-followers. He loves people and invites them in. He came "to save that which was lost" (Luke 19:10). Like the woman caught in the act of adultery, He ended their startling interaction with an empowering and challenging word: "'I do not condemn you, either. Go. From now on sin no more'" (John 8:11). We are to speak "the truth in love" (Eph. 4:15) regarding this issue or any other. We are not to agree with any ideology that strays from the truth of Scripture. That would be unloving. In the case of homosexuality, the Scriptures are clear:

- First, God established His order in Genesis 2:24: "For this reason a man shall leave his father and his mother, and be joined to his wife; and they shall become one flesh."

- Jesus affirmed this foundational truth in Matthew 19:5: "'FOR THIS REASON A MAN SHALL LEAVE HIS FATHER AND MOTHER AND BE JOINED TO HIS WIFE, AND THE TWO SHALL BECOME ONE FLESH.'"

- In the moral law, we read in Leviticus 18:22, "You shall not lie with a male as one lies with a female; it is an abomination." That command is placed between the forbidding of child sacrifice and the forbidding of sexual intercourse with an animal. I don't think any rational person would argue against the forbidding of child sacrifice or the outlawing of sex with an animal. You would think the prohibition against homosexual activity would be viewed in the same light. It is important to note that God's moral law is unchanging. Jesus even raised the bar when he stated, "You have heard that it was said, 'YOU SHALL NOT COMMIT ADULTERY'; but I say to you that everyone who looks at a woman with lust for her has already committed adultery with her in his heart'" (Matt. 5:27-28).

- Leviticus 20:13 states, "If *there is* a man who lies with a male as those who lie with a woman, both of them have committed a detestable act."

- Romans 1:24-34 reveals: Therefore God gave them over in the lusts of their hearts to impurity, so that their bodies would be dishonored among them. For they exchanged the truth of God for a lie, and worshiped and served the creature rather than the Creator, who is blessed forever . . . For this reason God gave them over to degrading passions; for their women exchanged the natural function for that which is unnatural, and in the same way also the men abandoned the natural function of the woman and burned in their desire toward one another, men with men committing indecent acts and receiving in their own persons the due penalty of their error.

When the Bible uses the term, "God gave them over," it is a term of judgement. The peoples' disobedience cries out for correction.

- Jude 1:7 states, "Just as Sodom and Gomorrah and the cities around them, since they in the same way as these indulged in gross immorality and went after strange flesh, are exhibited as an example in undergoing the punishment of eternal fire."
- 1 Corinthians 6:9-11 states: Or do you not know that the unrighteous will not inherit the kingdom of God? Do not be deceived; neither fornicators, nor idolaters, nor adulterers, nor effeminate, nor homosexuals, nor thieves, nor *the* covetous, nor drunkards, nor revilers, nor swindlers, will inherit the kingdom of God. Such were some of you; but you were washed, but you were sanctified, but you were justified in the name of the Lord Jesus Christ and in the Spirit of our God.
- 1 Corinthians 7:2 states, "But because of immoralities, each man is to have his own wife, and each woman is to have her own husband."
- 1 Corinthians 6:17-20 states: But the one who joins himself to the Lord is one spirit *with Him*. Flee immorality. Every *other* sin that a man commits is outside the body, but the immoral man sins against his own body. Or do you not know that your body is a temple of the Holy Spirit who is in you, whom you have from God, and that you are not your own? For you have been bought with a price: therefore glorify God in your body.

- Hebrews 13:4 states, "Marriage *is to be held* in honor among all, and the *marriage* bed is *to be* undefiled."

- 1 Timothy 1:8-11 states: But we know that the Law is good, if one uses it lawfully, realizing the fact that law is not made for a righteous person, but for those who are lawless and rebellious, for the ungodly and sinners, for the unholy and profane, for those who kill their fathers or mothers, for murderers and immoral men and homosexuals and kidnappers and liars and perjurers, and whatever else is contrary to sound teaching, according to the glorious gospel of the blessed God, with which I have been entrusted.

God is sovereign. He is Love. He is holy. He is just. He is the Way. He is the Truth. Love never acts independently of these other traits. They are meshed as one. The Creator of the universe, the Savior of the world, has the right to direct His creation according to His will and His precepts. The Good Shepherd understands His sheep and knows what is best for them. He is to be feared. He is to be revered. He alone holds the power of life and death (John 5:24).

Who of us has not respected the coach who is demanding, who pushes his players to levels they would never reach otherwise? Who has not respected the high school chemistry teacher with his endless homework assignments, who helped us earn an "A" in college? Why would we expect any less of the One Who is perfect, the One without blemish, the One Who has created us? "There is a way *which seems* right to a man, but its end is the way of death" (Prov. 14:12). Wouldn't we be wiser to humble ourselves before the King of the universe, "the Alpha and the Omega, the first and the last" (Rev. 22:13) and humbly align ourselves with His Word?

If I were diagnosed with cancer, I would not want well-meaning people to tell me that I was okay. I would want to know the truth. I would want to know what lies ahead. I would want to know how I could win the battle that I am facing. Denial rarely, if ever, makes anything better. Rebelling against the truth only distorts our ability to prosper. How are we helping anyone by telling them that their actions are acceptable when the One Who created them clearly says otherwise?

If I have a desire for another woman when I am married, would you encourage me to act on that desire? If I am not married, would you encourage me to have sexual relations with a woman before I proved to her that I could be faithful to God by waiting for His timing? If I am filled with anger, would you encourage me to vent that anger with violence toward another? If a grown man has strong feelings for a young girl, would you encourage him to pursue her? I have found that any urge that I have that does not line up with the Word of God is a signal that something is off. That something needs to be addressed. That something needs to be repented. Dark clouds overhead indicate rain is coming. Smoke indicates a fire is not far away. Attractions to the same sex indicate that something has gone wrong. That my identity is not grounded as a son or daughter of God. That I have strayed from the will of God. That possibly, my fear of being alone is throwing me off-course.

My observations over the years have told me that many times, homosexuality is a bad reaction to pain. The individual has believed many lies about him or herself that need to be worked out with the help of knowledgeable counselors or ministers. Sin brings pleasure for a season (Heb. 11:25) but never brings lasting freedom. It is a bottomless pit that can never be filled.

Jesus once told the Sadducees (a group of religious leaders) that they were in error because they did "not [understand] the Scriptures nor the power of God" (Matt. 22:29). We are seeing that same error today regarding the sin of homosexuality and a culture's tragic response to it. Ignorance of God's Word and/or rebellion against it lead to a very sandy foundation that will lead to many problems (Matt. 7:24-27).

Reformed Presbyterian Church has a respect for the authority of the Word of God. They proclaim a message that will provide freedom, peace, and a foundation from which life can be lived well. RPC will not wow you with the beauty of its church building. It will not impress you with the size of its congregation. Most likely, anyone who visits the Durham, North Carolina, area will make a point to see the pristine, castle-like campus of Duke University. They will not likely stop on a small residential street in the shadow of a world-renowned humanistic institution to hear the truth of the Gospel of Jesus Christ. If they do, however, they will see a small group of people committed to Jesus and committed to each other. They will see a group of people who desire to see others set free, even if these people are not even aware that they live in bondage.

Opposition to God's ways produces bad fruit. Ignorance of His Word does the same thing. Satan came to rob, kill, and destroy. He is a deceiver, a liar by nature (John 8:44). He comes as an angel of light, though, not as a storm on the horizon (2 Cor. 11:14). If we are ignorant of God's Word, we are an easy target for him. Regardless of how the world responds to them, the people at Reformed Presbyterian will love you enough to share the truth of God's ways with you. Perhaps the next time you are in Durham, you may want to bypass Duke and join our brothers and sisters in Christ singing the Psalms, proclaiming God's Word, and being as faithful to God and His Word as they know how.

Leaving the state capital region of North Carolina, we left one group of faithful believers to spend time the following week with another group of believers almost four hours west and over one mile higher.

ON TOP OF OLD SMOKEY

BURNSVILLE, NORTH CAROLINA

It is time for a quiz. What is the highest point in the United States east of the Mississippi River? If you answered the Rockies, I worry you weren't paying attention in your high school social studies classes. It's becoming apparent, however, that I wasn't listening either. Three months ago, I would have answered Mount Washington in northern New Hampshire.

I had visited my older brother, Andy and his wife, Janet, to see their new home in Massachusetts. Two of our childhood friends—really more like brothers—Bill Lewis and Kurt Panzenbech drove up from Long Island, New York, to meet with Andy and me in the Bay State. With waist lines much wider than our former glory days, the four of us packed into Andy's car like sardines in a can. We drove roughly four hours north to the White Mountains to see what I thought was the highest point on the east coast. Two days later, my aching knees and I departed for the Palmetto State grateful to see my close friends, happy that I was able to reconnect with the White Mountains of New Hampshire but gravely misinformed about what I thought we had just accomplished.

The surprising truth is, I had not made it to the highest point in the East Coast as I had thought. But I was about to now. If you have driven the Blue

Ridge Parkway in the western parts of North Carolina, you can understand why the ride to Mount Mitchell State Park ignited very conflicting emotion inside of me—feelings of awe as Linda and I witnessed one beautiful mountain scene after another and of anxiety as we weaved our way through winding, narrow roads with no side rails to give us any reassurance that our lives wouldn't end prematurely. Before we would get to the highest point on the East Coast, however, we had some lofty heavenly places to attend to in Spruce Pine, a town of roughly twenty-two hundred residents about a half-hour drive from Mount Mitchell.

How would you like to earn four hundred thousand dollars in one day without even trying? The Bible gives us a hint of how that can happen. It reminds us that "with God all things are possible" (Matt. 19:26). It challenges us to keep our eyes on things above and not on the things of this world (Col. 3:2). If we seek first the Kingdom of God, all the other things that clamor for our attention will be given to us as well (Matt. 6:33). We just don't have to worry about them in God's economy.

Pastor Tom was not thinking anything unusual on that particularly memorable day. Like he did every month, he went to pay his church's monthly mortgage payment. The people of The Bridge Church of Western North Carolina (TBCWNC) gather each Sunday in a one-hundred-year-old former elementary school building. The edifice actually took the shape of a very large three-bedroom ranch with a two-car garage. The sanctuary, which had been remodeled, was an inviting, quaint room that does not have the musty smell that some older, one-story church buildings sometimes have. Like the people of the church, it had an unassuming 150-seat sanctuary. The carpet, comfortable chairs, and black raised ceiling made the atmosphere peaceful. The stage area contained an American flag on the left and an Israeli flag on the right.

Each Sunday service, Pastor Tom begins by praying for the United States, Israel, and then a third country which changes each week. The church has a food pantry that meets some of the needs of the residents who live in the area. Pastor Tom spoke glowingly of Dave, the wheelchair-bound, ninety-year-old who continues to serve faithfully in this food ministry despite the fact that he has been told he will not live much longer. Finally, the church runs a small Christian K-12 school, Tri-County School, attended mostly by non-TBCWNC children from the surrounding rural areas.

When Pastor Tom paid this particular monthly payment, the owner of the building made a startling comment to him: "I don't want to see another payment again." That was it. A four hundred-thousand-dollar mortgage paid in full. No effort. No negotiations. No manipulation. Only God's marvelous provision. God's blessing. God's seal of approval on a group of His followers who were seeking Him first, living their lives to advance His Kingdom. They wouldn't say that, of course. Like the people who responded to Jesus, "'Lord, when did we see You . . . thirsty, and give You *something* to drink?" (Matt. 25:38), the members of TBCWNC are humble people, keenly aware that they are serving a God Who has been abundantly gracious to them.

I can say that about them, however. The people here reminded me of the born-again believers I communed with when I was first saved at St. James Church in Franklin Square, Long Island, New York. In those days, St. James was a conglomerate of persons saved in the Catholic Charismatic Renewal, a small group of elderly Episcopalians, and a significant number of ex-drug addicts and/or alcoholics. It is difficult to feel like you are better than anyone else when your salvation is birthed from a life of substance abuse. Or when you are keenly aware of the forgiveness that a very merciful God has extended to you as you fail often, even as a follower of Christ.

The people of TBCWNC would have fit in perfectly at St. James. Pastor Tom shared that as a Christian, he had fallen into a seven-year period of drug dependence. He knew better. He paid the price. He reaped what he sowed. That humbles a person. It makes you more compassionate to others. It makes you acutely aware that a life in Christ is the best life a person can live. It is the reason you would want to extend the good news of salvation to others. To people who are where you have been. People who don't have the capability right now to see what you see and know what you know. It is the reason you persevere in prayer, knowing that God's will is that none should perish, and that all would come to a saving knowledge of Jesus (2 Peter 3:9).

After Ryan, the worship leader, led the congregation through a time of worshipping God, Pastor Tom gave the message. He said that of the three eternal values, love is considered the greatest. While we are to earnestly seek the higher gifts of the Holy Spirit (1 Cor. 12:31; 1 Cor. 14:1), we must make love the driving force of our lives. Four things stand out about God's love and our response to it, he continued.

First, we need to "know it" (God's love). He first loved us (1 John 4:19). "God demonstrates His own love toward us, in that while we were yet sinners, Christ died for us" (Rom. 5:8). There is not a time in the Bible that Jesus did not accept anyone who humbly came to Him, seeking the life that only He can give.

Second, we need to "glow it" (God's love). The twenty-first verse of Jude tells us, "Keep yourselves in the love of God." We need to keep "fixing our eyes on Jesus, the author and perfecter of faith" (Heb. 12:2). Abide in Him daily, and He will remain in you (John 15:4). Worship Him for Who He is and what He has done. Give thanks to Him in all circumstances (1 Thess. 5:18). Walk in step with His Spirit. A life connected daily to Him will shine. It will reflect the very One Who has taken up residence in the believer's heart.

Third and fourth, we need to "live it and give it" (God's love). Paul said that we now carry a substantial role in this world, one that we need to take very seriously. "Let a man regard us in this manner, as servants of Christ and stewards of the mysteries of God" (1 Cor. 4:1). Paul further stated, "For the love of Christ controls us, having concluded this, that one died for all, therefore all died; and He died for all, so that they who live might no longer live for themselves, but for Him who died and rose again on their behalf"

(2 Cor. 5:14-15). Anyone who has been reconciled to God now has a ministry of reconciliation.

Paul expounds, "Therefore, we are ambassadors for Christ, as though God were making an appeal through us" (2 Cor. 5:20). As we ourselves go through the sanctification process, we are to intercede in prayer for others, extend compassion to fellow sojourners who are stumbling, and reach out to those who have not yet come to know Jesus as their Lord and Savior. Like a parent to a child, we are to bear the image of the Savior, the image of the Creator Who took on human flesh (John 1:14).

As we left TBWNC, those lofty thoughts filled our minds as we drove through the towering terrain. I have heard the term "God's country" many times in my life. I am wondering if that term originated near Mount Mitchell, thirty-five miles northeast of Asheville, North Carolina. The peak of the mountain stands at 6,684 feet, almost four football fields taller than Mount Washington in New Hampshire.

Entering the park, we began the ascent through the spruce-fir forest, driving to the parking area at 6,578 feet. The clouds seemed to meet us there as the sky became overcast. To get to the highest point, visitors must abandon their cars and make the remaining 106-feet trek to the peak by foot. While it pained me to miss this opportunity, the increasing infliction in my damaged right knee warned me not to go any further. Linda took the bad news like a trooper, seemingly just happy to be with her groom for the day. With the majority of my weight leaning heavily on my new wooden cane and with Linda's arm locked in mine, we retreated back to the car for our return trip home.

Despite the disappointment of not making it to the peak, we left the park with renewed resolve in our hearts. My body had failed me, but our spirits were soaring. We were grateful for the privilege of seeing such lofty things— the highest point east of the Mississippi River, Mount Mitchell, and the one even higher than that, The Bridge Church of Western North Carolina.

Could we find that same inspiration next week as we ventured to the land that birthed one of America's greatest evangelists ever?

BILLY GRAHAM'S ROOTS

CHARLOTTE, NORTH CAROLINA

Once called the City of Churches, the Queen City of Charlotte, North Carolina, was home for the world-renowned evangelist, Billy Graham. Drive around the outskirts of Charlotte and you will see many references to the Christian statesman to the nations. A sign on Interstate 85 informed us that the Billy Graham Parkway exit was approaching in two miles. An advertisement on the side of the highway invited drivers to the number one attraction in Charlotte, North Carolina, the Billy Graham Museum.

When Linda and I prayerfully decided to visit Calvary Church in Charlotte that Sunday, we had no idea Billy Graham's father was one of the founding members of Calvary in 1939. Seventy-eight years ago, the church was called Bible Presbyterian Church Unaffiliated. The church was located in uptown Charlotte at the old Central High School. As evangelism thrived and the congregation grew, a plan was proposed to build a five-thousand-seat worship center. A local developer gifted the church one hundred acres along rural Highway 51. In 1986, ground was broken, and a new church building was dedicated in December of 1989. The area is rural no longer.

Exiting off I-485 South on Pineville-Matthews Road, the four-mile trek to the church seemed like a drive through a world of endless malls and new subdivisions. It was obvious the area was freshly developed. Everything seemed bright and clean. No vacant buildings, no advertisements from real estate companies. Many cars joined us on our trek, making it feel more like a typical weekday than a tranquil Sunday morning.

Driving further on, we could see an expanse appearing to our right. The continuous buildings stopped suddenly. Through the limbs of a few trees that lined the street, we could see what the Daily Agenda calls, "The church that may have the most visually impressive exterior in all of Charlotte."[19]

The front outside of the church, facing the corner of the adjacent roads of Highway 51 and Pineville-Matthews Road, consisted of thirteen pencil-shaped high vertical windows with the points of each window all pointing to the sky. Linda thought it looked like a crown or a wedding ring. Whatever the architects had in mind, it was unique. A right at the traffic light that joined the two streets and we could see the expanse not only of the sanctuary but also the adjoining family life center as well. For some reason, the Scripture, "The LORD will make you the head and not the tail" popped into my mind (Deut. 28:13).

Cruising slowly into the parking lot while admiring the majestic edifice, I was about to face my greatest challenge to date of our weekly sojourns. Linda, thankfully, is much more civil than I am. When we travel in our casual attire each Sunday, she asks that I stop at a local gas station or hotel in order to change into her more formal clothes. More Viking-like, I prefer to change in the car, waiting coyly for the coast to be clear before I hurriedly do my best Superman impression, changing from my gym attire to my Sunday best as quickly as possible.

That day proved more challenging, however. Despite arriving a half an hour early for the service, the parking lot was filling up quickly. Worse yet, we were in the walking path from the cars to the church entrance. A

19   Andrew Dunn, "The 16 Largest Charlotte Churches by Membership and Attendance," CharlotteAgenda.com, https://www.charlotteagenda.com/20052/the-12-largest-charlotte-churches-by-membership-and-attendance (accessed October 14, 2018).

steady stream of churchgoers kept walking past the front of our car. The plot thickened. A man and his toddler were greeting people right behind our car. We were being sandwiched in. Sweat was beginning to become more prominent on my forehead. The steady stream of passersby was in front and the man and his toddler behind.

Phil, a soft-spoken and friendly parking lot attendant, spotted Linda and greeted her warmly as she opened the front passenger door. I was in a quandary. I looked quickly to my right and then to my left. Perceiving I had about ten seconds to change, I decided the basketball shorts would have to stay on. I hurriedly put my dress pants by the car brakes and rushed them up my legs while bouncing up and down to get more room for each upward movement. Not having enough room to put on my shoes without ripping my good pants, I stepped into the lot, scooted into my shoes, and with my suddenly red face, said hello to the man to my left. I knew it wasn't a complete victory when Linda encouraged me to tuck in my dress shirt.

The heroic effort was worth it. The building was more magnificent on the inside than it was on the outside. Larger than life organ pipes on the wall behind the altar area seemed to rise up like a skyscraper on a city street. Two large, horizontal screens made it possible for the people sitting in the second-story balcony to see the lyrics of the worship songs and the Scriptures referenced from the pastor's sermons. Four vertical, pencil-shaped windows stood majestically to the right and left of the screens, connecting the inside of the sanctuary to the open land beyond the church walls. The stage area was big enough to house the twenty-five-member orchestra and the chorus on raised benches. Ten rows of pews extended back to the rear wall, making the seating capacity seem like thousands.

As beautiful as the sanctuary was, the preaching of the Word was even better. Paul, the great apostle and writer of much of the New Testament under the inspiration of the Holy Spirit, wrote to his son in the Lord and his fellow worker, Timothy, "Preach the Word . . . " (2 Tim. 4:2). The Book of Acts tells us that the Christ-followers "were continually devoting themselves to the apostles' teaching and to fellowship, to the breaking of bread and to prayer" (Acts 2:42).

Two millennia later, Pastor John Munro gave those in attendance reason to be devoted to the Word that Sunday. Using Romans 8:28 as his text, the seventy-year-old former Scotland lawyer spoke with a confident authority. He stated that this verse is one of the best known and best loved verses in all of the Bible, and rightly so. It is the reason for hope when circumstances attempt to tell you otherwise. It is the path of peace when life seems to be confusing. It is a truth that is limited to a select group of people, however. It is not a universal truth that comes with the physical birth into this world. It is a truth only for those who have experienced a second birth, the spiritual birth into the family of God, a birth attained by faith in the finished work of Jesus (2 Cor. 5:17).

"And we know that God causes all things to work together for good to those who love God, to those who are called according to *His* purpose" (Rom. 8:28). This powerful, transformational truth is only true for those who have responded to Jesus by faith, those who are living for His purposes. It is not because we who have called upon the Savior's name are any better than anyone else. It is because a Power greater than ourselves is at work in us. This powerful God is able to make *all things* work for good. Good things. Bad things. Disappointing things. Yes, even evil things. To give eternal purpose to seemingly temporal things. To take suffering and mold the heart of the believer, leaving a likeness to the One Who created and redeemed him.

Pastor Munro quoted Corrie ten Boom: "There is no panic in heaven! God has no problems, only plans." The Gospel is multi-faceted. It gives assurance to the believer that he will be with Jesus forever. There needs to be no fear of death, no hoping to be good enough to warrant salvation. That work was accomplished two thousand years ago. The Gospel is also a great comfort for this life, knowing that a sovereign God Who is at work at all times, is working for the good of those who love Him, those who are called according to His purpose. What a great way to live. What a great God to serve.

Linda and I walked to our car at the conclusion of the service. Bill, the greeter who had graciously welcomed us to the church before the service, spotted me in the parking lot and drove over to say goodbye. He had treated me like I was Cliff Barrows, the former member of Calvary Church and close confidante to Billy Graham. He treated me like I was Norman Geisler, the great Christian apologist who had attended this day's service. He treated me like another Bill I had known all my life, my oldest brother Bill, who had led me to the Lord and who had cared for me like I was his own son, who exhorted me when my faith was faltering. The same brother who believed in me more than I believed in myself. The same older brother who had died a terrible, slow, heart-wrenching death just a few years prior, going from a vibrant, life-giving person to a man who could not talk or even move.

Despite the tears and the periodic grieving that comes with memories of Bill's death, I can hold on to the rock-solid truth that God, in His eternal goodness, in His ways that are far above mine, is even working Bill's tragic death for good for those who love the Lord and have been greatly impacted by Bill's horrifying demise. Somehow, on this glorious Sunday morning, I can picture Bill, Billy Graham, and all the heavenly host exhorting me and Linda to keep running the race that God has called us to run, to trust Him in all things, and to believe that He is working for our good in all things and at all times.

We continued to run our race the following week, seeing "that God causes all things to work together for good to those who love [Him]," even in a town like Las Vegas, of all places.

SMALL AND BIG

MIDDLEBORO, KENTUCKY

"Can anything good come out of Nazareth?" Nathaniel asked Philip when he was told that the possible Messiah had come from that remote town in Judea (John 1:43-46). That question could probably have been asked about Middlesboro in the 1930s. Known as "Las Vegas of the East," the small town in southeastern Kentucky was infamous for gambling, illegal betting, and brothels. Like the town of Nazareth, which quietly produced the most important Person in all of history, little-known Middlesboro unceremoniously produced another person who would give his life for the call of God.

William McElwee Miller became a Christian missionary in Persia (modern-day Iran). As a part of his missionary work, he learned Persian and studied Islam—particularly Shi'a Islam—Persia, and Persian culture. During his missionary work in Persia, he also encountered the Bahá'ís, a large religious minority there. Much of his ministerial work involved developing Christian apologetic responses to these religions. He would go on to write *Ten Muslims Meet Christ*. Miller knew that only two things last forever—the Word of God and the souls of human beings.

With a bonus hour of sleep in our tanks due to the end of Daylight Savings Time, Linda and I departed from chilly Greenville at 5:30 a.m. to begin our three-and-a-half-hour journey northwest to Kentucky. With no other cars to escort us, we covered a lot of ground before the sun began to make its appearance.

I made another traveling mistake that frosty November morning. Linda is never to be outdone by the temperatures. While she dressed more as if we were journeying on a trip to Alaska, I wondered if my t-shirt and shorts were going to be sufficient for the colder-than-normal temperatures. Driving in the dark, Linda announced that she was hot and lowered her window. I regretted not listening to that little voice of caution within me. I had to do something to survive. For the next two hours, I surreptitiously turned on the heat every time I saw her window coming down. Once I saw the window going back up, I quickly turned the heat off. One hundred and twenty bone-chilling minutes later, I rejoiced for the first time in my life when Linda asked if we could stop for a bathroom break. While she exited quickly for the Raceway bathroom, I made a bee line to the back of our van. With my newly secured sweatshirt now zipped as high as any zipper can go and with Linda's bladder much lighter, the now equally yoked couple marched on with a renewed zeal.

There is one thing we have learned about Tennessee in our weekly travels that really stands out. The rest stops are unparalleled. This particular building looked like a log home from the area's historic past. It fit in beautifully with the mountain roads and their striking views that had led us to it. One particular maple tree at this rest stop stood out. Its bright yellow leaves silhouetted against the clear blue sky, as if the sun were focusing all its radiance on this one particular tree.

Continuing on from there down Highway 26 East and 32 North through the Cumberland Gap, the trees with their multi-colored leaves seemed to be competing for our attention as the panoramic views continued for miles. Driving through the small town of Tazlewood, we continued on through the beautiful country side of eastern Tennessee.

Saying goodbye to the Volunteer State, we entered Kentucky. At once, we were greeted by a long tunnel, which took us through an entire mountain and ushered us forward to our destination in the Blue Grass State. The small town of Middlesboro, like many other small towns throughout the U.S., gives indications that its best years are behind, its main commerce displaced by the malls and businesses that line more traveled highways short distances away. Nevertheless, the feelings of nostalgia set in as the houses became more frequent, and we entered the commerce area of Main Street. The American flags reaching toward the street from the brick buildings reminded us of our country's rich heritage of Small Town, USA. Somehow, some way, it seemed like Norman Rockwell must have been here at some point in his life.

Leaving the businesses of Main Street, we continued on past the more elegant homes of the area. This is where the more affluent residents must have lived in the town's heyday. Driving further, we took a left on Thirty-Fourth Street and approached the day's destination, Shiloh Church.

Sitting in our customary back row seat, I was impressed with Pastor David King as he graciously greeted each person in the sanctuary while we waited for the ten o'clock service to begin. I got the feeling that his overtures were genuine, more than a weekly ritual that he was performing. He seemed to really care about people. That is a hard thing to fake. When he thanked us for visiting, I really believed that his sentiment was genuine.

His sermon extended from that heartfelt concern for others. He exhorted us to believe God for great and mighty things. Faith believes when it doesn't see. Faith persists when nothing changes. Faith works when it doesn't make sense. The former coal miner of ten years and construction worker for another ten seemed to be exhorting us like a coach encourages a struggling player: "Come on, you can do this. Come on, you can put your faith in this mighty God. You can trust Him. He is trustworthy. Take Him at His Word." With the final amen, we left the service, pondering the challenging things we had heard and trying to sift through them and connect them to some of our current struggles.

Heading back home, the views seemed even prettier than before. "Look to your right!" "Did you see that?" "Look how that water goes all the way down." "Wow, that is pretty!" After stopping at a rest stop that overlooked the path that Daniel Boone and Davey Crockett had trodden through centuries earlier, we decided it was time to attend to the calls of our stomachs. Disappointed that Lois' Kitchen had a line of waiting customers extended to the parking lot, we settled for a Wendy's. While Linda was not thrilled, I secretly rejoiced, knowing that all sizes of French fries were on sale for one dollar. Taking advantage of this great opportunity, I ordered two large fries, a double stacker, and a chili.

A very kind, older man graciously told me that I could order in front of him. The man tugged on my heart for some reason. Perhaps he reminded me of my elderly father, who had passed away five years earlier. When Linda and I were eating, the man walked by with his tray of food. Seeing that he was alone, I invited him to join us. Somewhat surprised by our overture, he accepted my offer.

Frank was eighty-four years old. His crew cut made me think he was "old school." I told him if my parents were alive today, they would have ordered a meal just like the one he had. It was a baked potato with cheese. His wife had been deceased for three years, and only one of his three grown sons lived locally. He had been a metal worker his whole life, just like Linda's dad had been. Our hearts were burdened for Frank.

Eventually, Linda asked him if he knew Jesus personally as his Lord and Savior. Frank said he did not. He explained that he had attended church many years ago but was turned off by people who proclaimed one thing but lived another. We agreed with him that hypocrisy is a turn-off. However, we also know that the poor example of others is not a sufficient excuse before God's Judgement Seat on our final day.

Linda's passion kicked in. It was obvious she desired that Frank be with Jesus forever and not separated from Him eternally. I felt the same way. Frank was a very polite man but definitely not a people-pleaser. If he were playing poker, you wouldn't know if he had a full house or all singletons. He wouldn't budge from his position. As a final gesture, I asked Frank if he would agree to read the Gospel of John at home with an open mind, asking God to reveal His truth to him. He did not promise he would, only conceded that he would consider it.

We said goodbye to Frank, sad that he hadn't responded to God's overture to him (yet). We felt privileged to have met him and to share our lives together, even if just for a short time. Unbeknownst to us, a young couple with their two kids had heard us sharing the Gospel with Frank a table away. They were praying for us the whole time that we were sharing with him. The woman conversed with Linda in the bathroom, her eyes filled with tears, grateful to us that we had reached out to Frank. Her husband came up to me by the soda machine, thanking Linda and me for what we had done. He said it had inspired his family. It made me realize that we never know the full impact of our words and actions. We left Wendy's with a great sense of purposefulness.

We really enjoyed driving through South Carolina, North Carolina, Tennessee, and Kentucky on that beautiful, chilly Sunday in November. But we really *loved* reaching out to Frank, sharing the eternal message of the God we have come to know personally. We really *loved* conversing, if only for a few minutes, with the young family that had prayed for us in Wendy's while we shared with Frank. Only two things will last forever—the Word of God and the souls of all human beings. Can anything good come out of Middlesboro? Plenty. Where the Spirit of the Lord is, *there* is liberty (2 Cor. 3:17)!

We would experience more of that liberty the next week in an "igloo" far from any snow-filled lands.

CHURCH IN AN IGLOO

KNOXVILLE, TENNESSEE

Brrrrrrr. This was our coldest morning yet. You may not know this about the Upstate of South Carolina, but early mornings can be surprisingly cold in the fall and winter months. This sub-freezing Sunday morning at 5:00 a.m. seemed to be even colder than normal. As usual, I was not prepared. But I humbly add, I do have an ability to adapt. I took out my library card and methodically scraped the ice off our windshield. I am not sure if Linda was being sarcastic or not, but she seemed to be glad to realize that a library card could be helpful in a time like this. With close to frost-bitten fingers, we began our three-hour trek back to Tennessee—this time to Knoxville, the home of the University of Tennessee and, even more importantly, to Northstar Church.

It was fitting that we were visiting Northstar on this particularly frigid morning. Next to perhaps Calvary Church in Charlotte, it was the most unusual church building that we had visited. From Sherrill Street, it looked like either an igloo, a Hershey kiss without the paper tail, or one of those outdoor, covered tennis centers. The white building was connected to another building that looked like a large house. This attachment is used for youth ministry and services. Inside the unusual-looking edifice, a large wall cut the igloo-like building in two. On one half was the lobby area and church offices. The other half was the sanctuary. With a kind of blue glow on the white walls, the rounded-shaped room had a cozy and comfortable feeling to it. Lights hung from the white covering with an elevated stage in the front. Three sections of chairs all pointed toward the center screen. None of the 550 chairs seemed to be unoccupied. I was told by an usher that the second service was the same.

In 1792, the first church established in Knoxville was First Presbyterian Church. The Gospel message was brought to a land that was still being explored and settled. Two hundred eleven years later, Pastor Scott Cagle and the congregation at Northstar "are fully convinced that the Father has a plan for us to be a part of a great Spiritual Awakening in the mountains of East Tennessee in the years to come!"[20]

Cagle announced to the congregation that Thursday would be the one-year anniversary of "Pray Knox." For a year, four churches in the area have partnered together to pray, asking God for an awakening that would transform the eastern part of Tennessee.

Many of us are not aware of the great Christian heritage of our country. The First Great Awakening in the United States ran from the 1720s to the 1760s. The Second Great Awakening covered the time period between 1790 and the 1850s. Thousands came to Christ during these great outpourings of God's Spirit. Benjamin Franklin, noting the effect of the first Great Awakening, commented:

> It was wonderful to see the change soon made in the manners of our inhabitants. From being thoughtless or indifferent about religion it seemed as if all the world were growing religious so that one could not walk through the town in an evening without hearing psalms sung in different families of every street.[21]

---

20 "Our Story: Sharing the Gospel of Jesus Christ," Northstar, https://northstarknox.com/our-story (accessed November 11, 2018).
21 Peter Marshall, *The Light and the Glory*, Grand Rapids: Revell, 303.

Pastor Cagle, a former starting tight end at nearby Carson-Newman University, a perennial division two football powerhouse, hopes for that same effect on the greater Knoxville area. He encouraged everyone at the service to attend Thursday's one-year anniversary prayer meeting.

I found it interesting that "only" four churches were connected for this outreach. I was reminded of Rick Joyner's experience with trying to unite local churches in a particular city. Joyner is the pastor at Morningstar Church in Fort Mill, South Carolina. When his effort to unite the churches seemed to fail, he sensed the Spirit of God speaking to him about the Scripture, "For where two or three have gathered together in My name, I am there in their midst" (Matt. 18:20). Joyner sensed God was telling him to start with two or three churches, not with an entire city. Perhaps it was that *koinonia* could only be realized with more intimate connections. Perhaps true community, fellowship-centered and rooted in the person and mission of Jesus Christ, could only be realized in this type of setting. I pay attention to respected leaders like Rick Joyner. In my mind's eye, I see him handing the baton to leaders like Scott Cagle.

Some people would not have liked the way Pastor Cagle entered the sanctuary on this particular Veteran's Day. When the uplifting time of worshipping God had ended, two of the back doors to the darkened sanctuary opened up with two powerful lights entering into the rear of the building. Driving down one of the aisles on his ATV, the pastor climbed with the vehicle up a short flight of stairs and onto the stage. From there, he took off his helmet, told the congregation laughter was good medicine for the bones, and continued his weekly series called, "Back to the Woods."

With a booming bass voice seemingly created for television work, Pastor Cagle gave us a glimpse of the life of Elijah and how the Old Testament prophet overcame the torment of his heart as he pondered the death sentence that the evil Queen Jezebel had placed on his life.

Pastor Cagle then went on to offer his congregation what he titled the "Twenty-One Day Challenge." This plan of action would help anyone in the midst of a heavy time in his or her life to rise above it. The first part of the challenge is to get sufficient rest. Seven to eight hours a night are needed for the average adult. The second segment is to eat healthy, clean food. The person needs to stay away from all processed food. Third on the plan is to drink at least sixty-four ounces of water daily. The body is made up of sixty percent of water. The fourth and final point—and, in my opinion, the most important—is to get in the presence of God daily. Nothing uplifts us more than to be in God's presence. The Word of God tells us that God inhabits the praises of His people (Psalm 22:3). Think about how our perspective changes when we choose to declare God's sovereignty, His majesty, His power, His goodness, His truth, and His faithfulness over the circumstances that are dragging us down and trying to rob us of the joy that is rightfully ours as a child of God. The circumstances that are trying to tell us there is no hope, no way out of our predicament. The circumstances that are deceiving us into thinking that our situation we are wrestling with is greater than who we are in Christ. No, God is greater than any circumstance we find ourselves in, any situation that we find overwhelming, even any wounds that are self-inflicted.

When we begin praising Him for what he has done and worshipping Him for who He is, it is as if we rise above the situation, soar into the place that we are meant to be, the realm of God's Spirit. Our circumstances haven't changed; only our perspective has. An idol has been put away. The Savior takes His rightful place.

The psalmist experienced this shift from heaviness to hopefulness centuries earlier. After bemoaning how unjust he felt his circumstances to be, his perspective changed quickly, in the twinkling of an eye, when he changed his focus from his present circumstances to his God, Who is above them (Psalm 73:17).

Like a grown son ending a visit with his parents many hours away, we bid farewell to Northstar Church with a bit of a heavy heart. Sad only because we would not be a part of the great things God will be doing in this part of

Tennessee, we rejoiced that He had been so gracious to allow us to experience His work there—if only for one day.

We also rejoiced that we did not need our library card the rest of the day. The bone-chilling dark morning had given way to clear, spring-like temperatures. The beauty of the landscape that was hidden in the darkness on our way to Northstar was now revealed in all of its colorful splendor as we drove through the Smoky Mountains and the Cherokee National Forest and over the French Broad River. With each week, we were getting more and more encouraged of the state of the Body of Christ in the Southeast.

We would become even more excited as we ventured to Anderson, South Carolina, one week later.

OLD SOUTH AND NEW SOUTH

ANDERSON, SOUTH CAROLINA

The Old South and the New South. I had heard that phrase a few times when my family and I were preparing to embark on our new adventure fourteen years ago. Despite a somewhat intellectual understanding of how the South had changed through the years, our hearts would experience a further understanding of the changes in "the land of cotton . . . Dixie Land."[22]

Our day in Anderson, South Carolina, this particular Sunday would give us a good picture of the meshing of the old and the new and how each plays a part in the charm and vibrancy of the region.

Traveling south on Interstate 85 from Greenville, South Carolina, to Anderson, South Carolina, that early Sunday morning, we said farewell to the sleepy highway at Exit 27. The next three miles of Highway 81 were a microcosm of the melding of the old and new. Typical of any interstate exit, the first to greet us were McDonald's, Arby's, BP, and Exxon—among a few others. Big Zach's Fireworks propelled us further down the road, past the open countryside that surrounded an old farmhouse that looked like it had been around before World War II.

---

22   Daniel D. Emmett, "Dixie Land," 1859, Public Domain.

A little further south on 81, and the "new" really made itself present. The Bosch Group, an international company, makes many of its automotive electronic components at this manufacturing plant, employing over fourteen hundred people in the area. Advanced Manufacturing is becoming a leading industry in South Carolina. Many companies are moving to the state, taking advantage of lower state taxes and less expensive land. With the exception of a few companies, the textile industry is all but gone, only "mill homes" in the area reminding us of the great impact it once had.

With a right on Concord Road, we caught our first glimpse of the day's destination, NewSpring Church of Anderson. NewSpring is quite a phenomenon in South Carolina. With fourteen campuses spread throughout the state, it is unwaveringly committed to its core mission—connecting people to Jesus and each other.[23] While affiliated with the Southern Baptist Convention, NewSpring's Sunday service does not resemble the Baptist services of a generation ago. No hymns, no organs, no church directory with family names and pictures. NewSpring is the epitome of the new South, the poster child of the "new church."

Even today's speaker, Dan Lian, resembled little of South Carolina's past. The middle-aged teaching pastor of Chinese descent from Down Under spoke with an Aussie accent that gave no hint of resemblance of the Southern drawl that I had first heard from University of Alabama Football Coach Bear Bryant many years earlier on television. He may not have sounded Southern, but boy did he sound biblical. The humble husband and father of four spoke with an anointing of the Holy Spirit that held his audience in complete attention—especially two former residents of New York.

Skillfully connecting with his audience on many common areas of interest, including college football (part of Southern culture), Pastor Dan then brought his audience to a higher dimension, urging us to move from where we are today

23 "About Us," NewSpring Church online, https://newspring.cc/about (accessed November 18, 2018).

to where we have the potential to be every day, regardless of our occupation or season of life. What will bring us to this place where only God can take us? The apostle Paul provides the answer: "Therefore I urge you, brethren, by the mercies of God, to present your bodies a living and holy sacrifice, acceptable to God, *which is* your spiritual service of worship" (Rom. 12:1).

Pastor Dan gave us a working definition of *worship*. Worship is to ascribe value to someone or something more than anything else. When you think about it, all of us are worshipping something. For some of us, it is our money. For others, it is a sport. For many, it is a boyfriend or girlfriend or any human being that consumes our thoughts and governs our actions. All of this makes sense. All of us, despite our differences, despite our backgrounds, are born to worship. After all, we were placed on this Earth to worship. But God desires to be the object of our worship. He alone is worthy of such affection. Colossians 1:13-20 tells us:

> For [Jesus] rescued us from the domain of darkness, and transferred us to the kingdom of His beloved Son, in whom we have redemption, the forgiveness of sins. He is the image of the invisible God, the firstborn of all creation. For by Him all things were created, *both* in the heavens and on earth, visible and invisible, whether thrones or dominions or rulers or authorities—all things have been created through Him and for Him. He is before all things, and in Him all things hold together. He is also head of the body, the church; and He is the beginning, the firstborn from the dead, so that He Himself will come to have first place in everything. For it was the *Father's* good pleasure for all the fullness to dwell in Him, and through Him to reconcile all things to Himself, having made peace through the blood of His cross; through Him, *I say,* whether things on earth or things in heaven.

Psalm 19:1 gives us further revelation, "The heavens are telling the glory of God; And their expanse is declaring the work of His hands." All of creation points us in God's direction. There is great reason to make much of Him. "Come, let us worship and bow down, Let us kneel before the LORD our Maker. For He is our God, and we are the people of His pasture and the sheep of His hand" (Psalm 95:6-7). When we worship God, we experience the deepest connection with Him. When we worship Him, we gain a fresh perspective that reminds us that "we are His people." As we gain new perspective, we garner new purpose. As our purpose gets refocused, we experience peace and a sense of well-being, knowing that we are covered and protected by the Ruler of the Universe. We realize that our lives matter. We worship a God Who is worthy to be praised (Psalm 145:3). It is right to give Him thanks and praise. As we give to Him what is rightly His, we receive perspective, purpose, peace, and protection in return. Suddenly, fear seems to subside; worries seem to lessen; and order seems to emerge out of confusion.

Not wanting to leave NewSpring, Linda and I tarried in the lobby area, basking in the revelations that God had graced upon us. My mind began to wander. Imagine what life would look like if we brought God into every situation? If we stopped and prayed before reacting? If we worshipped Him and sought Him before we said a word to a man? What if the entire Body of Christ did the same? Wow! We would see the glory of God shining in us and flowing from us. We would be a people who are truly led by the Spirit and not bound by our natural propensities. We would be a people who see as God sees and loves as He loves. Would we not see revival as never before?

Like Moses, we had to come down from our mountain. It was time for us to put our service of worship in practice, to live out in the laboratory of life (Rom. 12:1). Something else would have to come first, however. It was time to eat.

Driving through the town of Williamston, South Carolina, from one end of the main thoroughfare that faces a water tower on the opposite end, Linda remarked that it reminded her of one of the towns we see in the Hallmark movies. Continuing through the town, we came upon Mineral Springs Park, named for West Allen Williams, who discovered a mineral spring on his property around 1842.[24] Signs in the park area invited everyone to the Gospel

---

24   "Williamston Mineral Spring Park—Williamston, South Carolina," SC Picture Project. org, https://www.scpictureproject.org/anderson-county/williamston-mineral-spring-park.html (accessed November 18, 2018).

singing event that would take place at two o'clock. Families sat at picnic tables, while their little ones frolicked around the area. Christmas decorations looked like they were put on display recently.

Continuing on, we came to the small town of Pelzer. Looking to eat in a home-grown eatery, we came upon a restaurant called Mill Town Place. We didn't just see the best of the old South here; we experienced it. Dee and the rest of the waitresses made us feel like we were back in our hometown visiting for Christmas. Linda and Dee hit it off immediately.

While they were "catching up," I gave special thought to my order. Dee had recommended the chicken livers plate to me. I thought back to the delicious chicken livers my mother used to make my siblings and me when we were kids. This was the ultimate, I thought back then. Now as an adult, I thought the grilled chicken might be a healthier choice. Our waitresses, eager to please, never let our glasses of water make it past half-empty. The chicken and fixin's were out of this world. These two Yanks were grinnin' like a possum eatin' a sweet 'tater.

Rolling back up Interstate 85 North toward home, we couldn't help but think again how God continues to bless us with such good gifts (James 1:17). I never thought I would hear a profound message at a contemporary church that would challenge me to live on a level that I have never lived before. I would never have thought we would eat a lunch in a town that Andy Griffith could comfortably call home. I never imagined we would eat at a restaurant that would pay tribute to the glories of the Old South. I never thought I would experience the new and the old all in one day, all minutes from each other, "way down south in Dixie."

Something new and old would occur the next week as well as we delved further south and further into the supernatural.

OUTSIDE THE LINES

DAWSONVILLE, GEORGIA

Sometimes, God draws outside of our established lines. We can see this first in the Hebrew Scriptures (Old Testament). Naaman was commander of the army of the king of Aram in the time of the prophet Elisha. He was highly regarded because through him, the Lord had given victory to Aram. He was a valiant soldier, but he had leprosy (2 Kings 5:1).

Through subsequent interchanges, Elisha became aware of his condition and gave the following message to Naaman, "'Go and wash in the Jordan seven times, and your flesh will be restored to you and *you will* be clean'" (v. 10). Naaman did not like this directive. Elisha had sent him beyond his established lines. He went away angry and said, "'Behold, I thought *He would surely come out to me and stand and call on the name of the LORD his God, and wave his hand over the place and cure the leper.* Are not . . . the rivers of Damascus, better than all the waters of Israel? Could I not wash in them and be clean?' So he turned and went away in a rage (2 Kings 5:11).

Fortunately, Naaman had wise counsel from his servants. They convinced the warrior to submit to Elisha's instructions. Humbling himself, he went down and dipped himself in the Jordan seven times, as the man of God had told him, and his flesh was restored and became clean like that of a young boy (2 Kings 5:14).

We see this phenomenon in the New Testament as well. The Gospel of John records a similar story:

> After these things there was a feast of the Jews, and Jesus went up to Jerusalem. Now there is in Jerusalem by the sheep gate a pool, which is called in Hebrew Bethesda, having five porticoes. In these lay a multitude of those who were sick, blind, lame, and withered, [waiting for the moving of waters; for an angel of the Lord went down at certain seasons into the pool and stirred up the water; whoever then first, after the stirring up of the water, stepped in was made well from whatever disease with which he was afflicted.] A man was there who had been ill for thirty-eight years. When Jesus saw him lying *there* and knew that he had already been a long time *in that condition,* He said to him, "Do you want to get well?" The sick man answered Him, "Sir, I have no one to put me into the pool when the water is stirred up, but while I am coming, another steps down before me." Jesus said to him, "Get up, pick up your pallet and walk." Immediately the man became well, and picked up his pallet and *began* to walk (John 5:1-9).

For some born-again Christians, the "sign gifts"—the spiritual gifts of tongues, prophecy, miracles, and healings mentioned in 1 Corinthians 12 are considered outside of their theological lines. My brothers and sisters in Christ who believe this way may think my theological understanding on this matter is outside of biblical lines. This is not the place for me to argue for or against what I believe the Bible teaches on the matter. I will leave that to the theologians and pastors. The Holy Spirit has been impressing upon me the importance of unity in the Body of Christ (John 17). I feel it is my job to maintain that unity at all costs as it relates to issues of our common salvation in Jesus' atoning work on the cross and His resurrection from the dead to defeat the power of sin.

German Lutheran theologian Rupertus Meldenius uttered the following statement during the Thirty Years War (1618–1648): "In Essentials Unity, In Non-Essentials Liberty, In All Things Charity."[25] That plea for unity seems as appropriate today for the Body of Christ as it was for the church in that bloody time of European history.

In that spirit of humility, I liken myself to the blind beggar who was healed by Jesus (John 9:1-12). When some of the angry Jewish leaders questioned him about the details of his healing, he replied, "'The man who is called Jesus made clay, and anointed my eyes, and said to me, *Go to Siloam and wash*; so I went away and washed, and I received sight'" (v. 11).

While our experiences should never shape our theological understanding, they can influence them for sure. I, too, can only say, when my pastor, Orie Wenger, taught about healing, I had to question myself. Do I believe this or not? I then proceeded to take my sprained ankle off my seat and walked unhindered, without a sign of a limp, down and back in front of the stage area after the service had ended. My ankle was sprained no longer. I was restored to complete health. "Jesus Christ is the same yesterday and today and forever" (Heb. 13:8). That biblical truth came to life for me as I thought about my ankle being healed.

Loraine Pruitt of Macon, Georgia, had a similar experience that fall. She journeyed to Christ Fellowship in Dawsonville, Georgia, hoping for something big. Since February, Christ Fellowship has been experiencing what some are calling The North Georgia Revival. In February, she and her husband, Mark, made the two-plus-hour drive from their home in Macon, Georgia, hoping that God would heal her of her stage-four breast cancer. Her most recent PET scan gave a bleak picture that was worth a thousand rough words. In the natural, she had no hope. The doctors confirmed that dark prognosis, giving her little time to live. Loraine stepped into the baptismal waters at Christ

---

25   Philip Schaff, *History of the Christian Church*, Vol. 7, 2nd edition, New York: Charles Schribner's Sons, 1910, 650.

Fellowship with a pain-wracked body but a hopeful spirit. She was prayed for by the elders and then put under the water. She came out of the baptistery, slowly ascending the flight of stairs and out of the fount. Immediately, she noticed something was different. There was no pain. She moved her neck. Still no pain. Time seemed to stand still. She and her husband returned to Macon that night. A few days later, she returned to her doctor and had another PET scan done. The picture spoke a different thousand words. The lesions were gone. She had no breast cancer.

If we thrusted Loraine back in time to Jesus' day and placed her in the story of the healed, blind beggar, she could say to some of the angry Jewish leaders, "All I know is that I went into the water full of cancer. They prayed for my healing in Jesus' name. They then dunked me in the water and brought me back up. I left the baptistery knowing something was different. The pain was gone. I knew I was cancer-free!"

"Who healed you?" those same leaders might have demanded of her. "What do you have to say about Him?"

Unfazed and with complete gratitude, Loraine would have sighed slowly, then responded, "A man named Jesus healed me. All I know is that I had cancer a few days ago, and now I am cancer-free!"

The Bible warns us to test the spirits (1 John 4:1-3). It also tells us to evaluate the fruit of a person or group (Matt. 7:15-20).

Christ Fellowship currently has the following services:

Sunday:	Morning	Prayer	9:00	AM
Sunday:	Morning	Service	10:30	AM
Sunday:	Afternoon	Prayer	5:00	PM
Sunday:	Revival Service		6:00	PM
Monday:	Prayer		6:00	PM
Wednesday:	Prayer		6:00	PM
Wednesday:	Service		7:00	PM
Saturday:	Prayer		9:00	PM

Like the early church in its infancy (Acts 2:46), the people of Christ Fellowship and North Georgia are hungry for God. They are seeking His face, not just His hand of healing. They are sacrificing their time to pray corporately. They are interceding for others. They are giving glory to Jesus, the Author and Finisher of their faith, for all that is occurring in their baptistry. They are working together for the common purpose of seeing others set free.

At the Sunday service, Pastor Todd Martin prayed that he would not get in the way of what God was doing at Christ Fellowship. They are passing the test. They proclaim Jesus as Lord (1 Cor. 12:3). They are producing fruit that brings glory to God. Lives are being changed by the Gospel.

If Joyce and Jerome Swine are any indication, the people are also very kind. Joyce greeted us at the entrance of the massive 140,000-square-foot church building that looked more like an office building (minus the windows) than a traditional house of God. Joyce led us through the lobby area, down the long corridor that led to the sanctuary, and through the doors of the sanctuary itself. She and her husband, Jerome, retired from the oil industry, sat behind us in the service. After the Sunday fellowship ended, they spoke excitedly about what God was doing in their midst and how much they enjoyed their church.

Joyce quickly corralled Pastor Todd after we told her why we were visiting Christ Fellowship that Sunday. The former Alabama native politely asked us about ourselves, hoping that we would attend the revival service later that evening. Joyce also shared with Linda her testimony of how she had contemplated suicide years earlier. Having access to pills through her work as a pharmacist, she shared her dark plan with Jerome. He told her she would have to take him with her. She couldn't do that to him and changed her mind. Years later, the two septuagenarians are joyful, hopeful, and peaceful. They have purpose. The pills are safely locked away.

God moved outside of my lines that Sunday as well. I went to Dawsonville, Georgia, with preconceived notions of what the setting and church would be like. The internet told me that Linda and I would be visiting a small, rural, North Georgia town of 2,792 residents. Each October, the town celebrates the Mountain Moonshine Festival. It is noted as the hometown of former Houston Oiler Football Coach Jerry Glanville and the site of the Georgia Racing Hall of Fame. Outside my lines, however, we found Christ Fellowship seven miles outside of downtown Dawsonville. We found the people congregated not in a stereotypical-looking church building with bricks, white columns, and a steeple reaching to the heavens, but in a massive office building-like structure, tucked away behind other buildings off the main road. We were joined not only by members of Christ Fellowship but by people from all over Georgia; Moravian Falls, North Carolina; and Birmingham, Alabama.

We had been told awhile back that revival had broken out in Northern Georgia. We had been informed that God was healing people in the baptistery of Christ Church. Now we had seen evidence of it ourselves. Encouraged by what we had experienced, we drove home through the beautiful countryside of Northern Georgia with its rolling hills and cattle farms, excited that God once again expanded our understanding of Him and the vastness of His Kingdom.

That expansiveness would be evidenced again the next week—this time in an unlikely place—a public high school in downtown Greenville, South Carolina.

DON'T JUDGE A BOOK BY ITS COVER

DOWNTOWN GREENVILLE, SOUTH CAROLINA

Don't judge a book by its cover. The Gospel of Mark gives us a glimpse of this principle.

> And He sat down opposite the treasury, and *began* observing how the people were putting money into the treasury; And many rich people were putting in large sums. A poor widow came and put in two small copper coins, which amount to a cent. Calling His disciples to Him, He said to them, "Truly I say to you, this poor widow put in more than all the contributors to the treasury; for they all put in out of their surplus, but she, out of her poverty, put in all she owned, all she had to live on" (Mark 12:42-44).

We get further revelation from 1 Samuel 16:7: "For God *sees* not as man sees, for man looks at the outward appearance, but the LORD looks at the heart."

Normally, when I walk into a church with many people attending, I become excited, assuming that God is doing a great work in their midst. That may be the case with most large congregations who proclaim Jesus as Lord. It certainly seems to have been the case for the ones we have visited on our journey through the Southeast. When Linda and I walked through the doors of Beechwood Church in downtown Greenville, South Carolina, that Sunday, however, we saw something entirely different.

On Sundays, the auditorium of Greenville Senior High School turns into a church sanctuary. The school stage becomes a church stage. The windows, typical of the style of 1938 with their stately, tall arches, lack only the stained glass. The wooden, theater-type seats give a hint that money is most likely spent on the necessities first.

On this particular Sunday, only about fifty-five of the four hundred seats in the auditorium were filled. "If everyone were present, we would have about eighty-five here," explained Lead Pastor Doug, raised on the mission field of Ivory Coast, West Africa.

"The church is a people, not a steeple." I was reminded once again of John Nyhan's proclamation to his congregation in Long Island, New York, many years earlier. That statement has remained with me to this day. As I mature in my walk with Christ, it is taking on even deeper meaning. Today, it came to life for me.

While Linda and I entered cautiously into the sanctuary, we took our customary seats to the rear of the church. Since it didn't look like many people would be attending that day, we went up a little further than normal, yet still behind the last row of attendees. While sitting and surveying the scene, I spotted the teaching pastor, Corey, whom I have known for about ten years in a different capacity. In his Monday through Friday job, Corey works as an admissions counselor at North Greenville University in northern Greenville County. My work in neighboring Anderson County occasionally takes me to NGU, my favorite college in the state of South Carolina. Corey and I cross paths professionally about twice a year.

He was locked into his game-day preparations, so we planned to approach him later. A woman, also named Linda, approached us and welcomed us to Beechwood. Friendly, but reserved, she seemed like a person who would be a close friend if you got to know her. After a few more people welcomed us, a man that I recognized came walking toward me. I knew him for sure, I thought. But how did I know him? The context had changed. My bearings were off.

"Nice to see you, Mr. Kupec," he cheerfully greeted me. My heart sank. I hate not knowing someone's name when they know mine. In my world, stating someone's name is a sign of respect. It is an indication that I value the other person. I could tell you everything about this man. He was a real gentleman. Always went out of his way to greet me at the school where I work and where his seventeen-year-old son now attends. But our days go back further than that. This man had known hardship. He had known pain. His wife had left him years earlier, alone to raise his kids. His oldest son struggled through school. Our many parent-student-teacher meetings seemed to have no effect. The young man eventually dropped out of school, despite our attempts to keep him on board. When his son left school, the man thanked me for my attempts to help his son. He meant it. He grieved it. I could see it in his eyes.

A few years later, when we crossed paths again at a meeting in school for his younger son, he cheerfully told me that "Pete" was doing great. He had a good job at Toyota, was married, and had two kids. He was so happy to report this to me. It was like he was happy for me that my efforts were not in vain. He was also very proud of his son.

He said hello to my wife, and while they were talking, I had an epiphany. It finally came to me—Mr. Smith! Delivered from my anguish, I said his name again to myself. Mr. Smith. Then, like a young boy on Christmas ready to open his presents, I barged into their conversation, joyfully telling my wife, "Mr. Smith and I go way back together." I was so happy to remember his name. I said his name again. He deserved to have his name remembered. He deserved to have his name honored. He had given his family everything he had. He did the best that he could with what he had. He had "fought the good fight"; he had run the race; he had "kept the faith" (2 Tim. 4:7).

Walking with God is not meant to be easy. When the apostle Paul and Barnabas were exhorting the new Christians at Lystra, Iconium, and Antioch to remain true to the faith, they stated a powerful truth: "'Through many tribulations we must enter the kingdom of God" (Acts 14:22). Walking with God is the most exciting, fulfilling, and satisfying lifestyle to which a person could ever attain. It comes with incredible revelations, unparalleled purpose, and a true understanding of love. It also spurs failure, repentance, deeper self-awareness, sorrow, tears, testing, redemption, growth, and exhilarating joy. Above all, it provides the ability to see and experience things you could never have dreamed. I truly believe that hardship is the only way God can kill the flesh that rises up against Him, the same flesh that promises many victories but delivers very few.

Mr. Smith was asked to pray before we were to partake of communion. His voice cracked. He filled up. He thanked God for His mercy. He thanked Him for His grace. He held back the tears. These were not the prayers learned from some catechism. They were not words of theory. They were the cries of a heart that had been molded by "a consuming fire" (Heb. 12:29). They were the fruit of a man who experienced despair but did not lose faith in the One Who has the power to redeem everything. I took in the communion bread and wine, looking at Mr. Smith in one direction and his oldest son in another.

Corey's sermon drew from the Book of Daniel. I believe every Christian should become acquainted with Daniel's life. He is the perfect example of a godly man who remains true to his God in spite of all the ungodly influences and temptations of a secular society. Daniel remained steadfast. He bowed to no man nor succumbed to any ideology that raised itself against the Word of God. Daniel was used of God mightily. When the Babylonian leader King Nebuchadnezzar demanded from his advisors the interpretation of his dream, Daniel stepped forward and revealed God's future plans for not just Nebuchadnezzar, but for the world powers. Despite their seemingly invincible dominion, God would eventually destroy the world's superpowers—first,

Babylon, then Persia, Greece, and finally, the Roman Empire. No kingdom would last that extolled itself above the God Who created them (Psalm 75:7).

Corey exhorted us to get excited over this God, over this Kingdom that will have no end (Luke 1:33). Perhaps that is what true *koinonia* is. What true fellowship is. To push us forward in our pursuit of God, in the pursuit of things that matter to Him, and to encourage others to do the same.

The writer of Hebrews said it in a different way:

> Therefore, brethren, since we have confidence to enter the holy place by the blood of Jesus, by a new and living way which He inaugurated for us through the veil, that is, His flesh, and since *we have* a great priest over the house of God, let us draw near with a sincere heart in full assurance of faith, having our hearts sprinkled *clean* from an evil conscience and our bodies washed with pure water. Let us hold fast the confession of our hope without wavering, for He who promised is faithful; and let us consider how to stimulate one another to love and good deeds, not forsaking our own assembling together, as is the habit of some, but encouraging *one another*; and all the more as you see the day drawing near" (Heb. 10:19-25).

Jesus said that if "two or three have gathered together in [His] name, [He is] there in their midst" (Matt. 18:20). Beechwood Church does not have many members. It does not own a building to call its own. You may never hear of them again outside of this book. But Beechwood Church is rich in the eyes of God. They have Mr. Smith. They have his oldest son with his wife and their two kids. They have Pastor Doug, Pastor Corey, and other leaders who have worked for the Kingdom of God in this country and in others. They walk with God. They walk together, encouraging and exhorting each other as they go. They happen to congregate every Sunday at an historic high school in downtown Greenville. They have no steeple, but make no mistake about it, they are a people. Don't judge a book by its cover. If you do in the case of Beechwood Church, you may miss the God Who is among them.

You could also miss what God is doing on the beaches of South Carolina. Something truly different is happening there.

THE OCEAN

THE ISLE OF PALMS, SOUTH CAROLINA

Different. The word usually has a negative connotation. "That kid is a little different," we sometimes say. "It was . . . different," we hesitatingly comment when we really don't want to say it was bad.

The word *different* doesn't necessarily have to be negative, however. *Webster's Dictionary* defines the word *different* as "not the same as another or each other; unlike in nature, form, or quality."[26]

I first noticed something *different* when my family and I visited Hilton Head Island, South Carolina, back in 2005 for our first family vacation in the Palmetto State.

Thirteen years later was the second time I noticed something "different." Linda and I left Greenville at 5:15 a.m. with the stars shining brightly in the clear sky above. One particular planet seemed to be leading us through the darkness as we sojourned southeast on Interstate 385. Originally, the plan was to attend the 8:30 a.m. service at Seacoast Church in Mount Pleasant, South Carolina, and then spend a few hours on the beach of the Isle of Palms, a ten-minute drive away. The GPS told us this would not be a good idea, however, if we didn't want to be late for the start of the service.

---

26   *Merriam-Webster,* *s.v.* "different," https://www.merriam-webster.com/dictionary/different (accessed December 16, 2018).

Like a coach who makes adjustments at halftime, we altered our plans and headed directly to the Atlantic Ocean. The new plan was to walk along the beach on the Isle of Palms for an hour, take part in Seacoast's 10:00 a.m. service in Mount Pleasant, and then head back to the sand before returning to the Upstate of South Carolina.

I have heard people speak glowingly about the Isle of Palms. Now I could see why. The place was different—in a very good way. Perhaps swayed by the blue skies and brilliant sunshine after two weeks of snow (yes, snow) and rain in the Upstate, Ocean Boulevard seemed especially clean and bright. It seemed new. The buildings had not seen better days like many we have seen in our travels. Ocean Boulevard seemed to serve as the town's Main Street. With non-franchise hotels on the left, food places on the right, and small palm trees in between, we parked on the street with very few cars to compete with for parking spots.

We walked down an alley between two hotels and stopped halfway. There it was. That different sound. We heard it like a friend's voice we could never forget. We had heard that sound many times before on the beaches of Long Island, New York. Linda asked me to stop and listen. Ten seconds and two smiles later, we saw it. The Big Expanse—the Atlantic Ocean. Linda's smile and look of contentment spoke a thousand words.

Glad we had brought sweatshirts with us, we were awed by the beauty of the moment, only enhanced by the cold, winter morning. While the house for 6.3 million dollars further along down the beach was impressive, it paled in comparison to the amount of real estate our Father owns. What price could be placed on this incredible body of water? Or all the beautiful beaches that our eyes could take in as we scanned from left to right? The impressive, massive home suddenly seemed small and insignificant. Only the ringing of Linda's watch could take us away from such natural beauty. The main reason for our visiting the Isle of Palms was awaiting us.

Sea Coast Church, like its neighboring businesses and residential areas, was different. When we headed down Long Point Road and turned left into the church parking lot, it was the first time we saw the church. With most churches we have visited throughout the Southeast, we typically could see the church from a distance and approach it with both excitement and apprehension. Not so at Seacoast. Like the malls we had passed earlier, the property of the church was hidden behind trees and hedges that line its property. Everything blended in. The palm trees, Spanish moss, and other trees dominated the landscape. The stores sat behind them as if they were peeking out and wondering if visitors planned to come in. I am still not sure how businesses—and churches for that matter—secure any drive by patronage. I guess it is what makes the area so "different"—and, in my opinion, "better."

Even the parking lot at Seacoast was unusual. Trees were everywhere. Linda said she felt like we had ventured into a park. Even the church building itself was unique. No bricks, no steeples like older, more traditional church buildings. No large, white, rectangular, warehouse-type look like many of the newer and larger congregations. Like its surrounding neighborhood, it fit in. Large property? For sure! Large building? Absolutely. It seemed like you would cover a large distance if you planned to walk its perimeter. Classy, comfortable, picturesque. The mature trees that adorned it seemed to demand that you not get preoccupied with its presence but that you remember that it's part of the community.

That same attitude could be heard in the words of Seacoast's pastor, Josh Surratt. The low-key, humble, self-assured leader welcomed all attendees to the church. There were a lot to welcome. No seats in the twelve-hundred-seat sanctuary seemed to be empty, including the ones in the balcony on the second floor. Even the sanctuary seemed to be different. While the building had two stories, the side walls were not massive. The ceiling was surprisingly low, making a large crowd of twelve hundred seem like an intimate group of two hundred. The white, circular columns on the sides of the sanctuary connected the two floors. The television cameras that broadcasted the sermon to Seacoast's twelve affiliate campuses stood inconspicuously to the rear of the sanctuary, out of view to most persons participating in the service. Large windows to the right and left of the stage area gave just enough room for two large, wooden crosses to fit in nicely. The message, given by a young husband and wife team, maintained the calm atmosphere that the church exuded. While the message was given with a cool and calm delivery, the content was a heavy one—grief.

While the topic was not new for us, the way the church concluded its service was. Many evangelical churches have some time of ministry following sermons. It could be that leaders in the church are available in the front of the church to pray for anyone in need. It might be that with heads bowed and eyes closed, the minister prays for those who indicate by raised hands that they are in need of salvation or prayer. Seacoast was, well, different.

First, Pastor Josh told the audience that leaders were available in the back of the church for anyone who needed prayer. Then they did what we have not seen in our six months of attending services throughout the South. If anyone had a petition (prayer request), they could come up to the cross in the front of the sanctuary and tack their written petitions to the cross. All things are better when we take them to the cross of Jesus—His mercy, His finished work, His hand of victory. Then the pastor, explaining to the congregation that God did things through fire (i.e. Moses and the burning bush), invited his congregants to light a candle as a sign that God would intercede in the life of the person for whom they were praying. Finally, we noticed congregants helping themselves to the bread and wine of communion that were left near the rear of the church for anyone to partake.

Seacoast was different in many ways. One thing about them was not unusual, however. They carried the banner of Jesus that has been carried for two millennia. They worshipped the God Who created and redeemed them. They were committed to reaching as many lost souls as possible by being a Greek to the Greek, a Jew to the Jew, or in their case, a Mount Pleasant resident to a Mount Pleasant resident.

While it was time for Linda and me to say goodbye to this "different" church, we needed to get ready to say goodbye to our other "different" for the day, the one we rarely get to see because of our distance from it—the ocean.

Jones Beach on Long Island, New York, much further up the coast of this same ocean, was where Linda and I first spent time together back in 1992. We had both attended the National Day of Prayer in Hempstead. Linda's ride to the event asked if I would be willing to take her home since he had to return to work afterward. Since we both were off work for the day, I asked if she would mind taking a ride to the beach on that chilly May morning before I dropped her off. How could she resist?

Twenty-six years later, our union with Christ is truthfully the only reason that we are together today. With two strong wills and sometimes "quirky" demeanors, we have pushed God's grace to the limit way too many times. But His mercies are new every morning (Lam. 3:23). His cleansing is available with each confessed sin. His grace is our glue. His mercy is our hope. His "love never fails" (1 Cor. 13:8). Like the beautiful beach towns that we had visited, we, too, are "different." Fortunately, we have a God Who is unchanging (Num. 23:19), a God Who "*is* the same yesterday and today and forever" (Heb. 13:8).

We would experience that unchanging God again the next week as a large business expressed its Christmas spirit to us in an unlikely way.

THE HOLY CITY

CHARLESTON, SOUTH CAROLINA

I am not sure why they did it. Whether it is good for business or could actually have a negative impact on their profit margin, only God knows. But one thing I *do* know, I was glad to see their sign. There it was on the large AVX building in neon lights for all travelers on Interstate 385 to see: MERRY CHRISTMAS. Thank you, AVX. In a society that seems to be trying with all its might to relegate Christianity, and especially the biblical Jesus, to a non-influential role, it was a breath of fresh air to see a simple, yet powerful, sentiment expressed to all.

The message of salvation by grace in faith in Jesus' atoning and finished work on the cross alone is also expressed to all. It was done for all (John 3:16). It is not a message that was contrived by religious people two thousand years ago and perpetuated by like-minded people throughout the centuries that followed. The Bible says that Jesus came to fulfill the Law and the prophets (Matt. 5:17). His perfect life without sin qualified Him as the perfect, unblemished sacrifice (1 Peter 1:19). John the Baptist realized this truth when he saw of Jesus: "Behold, the Lamb of God who takes away the sin of the world!" (John 1:29).

Some scholars believe there are more than three hundred prophecies about Jesus in the Old Testament. These prophecies are specific enough that the mathematical probability of Jesus fulfilling even a handful of them, let alone all of them, is staggeringly improbable—if not impossible.[27] Here are just a few of them:

1. **The prophet Isaiah predicted this about 700 B.C.:** "Therefore the Lord Himself will give you a sign: Behold, a virgin will be with child and bear a son, and she will call His name Immanuel" (Isa. 7:14).

2. **The prophet Isaiah predicted this as well**: "For a child will be born to us, a son will be given to us; And the government will rest on His shoulders; And his name will be called Wonderful Counselor, Mighty God, Eternal **Father, Prince of Peace" (Isa.** 9:6).

3. **The prophet Micah predicted this between 750 BC and 686 B.C.:** "'But as for you, Bethlehem Ephrathah, *Too* little to be among the clans of Judah, From you One will go forth for Me one to be ruler in Israel. His goings forth are from of long ago" (Micah 5:2).

4. **The prophet Isaiah predicted this about 700 B.C.:** "Then the eyes of the blind will be opened And the ears of the deaf will be unstopped. Then the lame will leap like a deer, And the tongue of the mute will shout for joy. For waters will break forth in the wilderness And streams in the Arabah (desert)" (Isa. 35:5-6).

5. **The prophet Isaiah predicted this about 700 B.C.:** "The Spirit of the Lord GOD is upon me, Because the Lord has anointed me To bring good news to the afflicted; He has sent me to bind up the brokenhearted, To proclaim liberty to captives And freedom to prisoners" (Isa. 61:1).

---

27 Jesus Film Project, "55 Old Testament Prophecies About Jesus," JesusFilm.org, https://www. jesusfilm.org/blog-and-stories/old-testament-prophecies.html (accessed December 23, 2018).

6. **The prophet Daniel predicted this about 550 B.C.:** "I kept looking in the night visions, And behold, with the clouds of heaven One like a Son of Man was coming, And He came up to the Ancient of Days and was presented before Him. 'And to Him was given dominion, Glory and a kingdom, that all the peoples, nations and *men of every* language Might serve Him. His dominion is an everlasting dominion Which will not pass away; And His kingdom is one Which will not be destroyed" (Dan. 7:13-14).

7. **Zechariah prophesied this in about 540 B.C.:** "Rejoice greatly, O daughter of Zion! Shout *in triumph*, O daughter of Jerusalem! Behold, your king is coming to you; He is just and endowed with salvation, Humble, and mounted on a donkey, Even on a colt, the foal of a donkey" (Zech. 9:9).

8. **King David uttered this word about one thousand years before Jesus:** "My God, my God, why have You forsaken me?" (Psalm 22:1).

9. **The prophet Isaiah predicted this about 700 B.C.:** "He was oppressed and He was afflicted, Yet He did not open His mouth; Like a lamb that is led to slaughter, And like a sheep that is silent before its shearers, So He did not open His mouth. By oppression and judgment He was taken away; And as for His generation, who considered That He was cut off out of the land of the living For the transgression of my people, to whom the stroke *was due?*" (Isa. 53:7-8).

Pastor Kevin Giordano first heard biblical truth when he was a sophomore in high school in Myrtle Beach, South Carolina. Invited by a friend to a youth group meeting, a minister sat down with him and, using a napkin as a visual aid, shared how his sin (and yours and mine) separated him from God and how Jesus was the only way to bridge the gap. Three years later, as a freshman at the College of Charleston, Pastor Kevin accepted Jesus as his Lord and Savior. He had thought about the diagram on the napkin many times before his conversion. A marriage and four children later (and the death of a son), Pastor Kevin leads Charleston Baptist Church in this historic and charming city. It is also nicknamed the "Holy City. [This] designation stems from the numerous church steeples dotting its downtown skyline, as well as being one of the only cities in the original 13 colonies to welcome members of the French Huguenot Church."[28]

On this Sunday, two days before Christmas, Pastor Kevin spoke of the very first Christmas song recorded in the Gospel of Luke. Long before "Silent Night," "Hark the Herald Angels Sing," and "What Child is This," Mary, the chosen vessel through whom God would enter humanity, sang the following verse: "My soul exalts the Lord, and my spirit has rejoiced in God my Savior" (Luke 1:46). Mary, the mother of Jesus of Nazareth, is a great example for us today of how to hear the Word of God and respond to it with humility and reverence. That same humility also told Mary she was in need of a Savior. He would not only save her but also everyone else who would put their hope in "the Lamb of God who takes away the sin of the world (John 1:29).

Using the rest of Mary's song, Pastor Kevin spoke of God's grace, His faithfulness, and His holiness. Jesus is "the Alpha and the Omega," the first and the last, the beginning and the end" (Rev. 22:13). He is the King of kings and the Lord of lords (Revelation 19:16). He is salvation (1 John 5:12). Yet, despite His majesty and sovereignty, His heart is that none would perish (2 Peter 3:9). As the Good Shepherd, He leaves the ninety-nine sheep for the lost one (Matt. 18:12). He laments over an obstinate people that He would have gathered "as a hen *gathers* her brood under her wings" (Luke 13:34).

Leaving Charleston Baptist Church humming, "Oh, come let us adore Him," Linda and I headed down the Savannah Highway and over the Ashley River to get to our next destination, The Citadel, the military academy of South Carolina, before we would depart for home.

---

28 "SC City Nicknames Guide," SCIWAY.net, https://www.sciway.net/ccr/sc-city-nicknames.html (accessed December 23, 2018).

The Citadel is a landmark in Charleston and South Carolina that is noted for its educational reputation as well as its rich history. Founded in 1842, The Citadel has an undergraduate student body of about 2,300 students who make up the South Carolina Corps of Cadets. . . . The Citadel is best known nationally for its Corps of Cadets, which draws students from about 45 states and a dozen countries. The men and women in the Corps live and study under a classical military system that makes leadership and character development an essential part of the educational experience.[29]

According to their website, "30% of the graduating cadets commission into military service."[30] Even though the campus is historic—making us feel like we had gone back in time—the core values of The Citadel are what makes it shine so brightly in a self-centered society like we live in today. Their three core values are honor, duty, and respect.[31] Even these core values take us back in time when the prevailing culture extolled these characteristics and exhorted our young people to embody them. They were taught in church, in school, and in the home.

"Honor includes integrity; 'doing the right thing when no one is watching' . . . exercising the moral courage to 'do the right thing when everyone is watching.'" "Duty is . . . a call to serve others before self." It is why soldiers headed to Europe and Asia to fulfill their obligation to their country without thinking of themselves. "Respect means to treat other people with dignity and worth – the way you want others to treat you."[32] Respect doesn't demand certain behaviors from others before it will venture out on its own. It is concerned with how the person in the mirror is treating others, not on how he or she is being treated. I admire people

---

29 "Welcome to the Citadel!," Citadel.edu, http://www.citadel.edu/root/info (accessed December 23, 2018).
30 "At a Glance," Citadel.edu, http://www.citadel.edu/root/at-a-glance (accessed December 23, 2018).
31 "Core Values," Citadel.edu, http://www.citadel.edu/root/core-values (accessed December 23, 2018).
32 Ibid.

who possess these three qualities—honor, duty, and respect. I respect a college that makes them its foundation.

Leaving Charleston was not easy. The houses made us feel like we had journeyed back to the eighteenth, nineteenth, and twentieth centuries. The military college stands apart from the crowd. The uplifting message by Pastor Kevin reminded us that the Kingdom of God will have no end (Luke 1:33). Driving back on Interstate 385, I looked for the "Merry Christmas" sign on the AVX building, this time on my left as we headed northwest to Greenville. It was around 5:00 p.m. now. Despite the shortened days of winter, the sky was not dark yet. The greeting was not lit up in its neon best at the moment. My eyes had to squint a little more intensely to see it, but it was still there. The message was still clear for anyone who wanted to see it.

God's message is still clear to anyone with a desire to see it. In his letter to the Colossian church, Paul stated, "For it was the *Father's* good pleasure for all the fullness to dwell in Him, and through Him to reconcile all things to Himself, having made peace through the blood of His cross; through Him, *I say*, whether things on earth or things in heaven" (Col. 1:19). We are born to live. Jesus was born to die. Our sin separates us from God (Rom. 3:23). Jesus' sacrifice created a path back to Him (John 3:16). The ball is in our court. Is there room for Him in the inn of your life? If so, I want to join with my friends at AVX and wish you a Merry Christmas! If not, there is one more gift to be opened this Christmas season. It is the gift of eternal life through Jesus Christ. Only you can open it.

OUT WITH THE OLD

FORT MILL, SOUTH CAROLINA

This would be our last Sunday journey for the year 2018. We had seen a lot over the past six months traveling throughout the Southeast. I was more encouraged about the Body of Christ than I have been in my quarter of a century as a follower of Jesus. Granted, we were only seeing a bird's eye view of life in each church. But wherever we went, Jesus was being proclaimed. Whether in our western-most venture to Alabama or our eastern-most visit to Charleston, South Carolina, the Gospel message continues unabated. It is guarded by men who are called by God to steward that message of salvation. The services came in many shapes and sizes, but one thing was consistent: Jesus is the Head of His church, the Body of Christ.

Why the return to MorningStar Church in Fort Mill as 2019 approached? Since MorningStar emphasizes the prophetic (1 Cor. 14:3), we were hoping to get a sense of what 2019 might hold for us as we sought to glorify God and walk in the plan that He had for us. The day before we left seemed to fit into this desire to be led by God's Spirit. Linda and I spent a good part of Saturday afternoon relaxing by Greenville's Downtown Airport. On this unusually warm and sunny December afternoon, we watched as aspiring pilots practiced takeoffs and landings on their Cessnas and Pipers.

On our way home, we began interceding (praying) for others. At a red light, something unusual happened. As we were praying, I received from God a picture of a man with an angry fist clenched toward Heaven. At times, he began laughing. The meaning of the vision was clear to me. Humankind is arrogantly shaking its fists at God, mockingly telling Him that they know more than He does. Telling Him that they do not need Him. Telling Him that He doesn't even exist or, if He did, that He was distant and impotent. They would not humble themselves before Him. They prefer a religion on its own terms, devoid of any real power, devoid of any correction or intrusion.

Remarkably, Linda confirmed that word, saying that two days earlier, she had pictured a human Tower of Babel-like structure with human fists raised to Heaven in defiance. As the traffic light remained red, Linda and I began asking the Lord to forgive us (humankind) for our arrogance and folly. At that very moment, the driver in the car before us turned on her radio at a very unusually high volume. She then began to dance almost wildly in her idling car, making the car seem like it could tip over at any moment. We kept praying, realizing that we have an enemy who does not want us entering his turf. Before the light turned green, the driver took a right, sputtering off in a careless way, the car seemingly undecided about whether it wanted to go or stop. Linda and I felt humbled that God would include us in His work here on Earth. "For our struggle is not against flesh and blood, but against the rulers, against the powers, against the world forces of this darkness, against the spiritual *forces* of wickedness in the heavenly *places*" (Eph. 6:12).

I have grown to admire Rick Joyner, the President of MorningStar Ministries. I love listening to intelligent, Spirit-filled leaders who have experienced the depth of life's struggles, allowing their dark times only to lead them further into the heart of God. Like metal in the fire, they come out stronger, more tender, more steadfast in their commitment to Jesus and the Great Commission. Joyner encourages believers to operate in the prophetic. He wants them to hear from God. He seems willing to take risks when others might take a more conventional path. His goal appears to be that the truth of Ephesians 2:10 be fulfilled in each follower of Jesus: "For we are his workmanship, created in Christ Jesus for good works, which God prepared beforehand so that we would walk in them."

MorningStar was in the middle of their three-day "Vision Conference" when we arrived on the second-to-last day of 2018. Their two Sunday services were part of this conference. We arrived for the 9:00 a.m. service early and excited about what lay ahead. As the worship team prepared for the service, I noticed a thin man my age with a kind of derby hat on his head and scarf around his neck. I am embarrassed to admit it, but I thought to myself, "A music star wannabe." When the worship team began the service, I noticed that the "wannabe" was not on stage. In fact, he was nowhere to be seen. With that distraction gone, I put my focus where it should have been in the first place. Always longsuffering, God was touching my heart through the worship time. When the lead singer sang, "You picked up all my pieces, put me back together, You are the Defender of my heart,"[33] I filled up. I became very aware of God's holiness. His goodness. His grace. Suddenly, I was not the issue. He was. That is the way I want it to be. I am tired of me. I am tired of being self-conscious, afraid of what others might be thinking of me. The Word of God tells us, "The fear of man brings a snare, But he who trusts in the LORD will be exalted" (Prov. 29:25). The healthy fear of God leads to wholeness, peace, a sound mind, good decisions, order. It leads us to a place where we can genuinely love others. He is the Potter; we are the clay (Rom. 9:21). We do very well when we let the Potter mold us, however that molding might take place.

When the time of worshipping God ended, David Herr, a retired pastor from Utah, spoke to the audience about MorningStar's heritage community. He spoke of the power of community. He quoted from the Book of Hebrews of the importance "to stimulate one another to love and good deeds" (Heb.

---

33   Rita Spring, "Defender," *Battles*, Gateway Publishing, 2017.

10:24). As part of its many-faceted ministry, MorningStar manages apartments and condominiums for eighty-plus residents on site. He said the emphasis on this stage of a person's life should be "refirement," not retirement. Seniors can get "refired" as they walk in God's plan with other like-minded brothers and sisters in Christ.

As Dave was finishing his talk, I noticed something odd going on behind him. The "wannabe" I noticed earlier was doing something with the drum set on the stage behind Dave. When he completed his tinkering, he waited patiently for Dave to finish. As soon as Dave exited, "Wannabe" came forward and took the microphone! He shocked me with his first utterance. Before he would give today's message, he said, he had a solo on the drums to perform for us. As I have been humbled many times in the past, I would become humbled once again. Daniel Donnolly is no "wannabe." His stage name is "Zoro." He is known as "The Minister of Groove." He has performed with the likes of the Temptations, Frankie Valli, Lenny Kravitz, Bobby Brown, and Phillip Bailey— to name a few. Today, he is a motivational speaker, author, life coach, and drum instructor.

Zoro's life story was almost difficult for me to believe. His single mother raised him and his six siblings in poverty. They bounced around from apartment to apartment and from town to town. Never did Zoro depart from the simple, childlike faith in Christ that his mother had instilled in him as a child. With no father or any male role models in his life, he learned to forge on, to persevere, to work hard. Zoro's final admonishment was his best: "Bury your disappointments, keep your childlike faith, and work hard . . . God has dreams for this season of life. What is your vision for now?" He then ended with the following quote: "Live each day of your life like it will be your last. Someday, it will."

Humbled by a great message from a man I had incorrectly judged, Linda and I looked for Dave Herr when the service ended. Even though he had said he would give tours of the apartments and condominiums at 1:30 p.m., I was hoping he would show us one of the rooms if he had extra time. The kind, yet authoritative, gentleman complied, taking time out of his schedule to show us three condominiums. Linda and I wondered if we would end up here someday. It definitely looked like a great opportunity for an elderly person to get involved in a vibrant, growing community focused on the purposes of God. We left MorningStar asking God to lead us to another good place—this time for lunch.

The part of Fort Mill where the church resides looked like it had grown exponentially over the recent years. New housing developments and places of business dominated the landscape. We landed at one of our favorite places to eat—IHOP. More importantly, we hoped for an opportunity to share Jesus with someone as we entered.

That opportunity turned out to be our waitress, Samika or "Sam." It was obvious that she was intelligent, confident, and well-organized. After we ate, I told her just that. She smiled and thanked me profusely. She told us that she was a student at Johnson and Wales University in Charlotte, majoring in Hospitality Management and Event Planning. I further told Sam that she would be very successful someday. I told her that I have learned that the greatest success anyone can have is to be in Christ. Linda encouraged her to "seek first the kingdom of God" and that all things she would need in life would be given to her as she does that (Matt. 6:33). We said goodbye to Samika and Fort Mill, wondering what place the powerful and impactful MorningStar Ministries would have in our lives in the future.

We didn't get a specific word for the upcoming year like we had hoped. Instead, we came away with a strong sensing of what God was speaking to us about our lives and how we were walking with Him. I had heard Rick Joyner say that the Holy Spirit is the Helper, not the Doer (John 14:26). He said it again on that final Sunday in 2018. I realized I have a bigger part to play in my walk with God, to actively yield to Him in all things and at all times.

The goal is less what can we do for Him, but with Him. Or better yet, what He does through us. When we live by beholding the One Who is above all rule and authority and dominion, when we live our lives focused on the One Who upholds the universe with the word of His power, we, too, will rise above the usual to live in the realm of the supernatural. Hopefully in 2019, the supernatural would be natural.

Our final quest for the supernatural would be challenged by something very much in the natural the following week.

CAR TROUBLE

DOWNTOWN GREENVILLE, SOUTH CAROLINA

Uh oh. I am not mechanically inclined, but I do know one thing. When the orange line on the dashboard is standing on the "H" (overheating) and not in between the "C" and the "H," something is wrong. Very wrong! Normally, I kind of go into denial and push forward, somehow hoping that everything will turn out all right in the end. However, with a two-and-a-half-hour ride through the mountains of Upstate South Carolina, Western North Carolina, and Eastern Tennessee ahead of us, even I knew it was time to raise the white flag. Hesitantly, I told Linda we had to head back home. The twenty-minute return ride was a nail-biter for me. *Am I damaging the car by continuing to drive it?* I wondered. *Should I stop now and call a tow truck to get us? Is this the end of our journeying?* The questions raced through my mind.

Linda did not seem happy about the turn of events. In fact, she seemed very disappointed. When she gets disappointed, her sentences become shorter, her cadence sharper. "No." "Whatever." "Oh, well." The normally many-syllabled words are reduced to short fragments. The look on her face betrays the words that are being spoken. We pulled up the driveway and stopped the car. It seemed like we could not have gone an inch further. Smoke began to emerge from the hood. I got out and heard an ungodly clicking sound in the front. We went into the house, not saying a word. And not sure what to do.

Linda went out on the deck to get a glimpse of the rising sun as it spread its orange splendor behind the leafless trees. She asked me to come outside and join her. She seemed to come to life, despite the disappointment of the morning. She came up with the idea of attending Grace Church down the road from us, the one whose Sunday night service we had attended when the snow storm had shut down all the area churches' Sunday morning services. Not wanting to duplicate a trip, I recommended we visit Grace's downtown Greenville campus instead. Linda liked the idea. It was settled. Taking Linda's car and not the regular minivan, we headed for downtown Greenville, the former stomping ground of "Shoeless" Joe Jackson, associated with the famous 1919 World Series baseball scandal.

Downtown Grace has a stately and prominent-looking building. It looked like many of the First Baptist churches we had seen throughout the Southeast. Steep, outdoor steps rose as if to Heaven. Large, white columns in front claimed an authority derived from the Creator Himself. It boasted high, thick, and heavy wooden doors fit for a king and his court. The church complex took up an entire city block. Inside, there was a high ceiling with crown molding around the perimeter. Lights hanging from white chains looked like crowns turned upside down. Three sections of cherry walnut pews all sloped downward toward the stage in front. Five vertical, stained glass windows were on each of the side walls. It had that "First Baptist" look for good reason. Grace Church had taken over the building that First Baptist of Greenville had once called home. From what we were told, when First Baptist left for their new sanctuary a short distance away, they gave the old building to Grace. Interestingly, Grace's main campus on Pelham Road was also given to them by a church that had vacated the property.

The only thing that did not seem historic about Grace were the people who filled the pews that Sunday morning. In fact, the youthfulness of the church was noticeable. Linda and I stood out like sore thumbs. It was the most twenty-to-forty-year-old crowd we had seen in our six months on the road. Nonetheless, it was refreshing to see young people engaged in worshipping God, engaged in the message given by Scofield Foster, normally the Students' Director at Grace's Pelham campus.

The down-to-earth speaker gave such a great message that the concerns for our minivan slipped from my mind like a fog disappears from the ground. Using his smartphone as his teaching tool, he shared how even something good can lead to an unhealthy dependence on it if we let it. The cell phone is a neutral object. It can be used for good—obtaining needed information, communicating with others, etc. It can also become an idol—the owner of the phone living as if he or she cannot go on without it. Scofield has known people who had planned to attend a church retreat but canceled due to the fact that the participants' cell phones would have to be turned off during the time away. We have a tendency to do this with many things in our lives, not just with cell phones.

We tend to make idols out of the things we depend on too deeply. We begin to form our identity around the object or person rather than on our Creator. Any time we rely on anything other than God to determine our significance, satisfaction, and security, we are setting ourselves up for trouble—maybe not now, but certainly down the road. Jeremiah, the prophet, stated:

> "Has a nation changed gods When they were not gods? But My people have changed their glory For that which does not profit. "Be appalled, O heavens, at this, And shudder, be very desolate," declares the LORD. "For My people have committed two evils: They have forsaken Me, The fountain of living waters, To hew for themselves cisterns, Broken cisterns That can hold no water (Jer. 2:11-13).

The cistern was the object to hold water in ancient days. The people of God in those times were trying to draw water from cracked cisterns. The problem was not that the Israelites were thirsty. The issue was how they were trying to satisfy that thirst. The water from cracked cisterns would be muddy and unhealthy. The imagery is appropriate for us today. The cracked cisterns we seek to draw from are people's affirmation and approval. It is not wrong to seek approval; we just need to seek it from the One Who satisfies, the Fountain of Living Water (John 7:37).

Another way we attempt to draw water from cracked cisterns is to substitute entertainment for purpose. Are we captivated by God's mission (Matt. 28:16-20) or by the latest episodes on Netflix? Do we have a mission for our own lives? For that of our family? Does it align with God's purposes? Or are we living day to day, holiday to holiday, seeking to quiet that still, small voice that says something is missing, that something is incomplete?

A third way that we can attempt to draw water from cracked cisterns is by substituting spiritual activities in place of Christ. This is subtler, less obvious to the naked eye. We can go through the motions, even fruitful ones, but neglect our relationship with Jesus—not spending time with Him or in His Word. Just as a branch receives its life from the vine, so Christians are to receive their life from Jesus. Our spiritual activities cannot replace our time with Christ. When they do, they can become idols. When they supplement our time of intimacy with Him, they become life-enhancing moments, taking their rightful place in our lives and producing fruit that will benefit ourselves and others.

Not drawing water from cracked cisterns requires self-awareness and honesty. What are our tendencies? Are we willing to confront them and turn away from them? Jesus' encounter with a Samaritan woman who was looking to draw water from a well gives us revelation on how we can adjust our lives. While she was seeking earthly water, Jesus offered her something far greater. He said to her, "Everyone who drinks of this water will thirst again; but whoever drinks of the water that I will give him shall never thirst; but the water that I will give him will become in him a well of water springing up to eternal life" (John 4:13-14).

Imagine what life would be like if we were free of an unhealthy need of people's approval and, instead, became satisfied in the approval of the Lord. God created us. He died to secure for us a sense of belonging, a sense of significance. He can satisfy our souls in a way that no other can. Many times, we don't realize we are trusting in cracked cisterns for our identity and purpose. Rarely, if ever, will we become aware of them when we are isolated from others. We often become aware of our cracked cisterns when we interact with others. We can see it in the way we react, in the way we are triggered, in the way we lose our peace so quickly. These are the times, however, that we can see that something is wrong, we can seek the freedom we so desperately need, and we can finally look to our Savior, Who is waiting patiently to affirm us and set us free. We can lay those cracked cisterns aside and look to the One Who was meant to provide us our identity and our purpose.

We can agree with Helen Lemmel, who penned the following lyrics to her 1922 hymn: "Turn your eyes upon Jesus / Look full in His wonderful face / And the things of earth will grow strangely dim / In the light of His glory and grace."[34]

When the service ended, we walked through the stately doors, past the high, white, vertical columns and down the steep steps to the streets of Greenville. Our minds were on heavenly things, grateful that car troubles had changed our plans and brought us to the message that we needed to hear that day—a message that we need to be reminded of daily. Suddenly, the deadlines of Monday seemed far off in the distance. The need for man's approval seemed almost silly. "Blessed *be* the God and Father of our Lord Jesus Christ, who has blessed us with every spiritual blessing in the heavenly *places* in Christ" (Eph. 1:3).

Those blessings would continue the next week as we encountered something we had never seen our entire lives.

---

34   Helen Lemmel, "Turn Your Eyes Upon Jesus," Public Domain.

THE PAST AND THE FUTURE

BARNWELL, SOUTH CAROLINA

The past and the future crossed paths that day. The old and the new were reacquainted. Leaving behind the ever-expanding hustle and bustle of the Upstate of South Carolina and the excitement generated over Clemson University's second national championship in college football in three years, Linda and I headed for the peace and quiet of the small town of Barnwell, South Carolina. Barnwell is an hour's drive southeast of Augusta, Georgia; an hour and forty-five minutes from Savannah, Georgia; and a two-hour drive from Charleston, South Carolina.

In other words, it is in the middle of nowhere! Nowhere is a subjective word, however. The more we drove on Routes 321 South and 3 West, the more interesting "nowhere" became. Traveling quickly on the single-lane country road, few cars joined us on our jaunt through the wide-open terrain. Looking to our left as we continued on, we saw something that looked like snow on small plants that were maybe one-to-two-feet high above the ground. The plants appeared to be in the thousands. They seemingly went on forever, going far back from the road on which we were driving. Then it hit Linda and me simultaneously. Cotton!

We both had never seen cotton plants before in our lives. Apple orchards, peach orchards, grapevines—yes. Cotton farms—never. Little did we know at the time, but we would go on to see more and more cotton farms as we traveled on to Barnwell. Suddenly, I didn't have to "wish I were in the land of cotton . . . ," I was in it! The more we looked, the more cotton we saw. Something felt different. Even surreal. We were in a part of the Deep South that we had not experienced before.

Suddenly, all of those U.S. history lessons learned through the years from grade school teachers and textbooks became easier to picture. Slaves working the land leading up to the War Between the States. Bleeding fingers, sweat pouring from their brows. Eli Whitney and the cotton gin. We were in awe, thanking God for the new blessings that He seemed to thrust upon us as we continued our weekly journeys. The blessings were just starting, however.

Passing through the small towns of Swansea and Springfield, we came to our prize destination for the day—Barnwell. Unlike some towns we had passed through, Barnwell looked like it hadn't worn through the years. Despite the cold, overcast day, it had a vibrancy to it. The basketball court was in the middle of town. Cars seemed to be on important excursions.

Looking for a place where Linda could change into her Sunday best, we settled on the local CVS. While Linda went inside, I quickly went from Clark Kent to Superman in our van. Fortunately, no one could see my chiseled body.

With Linda back on board and my identity intact, we proceeded with our journey. The center of the town of Barnwell had a typical Main Street area. A square, green area with park benches in the center was surrounded by stately looking brick buildings on all sides. Only the Subway restaurant seemed out of place in this Norman Rockwell-like setting. Moving on, we took a left on Hagood. There it was. The Holy Church of the Apostles!

This Episcopal Church exuded history. The old tree in front with its thick, wide trunk looked like one of those old football linemen from days gone by with the oversized necks. Its limbs were clothed with Spanish moss.

The graveyard to the right had some old tombstones that were difficult to read. We found the tombstone of Charlotte Patterson, a confirmed slave who lived from 1793-1878. On the other side of the cemetery was the tombstone of Johnson Hagood, a Confederate general in the Second Battle of Fort Wagner, where Robert Gould Shaw was killed leading the all-black 54th Massachusetts regiment, whose story was portrayed in the 1989 film, *Glory*.

> Founded in 1848, the church building was added to the National Registry of Historic Places in 1972. Built . . . of pine in the typical Gothic style of the English Parish Church . . . this . . . sanctuary was used as a stable for Union horses by Gen. Kilpatrick during Sherman's 1865 march of destruction. The large baptismal font, believed to date from medieval times, was used as a watering trough for the horses. The altar window was a gift of Gov. James Hammond and was saved from Sherman's troops by being removed and buried along with the church silver.[35]

The Rector of the Church of the Holy Apostles, Rev. Robert Horn, later told us that hoof prints of the horses that had marked the church floor during this time of occupation were erased years later when the church was refurbished. Most of the church members were not happy when they discovered the missing prints.

When we entered the sanctuary through the heavy wooden double doors, Linda and I felt like we had stepped back in time. We felt a warmth that went beyond the temperature of the room and felt drawn in to the welcoming ambiance. The inside was as historic as the outside. The high, inverted, triangle-like ceiling was made of rich, dark wood. The two side walls were adorned with vertical, stained glass windows with rounded tops. The front wall, hollowed out by an arched opening gave way to the altar area backed by the back wall of the church. The stained glass window on the wall behind the altar area was traced with a stately looking beige molding that seemed to

---

35   "Church of the Holy Apostles: Thoroughbred Country," DiscoverSouthCarolina.com, https://discoversouthcarolina.com/products/1540 (accessed January 13, 2019).

give this stained glass window special importance. It kind of beckoned its observers to look in its direction. Two sections of dark, wooden pews went back seven rows. Only one aisle separated the two. The pews each could seat around four to five people in them. In addition, the balcony on the second row offered more seats, most likely for Christmas and Easter services.

On this particular Sunday, about forty people were present to celebrate. The majority of them welcomed us warmly, inviting us to the covered dish lunch that was to follow after the service.

While the liturgical aspect of the service was unusual for us, we enjoyed the singing of Psalm 89 (verses 20-29) and the reading of the Nicene Creed. I especially enjoyed Rev. Horn's sermon on baptism. He took us through John the Baptist's call for repentance in our lives. Repentance opens the door to God's grace, he explained. He then portrayed Jesus' humility in identifying with our sinful condition even though He had nothing to repent. He Himself was baptized to fulfill righteousness—a legal term that made someone right with the law, right with the judge, and right with the people. He finally expounded on the baptism to covenantal life with God and with His Body, the Church.

While Linda's hip injury kept us from staying for the luncheon, we had a quick time to converse with Rev. Horn. We actually have a connection to our past as well, and I wondered if it would be rekindled in the present. When Linda and I were members of the charismatic, evangelical St. James the Just Church in Long Island, New York, we became ministers in a ministry called VMTC (Victorious Ministries Through Christ). VMTC is designed to bring the believer into total commitment to Jesus. Many of us have sins and wounds from our past that block us from receiving God's fullness in the present. Through the guidance of a male and female-trained ministry team, the recipient of the ministry is led through times of forgiveness of others (including self), the confession of sins, and the renouncing and repenting of ungodly ways and beliefs.

I was a recipient of this Spirit-filled ministry on multiple occasions, as was Linda. Each time, God delivered me of blockages that had kept me from experiencing the abundant life that He desired for me. I subsequently was trained as a minister in the ministry. That ended when we moved to South Carolina. When we finally settled in the Palmetto State, I was informed that VMTC knew of only one person in South Carolina who was actively involved with the ministry—Robert Horn. At that time, I phoned him to inquire about the ministry, but the three hours that separated us and our responsibilities in our burgeoning household kept us apart. Until that day.

Rev. Horn informed us that he was still active in VMTC and gave us his email address to contact him if we were interested in resuming our involvement in the ministry. We plan to. But for now, it was time to return to our home in Greenville, two hours and forty-five minutes away.

Passing through the cotton farms again, this time we noticed a new kind of farm—a solar panel farm. A huge solar panel farm. The largest group of solar panels I have ever seen in my life. Cotton fields on the left. Solar panel farms on the right. An evangelical Episcopal church in the past that had shaped me as a new believer. An Episcopal church in the present that offered a bridge to past ministry. And a bridge to a possible future ministry. The God of the past and the God of the future is One. He is constantly leading, constantly calling us forward. I am thankful it took a trip to the past to help me get a glimpse of my future.

That phenomenon would continue the next week as well, as we reconnected with our past one more time, this time in a much more personal way.

BABY MAKES THREE

DALLAS, GEORGIA

For the first time in our weekly sojourns, we were joined by a third person. Twenty years ago, this same person joined our journey as well, expanding a husband and wife team of two to a family of three. Josiah (Joe for short) Kupec's seventeen-year-old birth mother asked Linda and me to adopt Joe two decades earlier. On this day, we were dropping Joe off at his biological mother's home to spend some hours together in Dallas with her and her family of six. No, not *that* Dallas. This Dallas is in Georgia, the Peach State.

A lot has happened in these past twenty years since we held that little baby in our arms. Through it all, I have learned much about marriage and raising children. Some of it has been learned through my failures and mistakes. All of it has been followed by an increased understanding of God's grace and His merciful heart.

Above all else, I am convinced that the beauty of marriage lies paradoxically in what it kills. A selfish man falls in love with a selfish woman. They naively tie the knot, thinking that this ultimate relationship will bring them peace and happiness. That can be the case later, but much later. Before that can take place, however, there are many deaths that must occur if the marriage will truly become what God intends it to be. Some submit to this process sooner than others.

Unfortunately, Linda and I were from the "others" camp. Marriage exposes self-centeredness and selfishness. If a person humbles himself and looks into the mirror, he sees that the cause of most of the problems in the marriage are staring right back at him. She is not the problem—he is. Conversely, he is not the problem—she is. When each party stops trying to take the splinter out of the other's eye and instead takes the time to remove the plank from his/her own eye (Matt. 7:5), the marriage has promise. "For GOD IS OPPOSED TO THE PROUD, BUT GIVES GRACE TO THE HUMBLE" (1 Peter 5:5-6). It is in humility that abundant life is discovered. Like a seed that is planted, the flower begins to emerge and take the shape and form that it was destined to take. Many marriages today end before the couples have the awareness to take the pointing finger and curl it right back at themselves. Once this critical change occurs, the marriage has a chance not only to survive but also to thrive. This is the first death that leads to life. The second death is the raising of children.

Joe was a contributor to my second death. That is not an indictment on him, but a truth to which any parent can attest. Waking up at unseemly hours for the 2:00 a.m. meal. Trying to live a godly life to set an example for young eyes. Sacrificing time and energy for the things that are necessary for his growth and development. Worrying about his safety and a future that I now realize I have very little power to control. Joe was God's long before he was mine.

The Bible says that children are a blessing from God (Psalm 127:3). The only problem is that God's idea of blessing is a little different from mine. He wants the flesh to die and the Spirit to gain control. He knows this is best for us. He is right, of course. "Truly, truly, I say to you, unless a grain of wheat falls into the earth and dies, it remains alone; but if it dies, it bears much fruit," Jesus explains in John 12:24. The raising of children leads to our death— if we are fortunate, that is.

Don't get me wrong—I still fill up when I think of some of the things Joe said and did through the years. "What's your favorite dinosaur?" he asked his new principal on the first day of school. "No, thanks!" he responded innocently to his teacher when she announced that the class would move on to math. "Do it again," he joyfully exclaimed as a toddler when I hurled him off my back and onto the couch when I was the camel giving him a ride around the living room. When I look at my twenty-year-old son with his full beard and his newfound, CrossFit body, I still see the cute little tike I called "Joey Boy."

I have learned a lot about adoption through the raising of our three adopted sons as well. Each child is different, with different needs and different reactions to the whole scenario of adoption. I wish I could have seen then what I can now see so easily. I missed a lot of cues back then that would have helped our children, not to mention Linda and me.

Our oldest son, Austin, was actually our second son. "The Bopper," also known as "Austy Boy," made our family four when he was two-and-a-half years old. Despite my love for him and our close relationship, I failed to see things from his perspective. I remember excitedly telling people his story, how God had spared his life from abortion and how He placed him in our family through many whirlwind events. That story was actually my story, or at least, how I saw the unfolding of events. I assumed Austin shared my joy and my perspective. But he didn't. His perception of events differed greatly from mine. To him, adoption meant pain. It meant being rejected. It made him insecure—understandably so. I should have seen this in the way he reacted as he stood by when I shared his story. He never looked comfortable. He almost looked embarrassed. His body language spoke volumes. I can see that now in hindsight. But I didn't then. I wish I had. I think I could have brought him more comfort had I the eyes to see and the ears to hear from his vantage point. I think he would have been healthier today if I had.

Our third son, Isaiah, almost seemed indifferent to the whole concept of adoption. As a generally laid-back person, life was what it was. I had asked him if he had any desire to see his biological parents, but he never expressed any desire to do so. Zaybo, or Mr. Zabinsky, did, however, have fond remembrances of his last foster mother in New York City, Ms. Walker.

Regardless of their reactions to the adoption process and all of its many complications, I do hope the boys know that their parents love them. Someday, I hope to write a children's series based on their lives. If you ever see the title *The Three Boys Go West,* you will know that I did. It may never rival *The Hardy Boys* or *Adventures in Odyssey,* but it will come from my heart. But that is for the future. On this particular day, we had something else on our radar—West Ridge Church in Dallas.

Dallas, Georgia, is nothing like the other "Big D." Located about a twenty-minute ride northwest of Atlanta, it has an old, charming downtown area that seems to be surrounded by the overflow of the life that has extended from the state capital. New subdivisions. New strip malls. New highways that eventually connect to the twelve lanes of Interstate 85. Off one of these newer-looking highways was West Ridge Church.

Driving down Hiram Acworth Parkway, we took a right into the entrance of the church parking lot. To our great surprise, West Ridge was a very large, rectangular, modern-looking edifice. Arriving an hour early for the 12:45 p.m. service, the last of three on that day, we circled around the building until we found a parking spot right in front of the church's main entrance. The building was so wide that I could not capture it all in the picture I was trying to take. After that failed attempt at photography, we entered the building not knowing what to expect.

Like many modern, expansive church buildings, West Ridge has a large foyer with a coffee station, an information station, and a place for visitors to obtain information about the church. Unique to West Ridge, however, was the second story entrance that Linda and I entered, which overlooked the foyer area. As we waited by the railings for the second service to discharge, the doors to the sanctuary opened, releasing the second service congregants into the foyer below us.

When I took a picture of the people, I didn't realize at the time that a larger-than-life chandelier hung between the crowd and my iPad. When Linda and I looked at the picture, it looked like a scene from the Book of Acts. The lights in the chandelier looked like tongues of fire falling on the people below just as it might have looked on the day of Pentecost. We pray for the people that they will experience the fullness of God's Spirit like the early church did following Jesus' death, burial, resurrection, and ascension into Heaven.

The speaker was Paul Richardson, the lead pastor of ministry for the church. Looking like a younger version of former basketball star Danny Ainge, the minister delivered a great message to the congregation the way the former Boston Celtic point guard used to deliver passes to Larry Bird and Company back in the 1980s. Mr. Richardson's text was 1 Peter 5:6-10:

> Therefore humble yourselves under the mighty hand of God, that he may exalt you at the proper time, **casting all your anxiety on Him, because He cares for you**. Be of sober *spirit*, be on the alert. Your adversary, the devil, prowls around like a roaring lion, seeking for someone to devour. But resist him, firm in *your* faith, knowing that the same experiences of suffering are being accomplished by your brethren who are in the world. After you have suffered for a little while, the God of all grace, who called you to His eternal glory in Christ, will Himself perfect, confirm, strengthen *and* establish you.

Coincidentally, for the first time in my years of being a Christ-follower, I have begun to consistently cast my cares upon God. For most of my life, I have not done this. A subtle worrying had become a steady part of my life without my even being aware of it. This has been a sinful pattern of my life of which I am now repenting. Jesus carries my burdens much better than I could ever hope to carry them. His shoulders are broader than mine. It is one of His many promises that are ripe for the picking. It is comforting and empowering to have His mighty hand come upon me as I am beginning to make this great transfer, as Mr. Richardson aptly described it.

It was also nice to have Joe join us on our weekly travels. He enjoyed his time with his biological mother and half-brothers and sister. Twenty years later, it was his turn to give someone a piggyback ride. First, his little half-sister, Lizzy, on their walk to the park near their home. And then his half-brother, Daniel, on their way back home. "Do it again," I could hear them saying to big brother Joe. "Do it again," I hear myself saying to our big and intimate God. He always seems to come through. He continues to do it each week. This time in Dallas, Georgia. This time with a group of three.

We would see Him "do it again" the next week—not once, but twice.

LET'S PLAY TWO

ATLANTA, GEORGIA, AND

LAWRENCEVILLE, GEORGIA

We might as well dedicate this Sunday to former Chicago Cubs baseball great, Ernie Banks. The Hall of Famer is known for the famous quote, "Let's play two," meaning he wanted to play two games of baseball, a double header, instead of one on the same day. With that spirit in mind, Linda and I departed that day with our sights set on not one church, but two.

The idea of attending two services began the previous week when we were heading home from the "Little D,"—Dallas, Georgia. Driving along Interstate 85 North, we had seen two churches on our left that seemed to call for our attention. The first because of its pastor—another Hall of Famer of a different type—and the other because of the church's physical uniqueness, as if calling out to us from the highway to include them in what we were doing.

In 1985, Dr. Charles Stanley was inducted into the National Religious Broadcasters' Hall of Fame. He is the founder and president of *In Touch Ministries* and also served two one-year terms as president of the Southern Baptist Convention from 1984 to 1986. He has authored over sixty books, including a few New York Times best-sellers. Most importantly to us, the eighty-six-year old preacher is the senior pastor of First Baptist Church in Atlanta, Georgia, our first stop of two for the day.

If you have ever heard Dr. Stanley on television, you probably have heard his infamous declarative "listen" right before he was to deliver one of his main points in his sermon. I "listened" through the years. So have countless others. Before we would listen on this day, however, we would need to get out of the massive parking lot and into the church building.

The outside of the building, though large, did not give any indication of how big the building actually was. When we entered the front doors, it was as if we had entered a very stately building, one that was important, almost larger than life. We could see down the extremely long hallway to the other end with its windows having that long-distance away sensation, like houses from an airplane thousands of feet above. Another octogenarian, Frank Stanley, no relation to the pastor, told us it was two football fields to the other end of the hallway. To you non-football enthusiasts, that is two hundred yards or six hundred feet. The ceiling was at least twenty feet high. When we walked from one end to the other, it seemed like we were strolling down an elegant hotel corridor or ballroom.

A large mirror immediately to our left captured our attention. Most likely twelve feet by eight feet, the mirror had a gilded frame. It looked like something King Solomon might have had in the temple in Jerusalem. Walking further, we came to the rotunda. Had we turned right at this juncture, we would have walked into the kids' ministry area. Instead, we took the left toward the sanctuary. The large, three-thousand-seat sanctuary reminded us somewhat of a very large courtroom. The dark, intricately carved wood of the railings, columns, and backdrop for the sanctuary area exuded a classic feel, as if many important persons had graced this meeting place over the course of many years. The front stage area was backed by the familiar picture of a worldwide map superimposed by six white columns (three on the left and three on the right) and a cross right in the center. The inference was clear:

"All authority has been given to Me in heaven and on earth. Go therefore and make disciples of all the nations, baptizing them in the name of the Father and the Son and the Holy Spirit, teaching them to observe all that I commanded you; and lo, I am with you always, even to the end of the age" (Matt. 28:16-20).

A picture is worth a thousand words. These fifty-nine words could be "heard" from the view we were taking in.

About twenty-five hundred joined together for the 9:00 a.m. service to worship God and receive instruction from Dr. Stanley. Two things stood out about the congregants we had joined. First, this was a "wear your Sunday best" type of crowd. Ties and jackets for the men and dresses for the women. They dressed as if they were attending something very important. Like this was the most important day of the week. My button-down shirt and polyester dress pants seemed to fall a little short for such an occasion. Second, this was the most diverse crowd we had witnessed in our thirty-one weeks to date. Black and white had gathered—not to discuss any differences they may have, but to unite over the Savior Who had modeled what it was to respect the dignity of each man and woman, the One Who had died for all people, the One Who prayed for the unity of His church two thousand years earlier.

"I do not ask on behalf of these alone, but for those also who believe in Me through their word; that they may all be one; even as You, Father, *are* in Me and I in You, that they also may be in Us, so that the world may believe that You sent Me. The glory which You have given Me I have given to them, that they may be one, just as We are one; I in them and You in Me, that they may be perfected in unity, so that the world may know that You sent Me, and loved them, even as You have loved Me" (John 17:20-23).

The diversity of the church could be seen in the two-hundred-member choir and twenty-member orchestra as well. Regardless of their backgrounds and makeup, there seemed to be one constant among each of the congregants— their respect for their ageless leader.

Dr. Stanley alternated between standing and leaning against his raised chair or high stool while giving his sermon that day. Though the voice was not as commanding as it once was, his voice did not have that quivering, congested sound that many seniors have. His hair was still solid, giving every indication that it planned to be with Dr. Stanley for the duration. That is not said irreverently at all—in fact, just the opposite. Since the days when my hairs began to go their separate ways at the age of twenty, I make it a customary practice to quickly scope the dome of every male I encounter. To have a full crop at eighty-six is quite an accomplishment.

Much more importantly, Dr. Stanley gave his customary, biblically based, life-changing message for anyone with a heart for God and a heart for His Word. Dr. Stanley encouraged all of us to walk in the plan that God has for each of our lives. When we do that, we will glorify God and experience the ultimate purpose in life that only God can give.

Being grateful that we were able to experience a day in Dr. Stanley's life, we ventured a half-hour northeast to Lawrenceville, Georgia, to join the people of 12 Stones Church.

The Body of Christ is the most diverse network of people you will find. Jew and Gentile. Black and white. African, Asian, European. Tie and jacket, t-shirt, and blue jeans. Ripped blue jeans was more the norm at 12 Stones than the exception. While they would be welcomed there, they would probably not choose to be a part of First Baptist of Atlanta. The eight-campus church is youthful, energetic, and seemingly hungry for God.

Arriving late for the 11:00 a.m. service (GPS's are not perfect, especially if you don't put in the correct address) we entered the sanctuary just after the time of worshipping God began. It was like we had stepped into a concert. The usher brought us to the front, where there were two empty seats. Because I am a man of significant size, I felt like a sardine in a can. Fish out of water, right? Wrong. It is not the style of music that leads us into worship, it is our desire to give God what he deserves that now motivates us. While I enjoyed the upbeat, rhythmic, electric guitar-less music of First Baptist more, the loud, electric guitar, drum-filled songs of 12 Stones were fine for these two really young, hip seniors.

The message from 12 Stones was just as fine. Kevin Myers, a transparent former marine and former atheist, shared many excellent points in his message. The Holy Spirit honed in on me one point in particular. While the pastor's sermon had many testimonial aspects to it, his sharing about a subtle complacency that had come into his life at one point bothered him. Where was the fire that he once had when Jesus first became real to him as a marine? Where was the desire to share Christ with others the way others had shared Christ with him? I could relate. Where was my compassion for the lost? Where was my willingness to share the Gospel with others at the risk of my being rejected?

We left 12 Stones feeling challenged. We left grateful that the Holy Spirit is present in a traditional setting like First Baptist of Atlanta and a contemporary one like 12 Stones in Lawrenceville. We were grateful that we had experienced what God was doing throughout the world through *In Touch Ministries* and throughout the metropolitan area of Atlanta, Georgia, through 12 Stones and its eight campuses. We left grateful that we had seen a Christian Hall of Famer like Dr. Charles Stanley in person and a man half Dr. Stanley's age who is carrying his mantle.

Yes, Ernie Banks, "let's play two." Each Sunday in northern Georgia, in two very different environments, within two different contexts, they are playing two. And when Dr. Stanley passes on to Glory, another will take his place. This game of two will never end.

The next week we would meet a group that wanted to play even more than two.

THIRST FOR REVIVAL

WALHALLA, SOUTH CAROLINA

I have heard that a Christ-follower is in need of revival every three days. I do not know who originated that premise, but I have seen it played out many times in my life over the years. The God Whom I had worshipped intimately on Sunday gradually became more distant to me by Wednesday—like a ship moving off-shore and far out to sea. This idea of the need for revival was brought to the forefront one Sunday as Linda and I ventured to Calvary Church in Westminster, South Carolina, a one hour and ten-minute ride from home.

In the midst of unseasonably warm temperatures, we coasted down Interstate 85 South for about forty minutes, the highway slicing through parts of Lake Hartwell in the process. The sign for Exit 11 told us we were heading toward Townville. A sense of heaviness seemed to come over me as I thought back to that dreadful day two years before when a deranged young man opened fire on elementary students playing on the playground of Townville Elementary School. One student died as a result. The killer took his father's life as well. Today, the new, post-massacre, black iron gates that surround the school property seem to remind us not only of the loss of a valuable life that can never be brought back, but also of the loss of innocence of a nation that seems to discard whatever it finds too inconvenient or bothersome.

Linda and I stopped to take pictures of the school, almost as if this were our attempt to honor the loss of the departed souls and pay homage to those who continue on in such challenging circumstances. With heavy hearts, we moved on.

The countless cows we passed on the way from Townville to Westminster seemed indifferent to our heavy thoughts. Some of them were gathered together as if having a meeting themselves on this day when Christ-followers in the northwestern most part of South Carolina would be gathering together. Some lay down on the ground as if enjoying the Sabbath rest that God has provided for us but few of us are heeding.

Driving on, we stopped in the old, sleepy town of Westminster. Unlike many small towns we have visited, Westminster's Main Street actually runs parallel to the main road that moves cars from one end of town to the other. Taking a right and quick left to get on Main Street, we could see the railroad tracks that run parallel with Main Street on the opposite side. I could only imagine the train stop on Main Street was once the hub of commerce in Westminster. Typical of these towns, the railroad probably runs seldom through these parts any longer.

With our fill of nostalgia, we continued on Route 24 for about four miles outside of town to Calvary Church. With very few homes or businesses on this side of town, we could see the church from a distance away. The unassuming, brick building with the steeple in front reaching to the sky gave no indication that anything out of the ordinary would happen here each Sunday. Linda and I were actually disappointed, wondering if we had made a mistake choosing this church as our place of destination.

Being very early, we decided to drive on, hoping to find some type of coffee shop to satisfy Linda's desire for a cup of joe. Realizing that the only chance of any kind of drink would be at the Hardees we had passed on the other side of Westminster, we decided it was too far to go back and risk being late for the service. Pulling into the church parking lot from a side entrance, we parked on a grassy area that was used for Sunday parking.

Getting out of the car, I noticed four pickup trucks to our left. Following the path of others who looked like regulars, it became clear that the church was not meeting in the main building near the main road we had passed, but instead, in a small, warehouse-looking type of building in the rear of the property. Some of the members of the church were gathered in small groups outside the building, seemingly catching up with each other from the last time they had gathered. We were definitely not interrupting many conversations, however. So many people greeted us that their names became a blur. I did catch Pastor Tray Brown's name, though. And Dorothy, whom friends call "DJ." She even walked us to two empty seats in the sanctuary. Inside, we met even more members.

With five minutes to go before the service, I surveyed the sanctuary. It was obviously new and inviting, not at all like the outside of the walls that were rather ordinary. The inside was much wider than it was deep. The two middle sections of chairs consisted of seven rows of ten chairs per row. Another two sections of chairs that flanked these two middle sections had roughly fifty chairs a piece. The stage area held the nine-member worship team with comfort.

The time of worshipping God began with the song, "Can't Nobody Do Me Like Jesus." It was followed by Christian artist David Crowder's "All My Hope," sounding more like an old country hymn than the contemporary song that it is. As a side note, a young man with a long beard playing the guitar while singing main vocals on this song sounded like he should be a country music star. Same thing with the young lady who sang alongside him. Just as I was about to get excited that we were at our first Southern Gospel-singing church, the next song, written and performed by Christian artist Chris Tomlin, dampened that excitement. Singing "How Great is our God," I began to focus on why we were here. Like the others who had gathered, I set out to worship God "in spirit and truth" (John 4:24).

When Pastor Tray Brown took the microphone for his sermon, there seemed to be an excitement in the air. The young preacher, husband, and father of two young children reminded me of a cross between Bill McCartney of Promise Keepers renown and Dabo Sweeney, the youthful and energetic coach of the Clemson Tigers national championship football team.

Pastor Brown started with the calm declarative, "We need revival." He stated that sin is rampant in our land. It has leaked inside the church. The Bride of Christ has lost its focus. It has reduced the fresh anointing of the Holy Spirit to a trickle. It has even become a breeding place of worldliness. It has substituted feasting for fasting, programs for passion, plans for prayer. Jesus denounced the religion of His day saying, "'THIS PEOPLE HONORS ME WITH THEIR LIPS, BUT THEIR HEART IS FAR FROM ME. 'BUT IN VAIN DO THEY WORSHIP ME, TEACHING AS DOCTRINES THE PRECEPTS OF MEN'" (Matt. 15:8-9). What is the answer?

Pastor Brown stated that revival means a people hungry for God. It means new wine for new wineskins. The old days of seeking revival are over. We don't need another church. We don't need a guest speaker. We need people who are hungry for more of God. For more of His working in our lives. Hungry people eat better. Hungry people for God experience His presence more; they receive revelations of Him; they grow in the understanding of their need for Him.

The Sons of Korah cried out:

> "Restore us, O God of our salvation, And cause Your indignation toward us to cease. Will You be angry with us forever? Will You prolong Your anger to all generations? Will You not Yourself revive us again, That Your people may rejoice in You? Show us Your lovingkindness, O LORD, and grant us Your salvation" (Psalm 85:4-7).

When have we cried out to God like that? Imagine if the countless believers all over this nation prayed with such passion? What would happen if we prayed with such a Kingdom of God focus? What if the "called out ones" we call the Church sought God with all their hearts? "Awaken the Sleeping Giant we call the church!" Pastor Brown cried out. "Why are we not more joyful?" Why are we not more grateful?" The fired-up leader then listed numerous victories the congregation had experienced over a short time period—the business that came back from bankruptcy, the return of a prodigal son, the healing of a marriage, the freedom of a member from a fifteen-year addiction. Pastor Brown then made an altar call, inviting anyone who was hungry for God to come forward to receive prayer.

Linda was very convicted by what she was hearing. She thought of the people she knew and loved who were not following Jesus. She went forward for prayer. Many others joined her. With a softer rendition of "All My Hope" playing in the background, Pastor Brown and a few elders prayed over those who were hungering for more of Jesus. As they prayed for Linda, she sensed God speaking to her about trusting Him more. She repented of things the Holy Spirit was pointing out to her. He was healing her at a deeper level of disappointment, of hopelessness, of a grieving sadness, of wanting to give up. She left the service tired, feeling like a wind-whipped piece of wet laundry on a backyard clothesline. She also felt relieved at the same time. She felt quietly refreshed, revitalized, and hopeful.

That was the main point that Pastor Brown had presented to all of us—that revival begins with me. It begins with you. It is the work that only the Holy Spirit can do in us and for us. We have to let Him show us the sin in our lives that keep us from experiencing His presence to the fullest. It is then that the power of the Holy Spirit can manifest in us and restore us to our rightful place of peace, passion, and power. It is then that we overflow with the abundant life that Jesus promises to all who call on His name (John 10:10).

When the service closed, we were greeted a second time by those who had spoken to us before the service began. In addition, a different gentleman approached me. He thanked me for being a part of the service and invited us back again. In a deep, Southern accent, he ended, "After all, you are family now." That touched me. There we were, two middle-aged Northerners with a group of Southerners, whose families probably go back many generations in these parts of South Carolina. That didn't matter, though. We were all brothers and sisters in Christ, seeking the same God, seeking His will for our lives. Seeking to please Him with lives that are wholly devoted to Him. Seeking His fresh touch.

Pastor Brown preached about revival for the entire month of February. The candle had only been lit. We don't want to be lukewarm and unfruitful (Rev. 3:16). We want to be hot. We need revival. In fact, we need it every three days.

The Word of God would provide us further revelation the next week as we would learn to turn a seed into a fruit-bearing tree.

I WANT TO LIVE

CHARLOTTE, NORTH CAROLINA

Quick, without thinking, say the first thing that comes to your mind when you hear the word "church." The churches that Linda and I visited each Sunday typically had standalone buildings on their own piece of land or possibly a group of buildings which are part of their own complex (sanctuary, youth group building, building used as a pantry to feed the poor in the community, etc.). Rarely were they located in a shopping complex like Mosaic Church in Charlotte, North Carolina. Then again, nothing about Mosaic seemed to be too traditional. Even the greeters in the parking lot seem to wave more emphatically than other church's greeters.

When we parked our car ten minutes early for the 9:00 a.m. service (the first of three at the church), we were met by Sierra, a personable twenty-something-year-old with a wide umbrella, whose assignment seemed to be to shield us from the periodic raindrops that were falling. As usual, I exited the car first. On this unseasonably raw Sunday morning, my short-sleeved, button-down shirt and dress pants were no match for the rigid temperatures. Sierra's umbrella helped out with the rain but made no provision for my goose-bumped arms.

As is our custom, Linda took much more time to get out of the car than I do, doing what women do when they reach their destinations. How much more small talk could Sierra and I endure as we waited for Linda? With Linda finally on board, Sierra escorted us past the Bouncy Store next door to the church and into Mosaic's new, bright, and chic church building.

Walking through the immaculate, small, two-story waiting area, we entered the sanctuary, feeling more like we entered a small theater instead of a traditional church building. The Jason Gray song playing in the background, however, reminded me where we were. In fact, it is one of my favorite contemporary Christian songs: "I want to live like there's no tomorrow / Love, like I'm on borrowed time / It's good to be alive."[36]

Why don't I live this way every day, I thought to myself? I am saved by God's grace through faith in His finished work on the cross. I am assured of eternal life, to be in God's presence forever. I am covered with the never-ending promises of God's Word. I have a purpose that has been given and ordained by the Creator of the Universe, Whose Kingdom will have no end. Why do I get off-focus so easily?

As always, the answers to my groaning were to be found in the exhaustive Word of God. The revelation of my soul-searching question is seen in Jesus' parable about the farmer and his seed:

> "Behold, the sower went out to sow; and as he sowed, some *seeds* fell beside the road, and the birds came and ate them up. Others fell on the rocky places, where they did not have much soil; and immediately they sprang up, because they had no depth of soil. But when the sun had risen, they were scorched; and because they had no root, they withered away. Others fell among the thorns, and the thorns came up and choked them out. And others fell on the good soil and yielded a crop, some a hundredfold, some sixty, and some thirty. He who has ears, let him hear." And the disciples came and said to Him, "Why

---

36   Jason Gray, "Good to Be Alive," A Way to See in the Dark, Centricity Music, 4, 2011.

do You speak to them in parables?" Jesus answered them . . . "When anyone hears the word of the kingdom and does not understand it, the evil *one* comes and snatches away what has been sown in his heart. This is the one on whom seed was sown beside the road. The one on whom seed was sown on the rocky places, this is the man who hears the word and immediately receives it with joy; Yet he has no *firm* root in himself, but is *only* temporary, and when affliction or persecution arises because of the word, immediately he falls away. And the one on whom seed was sown among the thorns, this is the man who hears the word, and the worry of the world and the deceitfulness of wealth choke the word, and it becomes unfruitful. And the one on whom seed was sown on the good soil, this is the man who hears the word and understands it; who indeed bears fruit and brings forth, some a hundredfold, some sixty, and some thirty" (Matt. 13:3-9, 19-23).

Four things can happen when an individual hears the Gospel. Two results are tragic; one is extremely unfortunate; and the last one is life-giving. The first is that the person hears the Word of God presented but does not understand it. The Evil One comes in quickly and snatches away the truth that was offered. The second is that the person responds to the Gospel and receives Jesus gladly. His newfound faith, however, quickly fades away at the first signs of opposition or trouble. The response was not a true conversion. The third possibility is that the person responds favorably to the Gospel. He receives God's provision for salvation and is saved from eternal destruction. His name is recorded in the Lamb's Book of Life (Rev. 20:12). All of Heaven rejoices over his conversion (Luke 15:10). But like a fog that sets in unexpectedly, a neutralizing factor slowly creeps in. The worries of this world and the pursuit of wealth prove to be too formidable an opponent for the believer. The tree is alive but produces no fruit.

I once heard that if Satan cannot keep a person from being saved, the next best thing he will try to do is neutralize that person. He will try to make him ineffective, keep him from displaying God's glory, prevent him from being used by God to either disciple believers or share the Good News of Jesus with others. Jesus said a person can't have two masters—he will love the one and hate the other (Matt. 6:24). Satan knows that if the follower of Christ produces fruit, his kingdom takes a hit. He knows that the Christ-follower is a vessel God uses to bring unsaved people to a saving knowledge of Jesus. He knows that the Christ-follower who is connected to the rest of Jesus' Body (His Church) will use his or her spiritual gifts to help strengthen the church and advance the Kingdom of God. He will do anything to keep the believer from that fourth possibility, that fruit-producing stage that brings God glory!

How many people who have heard the Gospel of Jesus are counted among the dead in the first two categories? How many are floundering in the third, barely keeping their heads above spiritual water? They are blown off-course by the worries of this world, a world that will end before we know it. A life so compromised from the abundant life that Jesus has promised to all who follow Him (John 10:10).

Think about it. How many of us knew our great grandparents? I didn't. How many of us knew our grandparents? I never met my grandparents on my father's side. They died before I was born. Fortunately, I have fond memories of my grandparents on my mother's side. Yet my grandmother died when I was about twelve, and my grandfather died when I was about twenty-three. I have been away from them forty-three years and thirty-two years respectively. The Bible says we are like a mist that is here today and gone tomorrow (James 4:14). All of us will share the same fate as them. What are we pursing? Why? Does what we are pursuing have any eternal value? Is what we're pursuing in alignment with God's will? Are we sure? Does His Word support that? Does His Spirit confirm it?

I am concerned that the majority of persons who have genuinely responded to Jesus' offer of salvation by grace alone are being neutralized by the distractions that compete for their attention. Bogged down by the worries of this world, rather than the things that matter to God. I am sad to admit that for too long, I have been a card-carrying member of this "third category" of followers of Christ. Of course, I couldn't see it through these wasted years. That is the essence of deceit. That is the essence of Satan's work.

But I can see it now. God's Spirit has revealed that to me increasingly over the past couple of years. Like a defeated player who realizes he just got beaten by a better player, I have to admit that my opponent is good at what he does. He is a deceiver and a liar, an enemy of God who has come "to steal and kill and destroy" (John 8:44, 10:10). But he is not great at what he does. He is no match for a God Who is faithful even when we are faithless (2 Tim. 2:13).

God is alive and well. He wants me to live the life that I have been called to live. He wants me to abide in Him, to be in vital union with Him. He wants me to bear fruit. Jason Gray captured my sentiment with the continuation of his song: "I won't take it for granted / I won't waste another second / All I want is to give you / A life well lived, to say 'thank you.'"[37]

I want to be in Christ in my home, at work, in everything I do. I want to be a person who studies His Word and has the mind of Christ (1 Cor. 2:14-16). I want to be a "doer of the word" (James 1:22), a person whose actions are spurred on by the Word of God and by the Spirit of God within me (Eph. 2:10). I want to be a brother in Christ who encourages and exhorts my brothers and sisters in Christ to remain true to the faith despite hardships that they are going to face (Acts 14:22). I want to be a person who shares the Good News of the Gospel of Jesus with others the way a lottery winner would share his newfound fortune with others less fortunate.

Today, however, my job was to hear the message of Mosaic's founding pastor Naeem Fazal. Pastor Fazal was "born and raised as a Muslim in Kuwait.

---

37   Ibid.

He came to the United States in 1992 after the Gulf War. That same year, Naeem had a supernatural experience with Christ that changed the course of his life."[38] Seventeen years later, the Scripture he used for his sermon was 1 Corinthians 13:4-8. Not only do the verses tell us what love really is, but it reveals the very nature of the God Who is the essence of love (1 John 4:8).

Thinking that we would have an early return home that Sunday, we soon realized (again) that God gives exceedingly more abundant than what we could ever ask or imagine (Eph. 3:20). As we were heading north on Interstate 85, I caught the sign that told us that the exit for Kings Mountain National Military Park was to our right. When Linda said she was willing to see the park, I quickly made a hard right just in time to make the exit. What a great impromptu decision that was! I had always heard about Bunker Hill; Lexington, Massachusetts, The Boston Tea Party; and all the heroes of the American Revolutionary War. I had heard little (or, at least, remember little) of the impactful battles that had taken place in South Carolina during America's quest for independence.

October 7, 1780, proved to be the day of the pivotal battle for the outcome of the War for Independence. The Overmountain Men of Virginia, Tennessee, North Carolina, and South Carolina had traveled by horseback with their own rifles and with very little training to take on the advancing British Army heading north in the rural area of Kings Mountain on the border of North and South Carolina. Against all odds, the mountain men crushed their red-coated opponents, brutally avenging the Waxhaw Massacre that had occurred roughly four months earlier. The many Carolinians who were loyal to the Crown before this battle now turned their allegiance to the Patriots and stopped fighting for the British. A short time later, the Red Coats were routed at Yorktown, leading to the Patriots' victory and the birth of an independent nation. Their heroic efforts laid the groundwork for our lives today.

---

38 "Lead Pastor, Naeem Fazal," MosaicChurch.tv, http://mosaicchurch.tv/lead-pastor-naeem-fazal (accessed February 17, 2019).

We had set out to see a church that was led by a former Muslim. In the service, we were met by the Holy Spirit speaking to us through an old song with a timeless message. God wants us to live our lives like there's no tomorrow. Live our lives as if eternity is at stake. Like the mountain men of Virginia who sacrificed their time and money for the cause of the Patriots, God is seeking those who will sacrifice for the ultimate cause—the discipling of all the nations. Let's not get caught up in the worries of this life and miss the life that only God can provide. A life of purpose. A life without equal.

And as we would see the next week, a life that could even impact a nation.

IF MY PEOPLE

FOUNTAIN INN, SOUTH CAROLINA

I love the United States of America. I have since I was a kid. When Mr. Lewis, our next-door neighbor, boomed patriotic music from his stereo for all the neighbors to hear each Independence Day, my grandfather yelled over to him to make it louder. *Yeah, play it louder,* I thought to myself. Three generations off to the wild, blue yonder.

Despite what is taught in too many history classes today, America has always been a beacon of light and an oasis for countless people bound by dictatorships, communist regimes, and Marxist and socialist governments that deny the liberty of its citizens. Despite its imperfections and blind spots, these fifty United States remain the hope of the world. A nation "under God" will always stand as a "city on a hill" for all other nations to see.

Yet in spite of its inherent greatness, the country has always been divided to some degree or another. In its birth pangs, the Patriots and the Loyalists (to Great Britain) were at odds with each other. In the time of the great conflict between the states, one side favored states' rights and slavery, while the other side favored a stronger federal government and the abolition of the "peculiar institution." The divide was so severe that modern estimates tally the loss of lives in the Civil War at roughly 750,000.[39] That is more deaths than those of World War I, World War II, the Korean War, and the Vietnam War combined.

Today, the chasm is over the very essence of life itself—the right of a baby to come to full term in his or her mother's womb versus the right of another to keep that life from being birthed. How do you compromise on an issue like abortion? Do we agree that you can legally take the baby's life up to four-and-a-half months but not one day after? Did counting blacks as three-fifths of a person make sense to a nation at odds with each other? How do you compromise sin? You don't if you truly want to remain united. Once we humans subjectively decide what is right or wrong, moral or immoral, trouble will not be far behind. The further we wander from our spiritual moorings, the more divided we will be as a nation. To clear the muddy waters, we need to find moral clarity and direction from the Word of God.

I once heard a person state that God's admonition to the Israelites recorded in 2 Chronicles 7:14 was just for the people of that day and for that time and not for our present day. It made me think. It made me question what I believed about the subject. But then a thought crossed my mind—*Isn't a truth for one generation the truth for a subsequent one? Is God's admonition to the Israelites following their miraculous deliverance from Egypt to "be holy just as I am holy" not as relevant today for our contemporary world?* I would have to say "of course" and a resounding yes.

So would the "Activist Mommy," Elizabeth Johnson. The homeschooling mother of ten children and wife of a medical doctor has been increasingly troubled by the blatant disregard for biblical morals in our contemporary American civilization. Her spark became a flame when a standing U.S. president supported the usage of bathrooms in public buildings by either sex. A grown man who "feels" he is really a woman can now use the women's bathroom. Bewildered, Ms. Johnson said enough is enough. She posted her

---

39   Guy Gugliotta, "New Estimate Raises Civil War Death Toll," NYTimes.com, https://www.nytimes.com/2012/04/03/science/civil-war-toll-up-by-20-percent-in-new-estimate.html (accessed March 3, 2019).

opposition to this new way of thinking on Facebook. She was not alone. Hundreds of thousands agreed. The flame became larger, now burning against other ungodly practices that were becoming more and more "mainstream" across this once Christian-influenced country.

God is the Author of Life. Isaiah the prophet knew this well. "But now, O Lord, You are our Father, We are the clay, and You our potter; And all of us are the work of Your hand" (Isa. 64:8). Again, he recognizes where life originates: "Thus says the Lord, your Redeemer, and the one who formed you from the womb, 'I, the LORD, am the maker of all things'" (Isa. 44:24). King David knew this as well: "Know that the LORD Himself is God; It is He who has made us and not we ourselves" (Psalm 100:3). He added, "For You formed my inward parts; You wove me in my mother's womb. I will give thanks to You, for I am fearfully and wonderfully made" (Psalm 139:13-14). Among the six things listed in Proverbs 6 that God hates, one of them is the shedding of innocent blood (Prov. 6:17). "You shall not murder" is crystal clear (Exod. 20:13). Yet, we live in a culture that has ignored the heart and mandates of God. We have made ourselves gods as a result.

That led to Linda's and my involvement on that particular day. Ms. Johnson organized an event in Albany, New York, called "A Day of Mourning." Thousands descended upon the Empire State's capital in response to the tragic decision by the New York State Assembly and signed into law by New York's governor to pass the euphemistically titled law, "The Reproductive Health Act."

Today, in New York, a baby's life can be terminated up until the day of his or her birth if the baby's mother desires. That is it. No questions asked. A woman decides the fate of another. One of the most beautiful relationships that God has ordained—the mother and child one—is distorted to pit one against the other in a totally one-sided fight. In a country that prides itself on "fairness," it seems barbaric. Tragically, a woman has replaced God as the determiner of life. The baby being formed—and fully formed in some cases—has no voice. A promising future. A violent, abrupt end. Just as God knew Jeremiah before the prophet was formed in his mother's womb, he also knew you and me (Jer. 1:5)—and the fifty million other American lives that have been cut short since a different tragic court decision in 1973 (*Roe v. Wade*).

Before we continue, however, I want to extend God's grace to anyone who has been connected to an abortion. I know many women who have. Many of them thought they had no other choice. Others acted out of ignorance. Some were pressured to abort by families, boyfriends, and medical professionals. Still others acted selfishly, choosing personal convenience over the sacrificing of another. Most of the women I know who have had an abortion have carried a heavy guilt. Deep down, they knew intuitively that what they were doing was wrong. Yet, for this sin, just like any other, God's mercy is available to the person who comes to Him with a humble and contrite heart.

The Bible is as clear about God's mercy as it is about His position on life. "If we confess our sins, He is faithful and righteous to forgive us our sins and to cleanse us from all unrighteousness" (1 John 1:9). That forgiveness includes the sin of abortion. No sin is greater than God's mercy. His desire is that we not only come to Him for the forgiveness of that sin but that we find healing from the effects of it as well. James 5:16 states, "Therefore, confess your sins to one another, and pray for one another so that you may be healed. The effective prayer of a righteous man can accomplish much."

Many pregnancy centers like the Piedmont Women's Center of Greenville, South Carolina, and Soundview Pregnancy Centers in Centereach, New York, and East Meadow, New York, have abortion recovery counseling to help women and men who are living with the effect of their abortions or their participation in them. The people serving in these centers are trained to be conduits of God's healing of broken lives.

"If My people who are called by My name humble themselves and pray and seek My face and turn from their wicked ways, then I will hear from heaven, will forgive their sin and will heal their land" (2 Chron. 7:14). While we did not take the thirteen-hour trek to Albany, New York, to join in the gathering, we settled for the next best thing—the twenty-four-minutes ride to Fountain Inn, South Carolina, for a simulcast of the event. While the four thousand-plus packed the Empire State Plaza Convention Center in Albany, about fifty of us gathered to add our prayers at Grace Reformed Baptist Church.

While we worshipped God in song, listened to speakers exhorting the troops to prayer and action, and asked God's mercy on us for our national sin, I could only think of those thirty-eight powerful words of 2 Chronicles 7:14. The revelation can be separated into seven categories: (1) If My people who are called by My name; (2) will humble themselves and pray; (3) if they will seek My face; (4) if they will turn from their wicked ways; (5) then I (God) will hear from heaven; (6) I (God) will forgive their sin, and (7) I (God) will heal their land. In Scripture, seven is the number of completeness and perfection—both physical and spiritual.[40] The Bible is clear that judgment begins with the household of God (1 Peter 4:17). Yes, we are to oppose barbaric laws like the one tragically passed by the New York Legislature. Yes, we are to advocate for laws that reflect the righteousness of God. Yes, we are to vehemently oppose any statute that threatens our nation's moral fiber. And yes, we are to prayerfully and financially support politicians who stand for life. If a public servant cannot see straight on the basic issue of life, how can he possibly lead us well on all other matters?

Above all this, however, the real answer lies with God's people. "IF MY PEOPLE . . . " We are the ones who should know better. We are the ones who should internalize God's Word and display it humbly for the lost to see. We are the ones called to be salt and light (Matt. 5:13-16). If we lose our saltiness, what good are we to a drifting nation? It is time for humility, prayer, seeking God, and repentance. That is our part. Then God will respond. He will forgive our collective sin. He will heal our land. That is His part.

---

40 "Meaning of Numbers in the Bible: The Number 7," BibleStudy.com, https://www. biblestudy.org/bibleref/meaning-of-numbers-in-bible/7.html (accessed February 26, 2019).

I love this country. I suspect you do, too. Its glory is fading, however, like the sun just before dusk. It's time we do something about it. The answer lies within us, the Bride of Christ. The answer is Christ Himself.

There's a church that we visited the next week that I am sure would agree with me.

JESUS SAVES

COWPENS, SOUTH CAROLINA

How could we not visit Mountain View Baptist Church? For years, Mountain View has played a significant role in our lives without our even taking one step on its campus. Mountain View was one of the first to welcome us to South Carolina when we ventured from the Empire State fourteen years ago. Every trip we took back North to see our families, Mountain View was there to send us off. With each return, it was there to welcome us back, late at night or just before the sun would begin to rise. For Linda's brother John's memorial service in Pennsylvania. For my parents' funerals in New York. For the bittersweet farewell to my brother, Bill, when he was called home to Glory. Mountain View was a calm in the storm. It provided stability when times seemed uncertain. It offered hope when death came suddenly and often. It was a steadying influence when waters became turbulent. Oddly enough, Mountain View didn't even know it was providing these things for me and my family.

It was actually the sign they put up that provided fuel for our empty tanks. Mountain View Baptist Church sits on Battleground Road, a quick walk from Interstate 85, our gateway between South Carolina and New York. Standing between the highway and the church stands a large, red cross with the clear, concise message, "Jesus Saves." You can't miss it. When you're heading south on 85, it stands proudly to the right. Heading north, it captures your attention from the left. The many billboards on 85 are no competition. The message on the tall, red cross is also the message of the church.

Linda and I have visited many Baptist churches throughout the years. Mountain View was different. We sensed it as soon as we entered the stately looking building and took our seats in the pew on the last row on the left. There was a buzz in the crowd. With a piano player and some orchestra members playing a very festive, upbeat Southern Gospel song in the background, the church members who had filled all the seats before the service began seemed to be busy catching up with each other. Their collective conversation sounded more joyful than noisy. They acted like they were excited to be in church, like they were genuinely glad to see each other, like they were the home crowd waiting for their winning team to take the field.

As if on cue, the seventy-five-member chorus sprang into song, the congregants staying right with them. Many hands were raised in praise to God. Scanning the audience, it seemed like there were more men in attendance than women. Ladies, I appreciate all you are and all you do, but I was really happy to see not just men, but also men who seemed like men's men. Men who work jobs. Men who take care of their families. Men who defend the Gospel. Not like the wimpy men that are portrayed on television, trying to make us believe that men today are clumsy, disengaged, irrelevant. I would bet my life that the men at Mountain View open the car doors for their wives, lead their families, and take their rightful place of leadership in the church.

The singing continued with its joyful, lively theme. The chorus and orchestra reminded me of a cross between the Gaithers of Gospel music fame and the Whitewell Metropolitan Tabernacle choir of Belfast, Northern Ireland, that Linda and I first heard on YouTube. The group singing ended appropriately with the song, "Jesus Saves."

As the chorus members filed out of the front and joined their families in the pews, one of the ushers led the church in a time of prayer. Totally engaged, the audience seemed to "hoot and holler" (sounds of support) with each sentence prayed. If you have ever visited an evangelical church, you may be accustomed with the chorus of amens that follow certain strong points delivered by the speaker. But this was something different. I had never heard those type of responses before. I strained to listen closely, like a person trying to hear a conversation in the next room. *What exactly are they saying*, I wondered. It made me think back to the past—how congregants must have sounded as they reacted to famous lines like Patrick Henry's "Give me liberty or give me death." Or Martin Luther King Jr.'s "I've been to the mountaintop." The members of Mountain View were either encouraging their brother praying, agreeing with his sentiments, or relishing the fact that a brother in Christ was praying according to the will of God.

That distinct voicing of approval continued as one family of four and then a family of five sang and played instruments while singing worship songs. The crowd approved. This was not a passive audience for sure! The thoroughly engaged audience continued their participation when it came time for the congregants to greet each other. Linda and I felt like we were the bride and groom at a wedding reception. I estimated about 350 to be in attendance. I think we shook 351 hands. I am still trying to figure out who shook our hands twice. It was *that* friendly a church. With each handshake and kind look in the eye, we *really* felt welcome.

Add to that young twelve-year-old Sarah sitting in the pew before us. She seemed to take a liking to Linda. Maybe even a tender, pastoral concern for her. When Linda sniffled, Sarah was there with a tissue. When Linda filled up with tears as God touched her during the service, Sarah glanced back at her, offering Linda a loving smile, her nods providing a wealth of comfort. Sarah even turned around and offered us both a Lifesaver. I hope there wasn't any reason for this beyond Sarah's generous heart.

When the time of giving tithes and offerings came around, all the visitors were asked to complete a visitor's card with identifying information and put it into the offering plate. On the bottom of the card, it asked how we had heard about the church. How could I fit our story in only two lines?

What I ended up writing must have caught Pastor Steven Griffith's attention. Right after the offertory hymn, he asked the audience where Tom Kupec was sitting. If you know me, I typically like to live my life under the radar. But how could I not respond? With an obedient, yet hesitant heart, I raised my hand. The pastor excitedly shared with the congregation what I had written on the bottom of the visitor card. "For many years, my family and I have driven past the church traveling on Interstate 85. Each time, we saw the 'Jesus Saves' sign. We had to visit a church with that kind of sign." The hooting and hollering followed in response.

The pastor then shared how the highway department had told the church that they would have to take down the sign because of the widening of the interstate. With a Jerry Falwell-type look, he added, "We'll just build a bigger one; that's what we'll do." Now I hooted and hollered!

Pastor Griffith then delivered his sermon for the day. No one will ever accuse the fifty-nine-year-old pastor of not giving his all. Mountain View has only had two pastors in its fifty-seven-year history. The first, Jimmy Robbins, nicknamed "a son of thunder," pastored for the first forty years of Mountain View's existence. Pastor Griffith has held the reigns for the last seventeen.

With Luke 15 as his text, Pastor Griffith expounded on the story of the prodigal son. He explained the father's heart toward his wayward son. When his son came to his senses and returned to his father, the father received him with open arms. He celebrated. He rejoiced. His son was lost, but now he was found. The father's heart in the story of the prodigal son gives us a picture of our Heavenly Father's heart for all of us today. When a person comes to his senses, repents of his sins, and puts his faith in Jesus' atoning work on the cross for his sins, God receives him warmly. In fact, Jesus said that all of

Heaven rejoices over one sinner who repents (Luke 15:7). Pastor Griffith then asked the audience if there were any present today who needed to be restored back to fellowship with God and with His church. A significant number responded by going forward to the front of the church for prayer.

We left Mountain View Baptist Church and headed for Cowpens National Battlefield Park, just a few miles down the road from the church. I was excited to be heading for another American Revolutionary War battlefield. The National Park Service has an eighteen-minute video on the entire War for Independence followed by a fifteen-minute feature on the Battle of Cowpens. Another "man's man," General Daniel Morgan, had led a group of Continental fighters, mountain men, and militia men to a commanding victory over General Tarleton and his Red Coats. The tide of the war was turning in the Patriots' favor. It wouldn't be long until the Battle of Yorktown and the final victory for the Americans.

I was filled with great appreciation for the service and courage of those who had sacrificed for freedom. It is a history we all should be proud of. I couldn't stop thinking, however, of the bigger battle we face that is timeless and for a freedom that is eternal.

I thought back to Pastor Griffith and his passionate message. I thought of Sarah and the role she is playing in God's army today. I thought of the people of Mountain View—their kindness, their welcoming spirit, their commitment to their church, and their commitment to the Great Commission. How many lives are they reaching through their collective efforts and through their big, red cross that stands quietly, yet loudly, by the highway? A simple, yet profound, statement. The answer to everyone's battle. The battle of our eternal state. The victory that God has provided through His Son and offers to all, regardless of their religion, regardless of their background, regardless of their family. It is there for the taking. "Jesus Saves."

THE WORD OF GOD

FOUNTAIN INN, SOUTH CAROLINA

The Word of God has a lot to say about itself. John the apostle tells us, "In the beginning was the Word, and the Word was with God, and the Word was God" (John 1:1). The writer of Hebrews tells us, "For the word of God is living and active and sharper than any two-edged sword, and piercing as far as the division of soul and spirit, of both joints and marrow, and able to judge the thoughts and intentions of the heart" (Heb. 4:12). The great apostle Paul rejoiced over those who accepted the Word of God, stating, "For this reason we also constantly thank God that when you received the word of God which you heard from us, you accepted *it* not *as* the word of men, but *for* what it really is, the word of God, which also performs its work in you who believe" (1 Thess. 2:13). Jesus made the most eternal statement of anyone concerning the Scriptures, "Heaven and earth will pass away, but My words will not pass away" (Matt. 24:35).

You would think that the Word of God would be important to us, too, would you not? It is to the people of Grace Reformed Baptist Church in Fountain Inn, South Carolina, a twenty-minute ride from our home in Greenville. As mentioned earlier in Chapter 31, we participated in the "Day of Mourning" event held at Grace Reformed Baptist via satellite from Albany, New York, about two weeks prior. That event was prompted by the tragic passage of the "Reproductive Health Act" by the New York State Legislature and signed into law by its governor, Andrew Cuomo.

For a few minutes after the event, Linda had a chance to talk with GRBC's leader, Pastor Gardner, and his wife, Marie. On the subsequent ride home that late Saturday afternoon, Linda filled me in on all that she had learned about Grace. I had a quick thought while she talked. Any church that would host an event like this was worth our investigating. We would make it a point to visit GRBC. That day had come.

Our entrance into the one room, storefront church building was uneventful. Apart from a few nods from some teenagers, we took our customary seats in the far back row without any fanfare. No greeters, no ushers, no welcoming committee. With the men of the church praying in a circle before the service began, the women seemed busy setting up the crockpots for the post-service luncheon. Back row or front row made little difference in this one-story room. There wasn't a bad seat in the house. Anyone looking to blend in with the crowd would have a difficult time here.

With a seating capacity of about seventy, I counted forty of those chairs filled. Eight of them belonged to Emily's family. The soft-spoken, yet alert, wife and homeschooling mother of six seemed pleased that we had attended the "Day of Mourning" event two weeks earlier. When I told her we had three adopted sons, it seemed to give us instant credibility with her. Her smile meant a lot. It was as if she knew what we had gone through, like she was affirming us for our labor of love. She showed a lot of interest in us, too, making us feel important and valued. She even mentioned knowing people who work with Cities4Life in Charlotte, a pro-life organization dedicated to reaching the lives of both pregnant moms and their forming children within. The service then started, the Word of God taking its rightful position of front and center.

Pastor Gardner led the congregation with an a cappella version of the "Doxology." He then read from the Book of Jeremiah. He noted that like a groom desires to be with his bride, God desires to be with His Church. Three hymns later, an elder of the church, Emily's husband, read the entire chapter of Hosea 10. Another hymn then led to corporate prayer. A man prayed for a fellow church member who was in Spruce Pine, North Carolina, for the day. I would not have recognized the name, Spruce Pine, if not for our visit to that small mountain town near Mount Mitchell a few months earlier. When the final amen ended the time of corporate prayer, another elder read the entire chapter of Mark 5. Pastor Gardner then delivered his sermon for the day, using Hebrews 11 and 2 Samuel as his main texts.

Pastor Gardner is an intriguing man. He is the owner of an engineering consultant firm and a full-time pastor. He is definitely a gifted teacher. I have not met many who have rightly divided the Word of God (2 Tim. 2:15) as well as he did that Sunday. Taking notes for his sermon was not an easy task. Feeling like I did when I read A.W. Tozer's *The Pursuit of God*, it was difficult to take in such great insights while still trying to write down each additional sentence. I felt like I was always a half-sentence behind. I felt like I was back in my college history class laboring profusely to write one sentence of notes while the professor continued on with other important anecdotes. Wondering if I should raise the white flag, lean back, fold my arms, and just listen to the sermon, I thought better of it and labored on with my harried notetaking. One cramped right hand and three pages of notes later, I am glad that I did.

The early Christians had difficult choices to make as well. Would they continue in their new faith in Christ in the midst of heavy opposition from their fellow Jews—enduring rejection, persecution, suffering, even death? Would they back down from the threats of the mighty emperors of Rome? Or would they give in to the pressures of the culture, rationalizing in their minds that it just wasn't worth the fight?

The Bible exhorts us to stay true to Christ regardless of the hardships that arise. Hebrews 11 lists noteworthy examples of men and women who lived by faith despite the most dreadful of circumstances and the severest of consequences. Pastor Gardner then brought us back in time to the days of Israel's first king, Saul. Having God as their King was not enough for the Israelites. They wanted an earthly king like the countries that surrounded them. Despite Samuel's warning of what would happen with a king other than God Himself, they insisted on their own way. Like we do today, they chose a way that seemed right in their own minds, but also a path that would lead to their own destruction (Prov. 14:12). God's Word was not enough for them. The world's appeal was too attractive. Like He does today, God gave them what they wanted (Rom. 1:28).

Fortunately, however, God does not leave us in our own demise forever. While the Israelites were reaping the consequences of their poor choices, God was working behind the scenes to provide a new king for the Israelites, a man after His very heart, a man who would do what God wanted Him to do (Acts 13:22). A leader who would act in the best interests of the Israelites.

The Bible tells us, "There is nothing new under the sun" (Eccl. 1:9). What about us today? What kind of leaders are we asking God to provide? Are we praying for our leaders as the Word of God commands us (1 Tim. 2:2)? Are we praying for our president? For our governor? For all those in authority over us? Are we praying that God would choose leaders for us? Or are we filling our minds with the people we think would be best for the positions? What exactly are we filling our minds with? If not the Word of God, then what? We all fill our minds with something.

Children, how about you? Are you obeying your parents? Are you interacting with other children who are influencing you away from the truth your parents have taught you from God's Word? The Bible promises that it will go well with children who obey their parents (Eph. 6:2-3). It will go well for children who forgive their parents when parents aren't acting in ways that are honorable.

And how about us adults? Are we obeying our Father in Heaven? We honor God by accepting His will. Samuel realized this in ancient Israel. That truth remains a challenge for us today. We are under a faulty impression that we deserve something. When God gives us something and then takes it away later, it helps when we remember that we didn't deserve it in the first place. It was God's grace that provided the blessing. What remains from that blessing is worth more than anything the world could provide. Are we living a life that is moral and religious but is lacking in grace? Does your Christianity seem like drudgery? Graceless? Miserable? When God is moving in your life, there is great joy. God didn't just free us from the penalty of sin; He saved us from the power and tyranny of sin in our lives.

The people of Grace Reformed Baptist Church value the timeless and eternal Word of God. You can see it in their eyes. You can see it in their behavior. The men have been taught to lead their families. I was mesmerized watching kids sitting in a two-hour service, listening to the pastor, no coloring books in sight, no impatient whining to their mothers wondering out loud how much time was left in the service. A seventeen-year-old girl quietly corrected her two younger brothers while their mother was occupied with the youngest sibling. I could hear it in their interacting with us after Pastor Gardner gave the final blessing. I could hear it in their invitations to us to eat with the church, to come back later for the six o'clock service, to join them for Wednesday's mid-week service, and to partake in the Friday's men's Bible study. I could envision it in their outreaches to community members who do not have the Word of God yet, who do not have the faith in God which comes from hearing the Word of God (Rom. 10:14-15).

Jesus said to His disciples, "Blessed are your eyes, because they see; and your ears, because they hear. For truly I say to you that many prophets and righteous men desired to see what you see, and did not see *it*, and to hear what you hear, and did not hear *it* (Matt. 13:16-17). The people of Grace Reformed Baptist Church are blessed. They know the Word of God. They are believing it, trusting it, and applying it. The Word of God was made flesh two thousand years ago. He's still forming and transforming lives today. Everywhere in the world, but especially, it seems, in Fountain Inn, South Carolina.

We would see the effect of the Word of God the next week as we traveled back in time.

I AM NOT WHO I WAS

GREENVILLE, SOUTH CAROLINA

A lot can happen in ten years. A young person trudges through middle school and high school, perseveres through four years of college, and begins a job that may carry him through the rest of his life. A wide-eyed rookie NFL quarterback becomes a seasoned veteran, leading his team to multiple Super Bowl appearances. A mother of three sons pinches her children's cheeks, blinks her eyes, and realizes her once-adoring children are now the object of other females' attentions. What have your last ten years looked like?

On Saturday, June 6, 2009, my family's world was rocked. Despite our church's many prayers, our beloved pastor, Orie Wenger, passed away after battling pancreatic cancer for about three years. Orie was a man of God. Not flamboyant or charismatic by nature, he was a man you could depend on. He made you feel special. He made you feel loved. He was humble, always looking to the Father, always encouraging us to align our lives with God's Word. He was transparent, never pretending to be someone he wasn't. Mount Zion Christian Fellowship felt his loss deeply. I asked the Lord why He took Orie to be with Him, and He impressed upon me the Scripture, "Truly, truly, I say to you, unless a grain of wheat falls into the earth and dies, it remains alone; but if it dies, it bears much fruit" (John 12:24). It was not an answer

I was expecting to hear. But it was the answer I needed to hear. Somehow, some way, in God's economy, Orie's death would lead to more life. Our tears were tempered with hope.

Two and a half years later, another beloved person, Helen Kupec of Syosset, New York, left this world on November 24, 2011, to be in her eternal home. Helen was a devoted wife and sacrificial mother of seven. I was her youngest. I can still see her sitting on the couch with a big smile as I entered through the screen door and entered the living room. She stopped everything, acting as if the most important person in the world had just walked in. She made me feel valued. She made me feel loved. She made everyone feel that way. I don't think there was a person who didn't like my mother. Well, let me take that back. There may be some of my mother's former bridge opponents who felt her competitive sting. One false double trump and you may have experienced her German side. Despite her being ninety-two years old at the time of her death, her loss was still impactful. It was unusual to see so many people at an older person's funeral. It was obvious she had touched so many lives.

February 14, 2014, was another sad day for our family. My dad, William Kupec, Sr., a teacher and principal for thirty-five years in Syosset, died at the age of ninety-four. The former World War II anti-aircraft sergeant had many admirable characteristics. The one that impacted me the most was his encouragement. Of all the football, basketball, and baseball games I played in my life, I always heard him say, "Good game, kid." His glass was definitely half-full on some of those observations.

There was only one other phrase he would say after a game that was troubling to me. I remember walking off the field after one game in my senior year of college, knowing that I had just played poorly. I just wasn't sure *how* poorly I had played. With my head low and my confidence shaken, I encountered my father an hour later. His bone-chilling comment? "Tough game, kid." I remember thinking, *Oh, boy. Was I that bad?* My dad was too kind to say anything negative about my performances. When he offered, "Tough game," the muddy waters became clear. The truth can be hard to live with!

Nineteen days later, another loss hit home. Bill Kupec, Jr. passed away after a four-year battle with Amyotrophic lateral sclerosis (ALS), also known as Lou Gehrig's disease. Despite our prayers for Bill's healing, the Lord decided to take Bill home. I have heard people comment that a person's entrance into Heaven is the ultimate healing. From a big picture standpoint, I agree wholeheartedly. From a more temporal position, I can't help but wonder if we missed something in our prayers for our beloved brother. In the final analysis, however, God knows best. His ways are above my ways (Isa. 55:8-9). I see in part; He sees completely (1 Cor. 13:9). He is holy; "I am a man of unclean lips" (Isa. 6:5). The only righteousness that I have was imputed to me by faith through Jesus' atoning work on the cross. Jesus lived a sinless and perfect life. Since He is the exact representation of God in human form (Col. 1:15), I can rest assured that His sovereign decisions are true and just. He is Sovereign in all things, even my brother's horrible death. He is good at all times.

I would rather focus on the beauty of Bill's life than on its disturbing end. Bill and I were the bookends of seven kids. Even though eleven years separated us, we became very close from my mid-twenties until his death twenty-five years later. God used my oldest brother to lead me to a saving knowledge of Jesus. It was a conversion that took many years. Bill was more than patient in the process. He was a stabilizing force in my life—exhorting me to go forward when my walk with God became stagnant, encouraging me the countless times I became disheartened, and always directing my attention to God's grace when I fell short. In Bill's eyes, I could do no wrong. He was my biggest fan. That attitude was not reserved for me, however. It was evident in his relationships with his wife, Gail, and his two children, Kerri and Daniel. They were the apple of his eyes. He was proud of them, prayed for them, laughed with them, and comforted them, always putting their best interests ahead of his own. It extended to the women prisoners he witnessed to in his job as a physician's assistant at Riker's Island in New York City, showing many of them a genuine, non-sexual interest—a first for many of them. It extended to the men and women he led in small groups throughout the years—the ones he exhorted to become all that God created them to be. It extended to his nieces and nephews of whom he always spoke in glowing terms.

I am happy for Bill that he is with his heavenly Father in his new spiritual body (1 Cor. 15:42-44). Still, I miss him a lot. I miss my parents, too. I think of all three of them daily.

Ten years later, on this particular Sunday and on this particular site, I was thinking a lot about Orie Wenger. Much has changed since he led the people of Mount Zion Christian Fellowship. The Christian school across the street bearing the church's name is no longer in existence. The building stands quiet, a larger-than-life "for sale or for lease" sign draped across it. The grounds of the church campus are still picturesque. The winding road leading to the parking lot up the gently ascending hill still slices its way through the two ponds that stand between Garlington Road and the church building. There have been some minor changes to the front of the edifice but nothing that would alter any memories of it. Only the new name on the church seems out of place—Bridgeway Church.

Linda and I walked into the service, definitely not the same people we were ten years earlier. If I am nothing else in this world, I am observant. Throughout the years, I have watched all types of people react to loss, disappointment, and turmoil in different ways. Some have become more hardened by life events, seemingly becoming more cynical about life, and with the people with whom they interact. A quiet bitterness has set in, like a morning fog that makes it more difficult to see. Like a drop of red dye into a bowl of water, the effect becomes obvious to others. The water is still there, but the purity of it has been altered. It is not as clear; it is not as inviting. On the other hand, some have taken a different path. Pain has not defeated them. They have become softer, gentler, more tenderhearted. They seem to have drawn closer to God in the midst of the upheaval, experiencing His embrace the way a mother comforts her little one. It is as if the process has made them more whole, more complete, more aware of their need for God and their utter dependence on Him. The pride that once raised its ugly head seems to have lost its place.

Linda and I took our customary seats in the back. I had expected to feel uncomfortable for some reason, but I didn't. I actually felt like I belonged— but not in terms of being a member of Bridgeway Church. While the church seems like a great place to be, I could sense it wasn't where God would have us settle down when our time of journeying through the Southeast ended. We belonged because we were in right standing with God. We belonged because we were learning to operate in true identity as children of God, not as a rite of birth but as a result of Jesus' finished work on the cross and His sanctifying work in our lives. We belonged because His mercies that are new every day have accumulated over days, weeks, months, and years. Ten years especially. We belonged because His grace is sufficient for us at all times and in all circumstances. Jesus stated:

> Therefore everyone who hears these words of Mine and acts on them, may be compared to a wise man who built his house on the rock. And the rain fell, and the floods came, and the winds blew and slammed against that house; and *yet* it did not fall, for it had been founded on the rock" (Matt. 7:24-27).

The winds blew hard on us these past ten years. God's faithfulness to us never tempered. A foundation on the rock. A human being rooted and grounded in Christ. It is the highest level of living to which a human being can attain. It is a life of purpose. It is a life of stability, yet exciting and unpredictable. It is a life of suffering but always followed by comfort. It is a life of repentance from our own finite and limited perspectives to faith in the One Who is above all (John 3:31-36), the One Who is "the same yesterday and today and forever" (Heb. 13:8).

In all my years of living, I have never once heard a person lament that he had surrendered his life to Jesus. On the contrary, I have only heard others say that if they could do it over again, they would have followed Jesus at a much younger age. For me, if I had to do my life over, I would have studied the Word of God daily, letting its power dwell in me deeply (Col. 3:16). I would have made it the rock from which I viewed life and made all my decisions. Unfortunately, it has taken me five deaths and many failures to seek God through His Word completely, not partially.

I would give anything to spend another day with Orie, my mom and dad, and Bill. Yet those reunions will have to wait for another time and a far more glorious place. For now, I forge on, humbler and more resolute than I was ten years ago. I am confident, because of God's abundant grace, I will not be the same person in ten years, either.

OBEYING GOD'S VOICE

POE MILL, SOUTH CAROLINA

According to the Census Bureau's population figures of 2017, Greenville, South Carolina, was the fourth fastest-growing city in the United States—growing by 5.8 percent from July the year before to 67,453 a year later.[41] Since the time my family arrived in Greenville in 2004, we have witnessed firsthand the effects of that exponential growth. Old buildings have been torn down. New condominiums have sprouted up throughout the city like wild flowers in early spring. Greenville is the place to be. You hear it in the German accents walking over the Liberty Bridge, the 4.5-million-dollar pedestrian bridge stretching across the thirty-two-acre, downtown Falls Park on the Reedy River. You hear it in the French accents walking down Main Street toward Fluor Field, the home of Greenville's minor league baseball team, the Greenville Drive. You hear it in the Northern accents, riding bicycles down the Swamp Rabbit Trail, a 19.9-mile, multi-use trail that largely follows the bed of a former railroad that had been nicknamed after the indigenous swamp rabbit. People from everywhere are coming to Greenville.

---

41 Maayan Schechter and Eric Connor, "Greenville named fourth fastest-growing U.S. city," Greenvilleonline.com, https://www.greenvilleonline.com/story/news/2017/05/25/greenville-named-fourth-fastest-growing-u-s-city/344009001 (accessed March 24, 2019).

Well, most parts of Greenville, that is. Very rarely do people venture into Poe Mill, the section of downtown Greenville that Linda and I visited on this particular Sunday. There is a story behind that, of course. The city of Greenville has a very long history in regards to textile mills and the communities that surrounded the mills. Greenville was once the textile capital of the world. That was yesterday. Today, nearly all of the textile mills in the city have been abandoned. Some of the textile mills have been left to be broken down by the elements.[42] That is the case of the Poe Mill neighborhood. The two remaining smokestacks stand both as a memorial to the textile days of old and as a symbol of the poverty that has seeped in like an unwanted nightmare. One longtime Poe Mill resident described Poe Mill as "the ghetto."

Griggs Memorial Baptist Church seemed to be no different than its Poe Mill neighborhood. Founded in 1936, the church almost died three years ago. Down to five members with no pastor, the small congregation turned to a seemingly unlikely candidate to revitalize its church. Pastor Mitch Miller reminded me of a younger version of the successful, quirky Washington State University football coach, Mike Leach. For non-football fans, a better comparison might be Lieutenant Frank Columbo, the unorthodox and persistent detective who starred in the television series *Columbo* from 1971 to 1978.

Like Coach Leach and Lieutenant Columbo, Pastor Miller gave the appearance of being somewhat unconventional. No tie and jacket and slicked back hair. No ripped jeans and sculpted body. Instead, an untucked, button-down shirt and wavy hair. While I can't say I saw it, I would bet my life he was wearing sneakers under those regular jeans. There was no angry look at the sound man when the speakers kept making a loud, jolting sound, interrupting first a guest from Gideon's International, Jordan McClarron, and then himself

---

42   "A History of Greenville, SC: The Textile Capital of the World," Upstate South Carolina News, https://upstatesouthcarolinanews.wordpress.com/tag/poe-mill (accessed March 24, 2019).

when he was giving the sermon. Instead, he stated, "I love when that happens" (I will explain what he meant by that later in this chapter). I believed him, too.

As he introduced himself to me, Mitch gave every reason to believe that he is the kind of leader who truly puts the interests of Jesus and the interests of his congregants before his own desires and agenda. He mentioned very early in the service that Griggs Memorial "loves Jesus, prays to Jesus, and is all about Jesus." That simple, yet profound, declaration is at the core of Grigg's mission—to make disciples in the Poe Mill neighborhood of Greenville, South Carolina. It is their clarion call. It fuels their strategies. Oddly, it is even evident in their church building, seemingly a reflection of the simple, yet resolute, people who are Griggs Memorial.

The inside appeared to have been remodeled recently. While fresh and new, the wood floors complemented well the rest of the building that was rebuilt after a fire in the 1960s. Two sections of fourteen rows of wood pews filled up the sanctuary. Five vertical windows spread across the two side walls. They seemed to be a mixture of stained glass and the soft pastels of a Monet painting. An old, large-print church covenant remained on the front wall of the sanctuary, as if a gesture and recognition of the work of others who paved the way for the work that God was doing today through them.

That work was impressive. To date, the church had delivered Bibles to seventy-five of the 320 homes that make up Poe Mill. Most of that had been done by Pastor Mitch and a small group of college students who are members of Griggs, some of them from nearby Bob Jones University. Church attendance was growing, slowly but surely. The church has a fifteen-passenger van that picks up the neighborhood kids and brings them to Sunday services. After having a block party for the neighborhood the previous summer and a family fun night in the fall, Griggs was having a spring block party for the residents of Poe Mill. At this outreach, the church would provide free lunches for all the participants and have games, prizes, and bounce houses for the children.

The church had plans to conduct a tent revival in Poe Mill in the late summer, reminiscent of meetings that were commonplace in churches throughout the South in generations gone by.

For this particular day, though, the main event was the preaching of God's Word. Alluding to the problematic sound system, Pastor Mitch said he wasn't interested in a smooth service but in the work of the Holy Spirit in our midst. As if on cue, he used Acts 9 as his text. Saul of Tarsus, later to become the great apostle Paul, set off on a 135-mile trek to Damascus to arrest his fellow Jews who recognized Jesus as the Messiah and had become part of "The Way." God intervened, however. He blinded the zealous Pharisee, knocked him off his horse, chastised him for persecuting Jesus (through His followers), and told him to go into Damascus and wait for further instructions.

God then spoke in a vision to another man, Ananias, a Jewish man who was a follower of Jesus. Jesus told Ananias to go into Damascus and lay his hands on Saul for his healing. Understandably, Ananias was cautious. He reminded Jesus who Saul was and what he had been doing to the followers of Christ. That was understandable. Can you imagine if God had asked you to go and lay hands on a notorious persecutor of the faith? A man who was responsible for the imprisonment and murder of many who shared your faith?

Pastor Mitch explained that it was acceptable to ask God for clarification. God did not rebuke Ananias' inquiry. In fact, He gave him further revelation. Sometimes, however, Jesus will ask you to do something odd, something that doesn't seem logical to your way of seeing things.

I am reminded of the ministry of Arthur Blessitt. While ministering to many drug addicted persons for years in Sunset Strip, California, he sensed God's call to carry a fourteen-foot cross from the Pacific Ocean in California all the way to Washington, D.C., Arthur obeyed. Then God called him to go to every nation in the world with the same assignment. From 1968 to the present day, Arthur obeyed God's directives. The man who could not graduate with a Bible degree because he could not pass a foreign language course was now ministering to people in the jungles of South America and Africa, sharing only one word with them in the process—Jesus.

If Jesus asks you to do something, Pastor Mitch explained, it is an honor to do it. It brings joy because it is the highest work possible for humans. Tragically, honor is not part of our culture any longer. It has been swapped for fun. Yet following Jesus is better than fun; it is an honor. It may bring rejection; it may bring suffering; but it will always be followed by God's comfort. First Peter 3:13-17 sums it up well:

> Who is there to harm you if you prove zealous for what is good? But even if you should suffer for the sake of righteousness, you are blessed. AND DO NOT FEAR THEIR INTIMIDATION, AND DO NOT BE TROUBLED, but sanctify Christ as Lord in your hearts, always *being* ready to make a defense to everyone who asks you to give an account for the hope that is in you, yet with gentleness and reverence; and keep a good conscience so that in the thing in which you are slandered, those who revile your good behavior in Christ will be put to shame. For it is better, if God should will it so, that you suffer for doing what is right rather than for doing what is wrong.

The truth is, we will all suffer in this world to some degree. Not walking with God only makes it worse. We reap what we sow, both good and bad. When God's Word and the leading of His Spirit are not the foundation from which we live our lives, we open ourselves to all of Satan's deceitful and destructive ways. Worse, we become hardened to God, rejecting the abundant life that Jesus promises to give to all who follow Him, all who take up His cross (Luke 9:23).

Many of the residents of Poe Mill are experiencing this slow death. Most are living in poverty. Many are leading lives dependent on alcohol and drugs, imprisoned by the very things that offer a temporary escape from the challenges of life. They are not experiencing the comfort that only God can provide.

The people of Griggs Memorial see the pain in Poe Mill. They are not running from it. In fact, they are running *to* it. They see the pain in the eyes of the residents that make up this community. With the comfort they have received from God, they desire to give that same comfort to others. They have heard the call of God on their lives and on their church. They, too, have come to Greenville—not for any suspension bridges or beautiful parks, but to share the message that can set people free for all eternity. Like a great college football coach, Pastor Mitch gave one final exhortation to his flock—to go forward with God's purposes, to obey Him, and to love each other. My hope is that people will come to Greenville to witness a mighty work that God is doing in a small group of humble people, doing only what God has asked them to do.

We would see another humble group the following week wrestling with a challenge that only God can answer.

WHAT DO WE DO?

ABBEVILLE, SOUTH CAROLINA

What do we do with all of this? I have thought this question myself many times throughout the years. As a Christian man who is aware of my duty (and privilege) to share the Gospel with others and as a father who has felt a protective urge to shield his developing sons from ungodly influences, I have wrestled not only with this question, but also with the appropriate response to it. It was nice to hear somebody else pose this challenging question for a change. It was just odd to hear it asked in Abbeville, South Carolina, a quaint and historic town of about five thousand residents an hour and fifteen minutes south from our home.

Like most historic towns, Abbeville has its glories and its skeletons. The glories of Abbeville are obvious to the naked eye. If it was not the prettiest town we had seen in our weekly sojourns, it was definitely in the top ten. Its downtown area—or Abbeville Square as it is known to the locals—seems more like a rectangle to me. The historic-looking brick buildings make for a sturdy-looking perimeter. Each building is two stories high, providing symmetry and a feeling that each building is expected to contribute to the whole, not place itself above it.

The brick-paved road, shaped like an oval, seems to have a built-in mechanism that causes the driver to slow down without even knowing it. The two ends of the oval provide an entrance into the square or an exit out of it. Inside the oval-shaped road are parking spots that face toward the tree-lined middle section. Standing at attention between the well-spaced trees are lamp posts with American flags jutting out from them about three quarters of the way up, waving in the breeze well above the cars parked below them.

Right in the middle of this Thomas Kinkadesque picture is the center piece of the town—an ascending, gray monument that seems to reach to the heavens, a tribute to Abbeville's fallen heroes of the War Between the States. It is easy to picture in this setting horse-drawn carriages in place of automobiles; women with modest, old dresses trimmed in lace, ruffles, and embroidery; and men wearing Victorian hats such as top hats or English Derbies. Perhaps these were items worn to Abbeville's most famous building, the Abbeville Opera House.

Abbeville was a railway stopover for "road companies" traveling the eastern seaboard from New York City to Atlanta. With a seventy-five-hundred-foot stage, the opera house was host to many live performances staged by traveling companies, including drama, minstrel shows, and vaudeville. Ten years later in 1918, "moving pictures" began to play alongside the stage shows. Live theater ceased when "talkies" arrived. Eventually, the Abbeville Opera House closed its doors in the early 1960s, only to be resurrected again in 1968. In 2002, it was designated the "state rural theater of South Carolina." It stands proudly close to one of the entrances to the square, next to the old hotel, The Belmont Inn, the itinerant home for actors and actresses before the railway called them away from Abbeville and on to their next destination.

Looking like it hadn't changed since its beginning, the Inn had a simple vertical "Hotel" sign on its corner closest to the square. Interestingly, because of some of the colors of the buildings, Abbeville reminded Linda of some

Caribbean towns she had seen and me of a town called Grenada in Nicaragua. The combination of tropical colors and historic buildings somehow worked. Perhaps that is what made it stand out from other towns we had visited.

Despite a strong temptation to linger longer, we knew the main event of our day was calling us. Friendship Worship Center on Carwellyn Road was a few miles out of the downtown area of Abbeville. Unfortunately, its pastor, Tony Temple, was away this Sunday with members of the youth group at a Fellowship of Christian Athletes event in Myrtle Beach, South Carolina. Doubling as an assistant football coach at Class AA state champion Abbeville High School, Pastor Temple coached his son for the last time the past fall. Nate Temple, a six-foot, four-inch defensive end and vocal team leader would play collegiately at the University of Pittsburgh the next fall.

Speaking in place of the senior pastor was one of FWC's elders, Steve Osborne. The calm and collected gray-haired leader of a blended family of six ("Got the Brady Bunch thing going in our family" is the way Steve described his family) comes from a law enforcement background. Even with all that he had seen over the years, he was still shocked by what he was seeing in American civilization today. Steve was the one who asked that million-dollar rhetorical question, "What do we do with this?"

The "this" was the drag queen library reading program. The "this" was taking the sacred union of one man and one woman and distorting it into the so-called "same-sex marriage." The "this" was the granting of the "right" of a woman to terminate the life of the one developing within her. The "this" was the demanding of others to accept and approve of the behaviors that God had clearly designated as sin. The "this" was the domination of state over church. The "this" could go on and on. What does a Christian do with "this"?

Steve was surprised where this search for an answer took him. God was showing him something he hadn't expected to see. He was beginning to feel convicted by the Holy Spirit about sin in his own life. A powerful Scripture came to his mind:

Why do you look at the speck that is in your brother's eye, but do not notice the log that is in your own eye? Or how can you say to your brother, "Let me take the speck out of your eye," and behold, the log is in your own eye? You hypocrite, first take the log out of your own eye, and then you will see clearly to take the speck out of your brother's eye" (Matt. 7:3-5).

Our hearts need to be in the right place when we venture out to comment on the lives of others. As born-again believers in Christ, we have been forgiven of all our sins by the incredible grace of God through faith in Jesus' atoning and finished work on the cross. We did not earn salvation, nor did we clean up our lives to be in a position to do so. At best, we were thrown a life preserver from a ship while we were about to go under the water for good, and we reached out and grabbed the life preserver for dear life. While we held on to it, God pulled us up and out of danger for good.

Sinners do what they do best—they sin. When a Christian culture was the governing power for many years in our country, most people either were sincere followers of Christ, or they were at least in submission to the laws that were dictated by the dominant group. Even my atheist grandfather, living in this Christian-dominated culture, made fun of any man who would live with a woman before marriage. "He is shacking up," he would comment derisively. Today, the biblical lid has been taken off completely, and a different ideology has taken its place—humanism: "doing what is right in your own eyes." "Shacking up" is a lost term.

Jesus gives us the best model of how to handle the "this" of today. Two thousand years ago, He faced a dilemma. The Pharisees, the powerful Jewish leaders of the day, brought before Jesus a woman who was caught in the act of adultery. Thinking they had him cornered, they asked Jesus what they should do. The Jewish law called for a woman to be stoned to death who was guilty of such an act. The crowd stood by, eagerly waiting for Jesus to respond. Taking his time, he stooped down and wrote on the ground with his finger. Perhaps he was praying. Maybe he was giving the conflict more time to fester, so His answer would have more of an impact on his hearers. He then delivered his verdict: "'He who is without sin among you, let him *be the* first to throw a stone at her'" (John 8:7).

One by one, they left until only Jesus and the woman remained. Jesus then pardoned and empowered her. "'Woman, where are they? Did no one condemn you?' She said, 'No one, Lord.' And Jesus said, 'I do not condemn you, either. Go. From now on sin no more'" (John 8:10). What can we glean from this encounter between the sinless Lamb of God and the one He had created in His image but was living her life apart from Him? The Pharisees offered only the law. Their message to this woman and to anyone missing the mark was to stop sinning. I will still take that declarative over the polar opposite that our culture offers today—if it makes you feel good, how can that be bad?

There is a better alternative, however. One that we can see in this passage from John's Gospel. Like the Pharisees, Jesus told the woman to stop sinning. But in contrast, He gave her something more life-altering than any force our world has ever known—Himself. He gave her His love. He gave her His mercy. He gave her His grace that is sufficient to live by. He gave her His genuine concern. He gave her a life-changing alternative to the men who promised love, but used her to satisfy their own lusts. He gave her the ability to leave her life of sin. He empowered her.

Linda and I drove through the beautiful countryside of Greenville, Anderson, and Abbeville counties. We witnessed grazing cattle, gently rolling hills, and flowering trees awakening after the long slumber of winter. We became reacquainted with Abbeville Square, remembering the charm and feelings of nostalgia we had experienced over ten years ago but had forgotten through the busyness of life. We left our home not knowing what God would have in store for us on this particular overcast Sunday morning one hour and fifteen minutes removed from our home. We encountered a church that had gone through some challenging times of its own but was persevering through hardships. We heard the Holy Spirit speaking to us through a law enforcement agent, who was subbing for his pastor.

We drove back through downtown Abbeville and back to our home feeling empowered. The world around us hadn't changed. The "this" that has become so prevalent around us and has even infiltrated the Church doesn't seem as daunting as it once was. Linda and I were committed to remove the planks from our own eyes, so we could see the specks of dust in others that still need to be seen. We will face the giants that are causing havoc in our culture, speaking the truth as the Bible reveals it, but offering the grace of God and the empowering love of Jesus that must go along with it. Repentance empowered by love is a force that can overcome any "this."

The next week, we would travel to the birthplace of the Savior who died for our collective "this."

A SAVIOR IS BORN

BETHLEHEM, GEORGIA

Merry Christmas! No, it isn't December twenty-fifth. And, no, I did not just watch a Hallmark Christmas movie in July. In fact, we were two Sundays away from Resurrection Sunday—four months after we celebrate Jesus' birth and three months before our nation's big celebration. Each week, Linda and I prayed about where we would be visiting on Sunday. Most times, we didn't hear God very clearly until very late in the week—kind of a game-time decision. Typically, before then, we googled a map of South Carolina and its neighboring states and tried to sense where God was leading us.

This particular week, I sensed an impression from the Holy Spirit to investigate towns in the United States named after biblical locales, such as Jerusalem or Israel. My inquiry led me to other names: Bethlehem, Calvary, and Antioch, to name a few. The sensing became much more emphatic. We were to visit Bethlehem, Georgia, on this particular Sabbath day. Jesus took on human flesh in the small town of Bethlehem. The Creator of the universe became the Son of Man. The world would never be the same.

Bethlehem Church is located on—you guessed it—Christmas Avenue. The town of Bethlehem is truly a little town (I am sorry) with about six hundred residents, according to the 2010 census.[43] Bethlehem is located about fifty miles northeast of Atlanta. Several historians agree that the town received its name from the Bethlehem Methodist Church, which was established in 1796. The suggestion for naming the town came from Judson L. Moore, a well-known Gospel songwriter and publisher who resided there. The street names in town are all names from the story of the birth of Christ.

Because of its biblical name and Christian significance, Bethlehem is always the scene of special activity around Christmastime. A live nativity scene is held each year in the town square. Sponsored by the First United Methodist Church of Bethlehem, the story of Jesus is narrated, with Christmas carols sung by the church choir. Afterward, refreshments are enjoyed in City Hall. Hundreds of people bring their Christmas cards to the Bethlehem Post Office in order to get the Bethlehem cancellation. Inked stamps stating, "Greetings from Bethlehem" are also offered for use to those sending cards. In 2018, the post office canceled more than 120,000 letters.

While embracing its past, Bethlehem Church forges forward with the timeless message it has been entrusted with—the life-changing Gospel of Jesus. Bethlehem Church was named as a "Top 100 Fastest Growing Churches" in the country in *Outreach Magazine*'s list in 2016, 2017, and 2018.[44] Its vision is to lead people to discover "New Life in Christ." Its mission is threefold and is best told by how it is stated on the church's website:

We are a people UNITED IN CHRIST.

---

43 "Bethlehem, Georgia," Ballotpedia.org, https://ballotpedia.org/Bethlehem,_Georgia (accessed April 7, 2019).
44 "Our Team," BethlehemChurch.us, https://bethlehemchurch.us/staff/ (accessed April 7, /2019).

In a world that divides, we will be different by being defined by what unites us. Our personalities, our backgrounds, and our culture divide us. Our common need for a Savior is what unites us.

We are a people FOR ALL PEOPLE.

In the community in which God has placed us, we are for all people. All people includes your neighbor. All people includes the next generation. All people includes people not like us.

We are a people BUILDING A BETTER COMMUNITY.

We, as Jesus followers, are actively rebuilding, restoring, and renewing the lives of broken people in our community and around the world.[45]

Bethlehem Church's mission seems to be resounding in many hearts. According to an usher with whom I interacted, the church had grown from 450 members four years ago to about twenty-five hundred today. The facilities appeared to have been constructed to meet the demands of this increase. The church's picturesque campus included a classy HGTV-looking church building with church offices and a 990-seat capacity sanctuary. It was backed by the new and impressive-looking Bethlehem Christian Academy, a school of 650 students in Pre-K2 through twelfth grade. The athletic fields behind the school included a football field with grandstands on one side and a well-manicured baseball field, including a professional-looking fence for home runs.

More impressive than its facilities, however, was the sense of excitement that exuded from the people of Bethlehem Church, the worship team, and its pastor. The people of Bethlehem had good reason to be excited. Chevas Phillips, one of the worship team members, gave a passionate testimony about how her husband, Josh, steadfastly and persistently prayed for her. While she would be in one room practicing her guitar for her next musical gig in a local

---

45   Ibid.

bar, he would put his hand on the wall in the next room, praying for her to know Jesus as her Lord and Savior. A year-and-a-half later, she surrendered her life to Jesus and found the abundant life she had been seeking in other places. Now she sang the praises of God and exhorted others to do the same each Sunday. She is not the same person she was.

That is the power of the Gospel, the effect of a life touched by the living God. Executive Pastor Matt Piland highlighted this phenomenon on this Sunday in the second week of his four-part series of the Gospel of John. As a side note, the husband and father of two reminded me of a cross between P.J. Gay, a former football teammate of my brother Matt at the University of North Carolina, and Danny Ainge, the president of the Boston Celtics professional basketball team. This was the second time a pastor reminded me of Danny Ainge. It must be a common look. More importantly, however, the pastor delivered his message the way Ainge delivered his crisp bounce passes to Larry Bird in the post.

Pastor Piland explained that Jesus turned Simon the fisherman into Peter the rock, the one who would make the bold proclamation that Jesus was "the Christ, the Son of the living God" (Matt. 16:16). Jesus turned the harsh, legalistic, law-minded Saul into Paul, the apostle of grace, the one who would expand the Gospel from the Jews—the Chosen People—to the Gentiles. In fact, only one Person ever lived a perfect life. That was Jesus. Today, the resurrected Christ, through the Holy Spirit, does perfect work through imperfect people. People think God can't use them because of their past mistakes. But the Gospel isn't who we were; it's who we are.

Pastor Piland then drew from the wildly popular HGTV shows that show the transformation of a "fixer upper" from its unpromising beginning to its almost miraculous rebirth six months later. Renovation is messy. It usually exposes deep-rooted problems that were hidden underneath walls and floors. In the middle of all the work, it is hard to look beyond the exposed pipes, the unpainted walls, and the old air conditioning unit covered with vines. But God always sees the finished product. He is always looking to whom we can become in Christ. He saw Peter long before Simon laid down his sword. He saw Paul long before he took the road to Damascus. He saw Israel walking with a limp long before he wrestled with the angel.

What's our part in this process? Paul's letter to the Romans maps it out: "And do not be conformed to this world, but be transformed by the renewing of your mind, so that you may prove what the will of God is, that which is good and acceptable and perfect" (Rom. 12:2). Fruit manifests when it is connected to the vine. Flowers blossom when they are watered and receive proper sunlight. Athletes are ready to compete when the pre-season preparations have ended.

The Christian becomes transformed when he does the following: First, he reads and studies the Word of God. The Bible "is living and active and sharper than any two-edged sword (Heb. 4:12). We gain God's perspective when we take in His Word. It speaks to us, exactly where we are. Second, we need to think about what we have read. What is God saying to me about Jesus through His Word? Where do I need to repent? Whom do I need to forgive? Next, we need to pray. Paul tells us to "pray without ceasing" (1 Thess. 5:17). Every situation is to be handled with prayer. As I have heard someone say, "Before you speak to man, speak with God." Finally, we need to live a life of obedience. We need to live according to our new nature, not the old one. We need to realize that when we defer to God's ways, we are taking not only the high road, but also the highest one possible.

After the final admonition by the worship team, Linda and I exited the sanctuary and walked slowly through the expansive building and its many hallways leading to other areas of ministry of Bethlehem Church. We then drove around the perimeter of the church property to see the Academy. I got out of the car one last time to see the football field and the baseball diamond lying quietly next to each other. It was as if I were trying to delay the inevitable. A part of me did not want to leave the grounds. I have felt this way many times before when I could sense that God had done something special in our midst. God was doing something great in Bethlehem, Georgia. A church in a small town of six hundred should not have twenty-five hundred people gathering for Sunday services. A church in a small town in rural Georgia should not be impacting lives the way it does. Then again, maybe it should.

Two thousand years ago, God did something great in the other Bethlehem, the one we sing about every Christmas season. He took on human form in a small, remote town of little significance. He lived the greatest life that was ever lived. He died, rose from the dead, and ascended into Heaven. Today, He takes on human flesh, this time through His Spirit in the hearts of humble men and women who call upon His name. He makes them a new creation. He gives them a new name. He sees only the righteousness that He has imputed from Himself. He sees the Peter in you. He sees the Paul in me. I am grateful that He took me back to the past, so I could clearly see my present.

Our journey this week brought us to Jesus' beginning. The next week would bring us to His end here on Earth.

DEATH VALLEY

CLEMSON, SOUTH CAROLINA

For a while, I have wanted to visit a church in Clemson, South Carolina. Surprisingly, Clemson and my childhood family from New York have a history together. In fact, the connection started when my second oldest brother and childhood hero, Chris, left Syosset, New York, at the age of eighteen for the Tar Heel State to play college football for the University of North Carolina. One of the things I remember Chris talking about when he came home during summer break was a stadium where it was very difficult for the visiting team to run an offense because of its deafening noise. The stadium? Clemson Memorial Stadium, popularly known as "Death Valley."

By today's standards, this may seem small, but back then, 41,400 fans in a sunken football stadium gave the home team a big advantage. In those days, the offense relied totally on hearing the quarterback call out signals to prepare for the snap of the football from the center to the quarterback. In Clemson's fifty-four to thirty-two victory over my brother's UNC team, the raucous crowd made life very challenging for my brother and his UNC teammates.

Four years later in 1978, Clemson again proved inhospitable to another Kupec member, this time my brother Matt. My third oldest brother, another childhood hero of mine, and his Tar Heel teammates lost a hard-fought battle in front of a boisterous crowd of 53,800. "Death Valley" again lived up to its reputation. On a few occasions when Matt would try to audible the play at the line of scrimmage, his teammates could not hear him because of the crowd noise. Matt then told the refs his predicament. Not sure what to do, the referees allowed UNC to regroup, and Matt changed the play in the huddle. Trying to survive in "Death Valley" took some moxy.

I did not realize *how* popular Clemson University and its football team were (and are) until my wife and three sons moved to the Upstate of South Carolina in 2004. We live about forty-five minutes from the Clemson campus. When my family moved to the Palmetto State, I took a pilgrimage to Clemson Memorial Stadium and walked out to the fifty-yard line. I wondered how my brothers must have felt when they stood front and center with the rest of their teammates in the middle of Death Valley. It's an experience no one can ever take away from them.

With the fond memories behind me, I looked to Clemson this time in more of a heavenly pursuit—a church where God would want us to visit. It would be a difficult choice, but eventually, an unconventional winner emerged—Downtown Clemson Fellowship.

Interestingly, DCF was started back in 1995 by a Clemson alumnus and a group of Clemson and Southern Wesleyan University students. They longed to create a safe place where their friends who were distanced from the church could connect with God and His people.

> Many students in their late teens and early twenties step away from their faith. Our hope was to offer the message of Jesus through living out the gospel together in practical ways, creating a safe place where those who felt distant from God could connect with Him and His people.[46]

---

46 "History," DCFClemson.org, https://www.dcfclemson.org/our-origin-story/ (accessed April 14, 2019).

Since its inception, the church has met in a bar, a hotel, a warehouse, and the basement of a restaurant. Over time, the church transitioned to a "house church" format. The main work of discipleship is done in the six house churches of DCF. Sunday is the day when all the house churches gather together to worship God corporately and to receive direction and vision from the lead pastor, Josh Spolestra. About one hundred gather each Sunday.

When Linda and I drove up to DCF's latest setting, the Holland Plaza on Clemson Highway in Seneca, it looked more like an extended log cabin than a church building. In fact, if the doors to the church were swinging doors of a Western saloon, we could have been back in the days of *Bonanza* or *Gunsmoke*. With a salon/spa on its left and two other stores to its right, the front entrance gave no indication of how expansive the inside of the church building would be.

We first entered the church's "living room." Like its name indicates, it truly does look like a large family space. Fully carpeted with couches and comfortable chairs all around, it was inviting. Part of me wanted to sit down and put my feet up. The "living room" is open during the week for people to meet, pray, or just relax. While enjoying the ambiance, Pastor Josh approached us to welcome us to DCF. The native of Washington State and former pastor of a church in Idaho for seven years sported a lip earring, tattoos on both arms, and a friendly smile. He seemed genuinely interested in our adventure, stating that our observations of the church might provide a fresh, outside perspective for them.

Leaving the living room, we sauntered into the expansive, yet cozy, sanctuary. The seating area of the sanctuary was covered by string lights. The raised stage section in the front was flanked by two hanging nets that reminded Linda of fishing nets that the apostles might have used in the time of Jesus. Three sections of chairs—the first four rows with cushioned seats and the last four consisting of metal folding chairs—made up the seating. Two aisles separated the three sections of chairs. Most importantly to a big man like me, there was ample space between each row of chairs. The perimeter of the sanctuary consisted of petitioned adjoining areas including a library, a sitting area, a few art galleries, and an art studio that people used as an expression of their worship to God.

I felt a twinge of Greenwich Village in the air. While it seemed like the atmosphere was created with college students and millennials in mind, these two baby boomers enjoyed the creativity and detail that went into transforming a five-thousand-square foot building into a welcoming home, where people could gather together to worship God.

The service on this Palm Sunday began with a worship song. It was followed with the reading of Psalm 118. The first verse and the final one, verse twenty-nine, were identical: "Give thanks to the LORD for He is good; For His lovingkindness is everlasting."

After more worship songs and a time for announcements, Pastor Josh delivered his sermon. While paralleling the final days of Jesus with the final days of the apostle Paul, he emphasized the importance of being filled with and being led by the Holy Spirit. The Holy Spirit indwells anyone who has accepted Jesus as Lord and Savior. He empowers the follower of Christ, teaching him, comforting him, leading him, and convicting him. A person cannot live the "Christian life" without the empowering of the Holy Spirit. Our lives are to be Holy Spirit-led, patterned after the life of Christ and His obedience to the Father.

Paul captures this sentiment in his letter to the Galatian church: "I have been crucified with Christ; and it is no longer I who live, but Christ lives in me; and the *life* which I now live in the flesh I live by faith in the Son of God, who loved me and gave Himself up for me" (Gal. 2:20). Paul explains the essence of being led by the Spirit as opposed to a self-directed life:

> But I say, walk by the Spirit, and you will not carry out the desire of the flesh. For the flesh sets its desire against the Spirit, and the Spirit against the flesh; for these are in opposition to one

another, so that you may not do the things that you please. But if you are led by the Spirit, you are not under the Law. Now the deeds of the flesh are evident, which are: immorality, impurity, sensuality, idolatry, sorcery, enmities, strife, jealousy, outbursts of anger, disputes, dissensions, factions, envying, drunkenness, carousing, and things like these, of which I forewarn you, just as I have forewarned you, that those who practice such things will not inherit the kingdom of God. But the fruit of the Spirit is love, joy, peace, patience, kindness, goodness, faithfulness, gentleness, self-control; against such things there is no law. Now those who belong to Christ Jesus have crucified the flesh with its passions and desires. If we live by the Spirit, let us also walk by the Spirit. Let us not become boastful, challenging one another, envying one another" (Gal. 5:16-26).

The word given to the prophet Zechariah for Zerubbabel, the head of the tribe of Judah during the time of the return from the Babylon exile, is appropriate for Christ-followers today: "'Not by might nor by power, but by My Spirit,' says the Lord of hosts" (Zech. 4:6). The goal is not to live our lives in our own power, but by the power of the Spirit of God within us. Paul gives us further revelation of the effect of the Holy Spirit not only for this life but also for the next: "But if the Spirit of Him who raised Jesus from the dead dwells in you, He who raised Christ Jesus from the dead will also give life to your mortal bodies through His Spirit who dwells in you" (Rom. 8:11).

At the conclusion of the service, Linda and I sauntered around the sanctuary and admired the artwork of Dionne White, a woman Linda and I had conversed with before the morning's service. She, too, was a transplant from up North. While I enjoyed the creative expression in the church, I had another form of creativity on my mind.

Linda and I departed DCF and headed to Death Valley. Driving to Clemson University and around the perimeter of the football stadium, the chained fence gates made it obvious I would not get to the fifty-yard line as I had hoped. Perhaps it was symbolic that my plan was deterred on this rainy, early

Sunday afternoon. The football days were over. They were exciting times for a young boy to see his brothers on national television and read about them in the newspapers. The faded newspaper clippings and the memories are all that remain from those days gone by. I play a different game now—fighting not to win on the gridiron but in the heavenly realms. I am running a different race, fighting a different fight—not by my own might, but by the Spirit of God within me.

That fight would continue the next week as we gave honor to the darkest day in history.

GREAT FRIDAY

GREER, SOUTH CAROLINA

I love Good Friday. I always have. Even as a kid who did not know what it meant to walk with God, I enjoyed the sacredness of the day. It was typically a warm, spring day in New York on Good Friday. The forsythias were in their full, yellow splendor. Something always felt different on that day. Our family did not watch television. It seemed quieter than normal. Like a hush had fallen on our home the way a new snowfall brings a town to a halt. I didn't even mind that my daily afternoon basketball routine was interrupted. Shooting baskets with my two-year older brother, Andy, at the park down the street sandwiched between Narcissus Drive and Cold Spring Harbor Road, I never complained that I would have to put the ball down for a couple of hours while my family and I attended the Good Friday service at St. Edward's Roman Catholic Church in Syosset. "Were you there when they crucified my Lord? / Were you there when they crucified my Lord? / Oh, oh, oh oh sometimes it causes me to tremble, tremble, tremble, tremble. / Were you there when they crucified my Lord?[47]

I was sad when the song ended. I remember wishing they would sing it forever. I felt at peace. I felt secure.

---

47   Johnny R. Cash, "Were You There (When They Crucified My Lord)," Kobalt Music Publishing, 1960.

This Sunday was no different. Forty-plus years later, I woke up hoping to leave the worries of life for a day and concentrate on the wonder of Good Friday. I wanted to soak in the meaning of it all, to be with the Lord only, the way a new bride wants to be with her husband. God has taught me many things about Him and His Word through the years. One of the best is that He gives us the desires of our heart. Not the things that we want for selfish gain, but the rich things that only God can provide, which bring lasting contentment and purpose, that bring perfect peace in a world that seems to thrive on chaos. My desire this day was fulfilled at a place called the Jesus Warehouse.

As the GPS guided us to our destination, I expected to see a large warehouse, like the size of the many manufacturing warehouses that have sprung up in South Carolina over the past ten years. When the GPS informed us our destination was on the right, I wondered how a group of people could fit into such a small building. Linda and I walked up the incline of the gravelly parking lot and entered through a side door. The forty feet by forty feet room was simple. About seventy metal folding chairs were lined up on the cement floor from the front of the room to the back. Two small, rectangular windows near the ceilings of both the front and back walls were visible only when you looked up. The front wall had a simple "Jesus Warehouse" sign on it. Tiny red and white Christmas-type lights provided a background for the sign. In the front of the room were three acoustic guitars. No drums or pianos were present. A simple four-foot-high cross stood quietly to the front left.

The people gathering this night were actually people from many churches across the Greenville area. Their purpose for gathering each Friday night is captured in the following statement:

> Jesus Warehouse is a ministry that exists to gather people together in worship and prayer unto an encounter with Jesus Christ! Come out with friends and family and fellowship with

us as we seek to grow in intimacy with God. We pray. We love.
We worship. We encounter.[48]

The people we joined with tonight seemed to represent people from all segments of life. The majority appeared to be from the mid-twenties to mid-thirties age group. The baby boomers (born 1946-1964) were not without representation, however. While many young people played in an adjoining room, still other pre-teens and teenagers participated with the adults. From the outset, it was clear that these people, regardless of their ages, were there for one reason—to worship and praise the Lord Jesus with all their might.

The first song appropriately dealt with the theme of the night: Jesus' atoning, sacrificial death on the cross. The chorus of the song is the following: "Jesus paid it all, / All to Him I owe; / Sin had left a crimson stain, / He washed it white as snow."[49]

The singing was loud and heartfelt. These people were not just singing a song at a church service. They were singing from their heart to God's heart. They had experienced the stain of sin and how it manifested throughout their lives like a cancer that spreads quickly through the body. They had felt the despair and regret that sin had never mentioned. But they had also experienced the amazing grace that God provides through Jesus' death on the cross. They felt the exhilaration of that weight being taken from them and tossed into the Sea of Forgetfulness.

I had first witnessed this type of heartfelt praise to God when I was a teenager visiting a Catholic charismatic prayer meeting with my oldest brother, Bill, and his wife, Gail. The people gathered that day had also experienced the mercy and new life that only Jesus provides. I remember sitting in the back and thinking to myself, *They have something I don't have.* I couldn't deny it. It was obvious. My pride wanted to push it aside and dismiss

---

48   The Jesus Warehouse, https://www.facebook.com/groups/JesusWarehouse/about (accessed April 21, 2019).
49   Kristian Stanfill, "Jesus Paid It All (with Passion)," Sparrow Records, 2006.

it altogether. But I couldn't. The elephant in the room was too obvious. I'm glad I didn't. By God's grace, I, too, made the plunge into the unfamiliar, a world that I had feared would take away my desires and ambitions. The pull of God was too hard for me to resist. I trusted in Jesus' atoning work on the cross for the payment of my sins. I accepted Him as my personal Savior. It was the start of a lifelong process of His becoming the Lord of my life. It's the only reason I could sing that day at the Jesus Warehouse.

When "He washed it white as snow" bridged to "Oh Praise the One who paid my debt / And raised this life up from the dead,"[50] I thought the roof of the building might come off. I have been to many basketball games where the home team had been way behind in the game and rallied heroically to go ahead in the final seconds before a frenzied home crowd. The noise level was off the charts. This time, everyone in this crowd had been behind in the game of life through their sin and wrong choices and had rallied back through the heroic efforts of the Star Player—Jesus. This time, the stakes were much higher. Basketball victories will fade away, remembered only by a few of the most connected to the event. Jesus' story will never end. It makes our story never end as well. His work brings those who trust in Him an eternity of bliss and complete joy. "O Praise the One who paid my debt / And raised this life up from the dead."[51]

The time of collectively worshipping God ended, and we all sat down for what I thought would be a sermon. Instead, one of the leaders, Danny, informed us that seven different people would share short testimonies or expositions on Jesus' last seven statements from the cross:

1. "Father, forgive them; for they know not what they are doing" (Luke 23:34).

2. "Truly I say to you, today you shall be with Me in paradise" (Luke 23:43).

---

50   Ibid.
51   Ibid.

3. "Woman, behold, your son! . . . Behold your mother!" (John 19:26-27).
4. "MY GOD, MY GOD, WHY HAVE YOU FORSAKEN ME?" (Matt. 27:46, Mark 15:34).
5. "I am thirsty" (John 19:28).
6. "It is finished" (John 19:30).
7. "FATHER, INTO YOUR HANDS I COMMIT MY SPIRIT" (Luke 23:46).

None of the presenters were ordained ministers. All had something significant to say. Two of the presentations stood out the most to me, however. The first was Beth, a mother of eleven children. She sang Psalm 22, one of many prophetic words that foretold of the suffering servant who would die for the sin of the world. The other was John, a middle-aged man who shared honestly about his struggles. Just that week, John had lamented to the Father about how he could praise Jesus with all his heart at a prayer meeting and then go home and look at pornography. How could he sing of his love of Jesus and have wicked things in his heart toward people? As John poured out his heart to Jesus, Jesus poured out His healing to John. Jesus' finished work on the cross is alive and well.

It was a long night for Linda. She was in a good deal of pain. Sitting on a hard chair for an extended period of time is challenging for her. Driving home, we tried to think of what Jesus went through in those six hours on the cross, His body not even recognizable. Worse yet, taking on the sin of the world when He had never strayed from the will of His Father. It is no wonder that the Bible instructs us to "[fix] our eyes on Jesus, the author and perfecter of faith, who for the joy set before Him endured the cross, despising the shame, and has sat down at the right hand of the throne of God" (Heb. 12:2). His work is finished. It's available to anyone who is willing, anyone who will humble him or herself before a holy and perfect God.

"Were you there when they laid him in the tomb . . .
Were you there when the stone was rolled away . . .

Oh, oh, oh, oh. sometimes it causes me to tremble, tremble, tremble, tremble, tremble
Were you there when the stone was rolled away?"[52]

I love Good Friday. And I love Resurrection Sunday!

We would see the timelessness of the death of the Savior the following week in the lives of three souls hanging in the balance.

52 Johnny R. Cash, "Were You There (When They Crucified My Lord)."

EASTER SUNDAY

HIGHLANDS, NORTH CAROLINA

Of all the significant Sunday excursions Linda and I had experienced over those past ten months, I would have to place this Sunday at the top of the list. Perhaps this particular day had an unfair advantage. It was Resurrection Sunday, after all—a day set aside each year to commemorate the culminating event of the most impactful three days in the history of the world. That event has impacted millions throughout the last twenty centuries. Countless lives have been transformed by the intersecting of Jesus' resurrection with the many hearts that have responded to it. We would see that miraculous intersecting in the lives of three young men that day in a small, picturesque town in western North Carolina.

Our selection of Community Bible Church in Highlands, North Carolina, came about a little differently than our previous choices for Sunday visits. This time, Linda was totally responsible for the venue. Two days earlier, Linda had visited the Facebook page of Dionne White, the sister in Christ we had met a week before in Seneca. Dionne had mentioned two churches in the mountains of North Carolina—Franklin Covenant Church in Franklin and Community Bible Church in Highlands. I was leaning toward Franklin, but

Linda kept coming back to Community for some reason. Because she had the stronger sensing, we went with her pick. I am glad we did.

Highlands was only sixty-four miles from our house on the map. Yet, it was a projected hour-and-fifty-minute drive, according to MapQuest. That had to mean one thing—it would be a drive through the mountains. To our surprise, we discovered that the mountains near Highlands were four thousand feet high. With the thermostat becoming more and more red recently, we were glad to get a reprieve from the mid-eighty temperatures that had settled over the Upstate of South Carolina. Even more surprisingly, the weather report was calling for temperatures in the low forties and a sunny sky for our estimated time of arrival in the mountains of North Carolina.

With no rain clouds in sight, we zig-zagged our way through the northwestern parts of South Carolina. Traveling in and out of a national forest, our jaws dropped as we looked to our left and saw some of God's finest art work. Even I had to stop the car so we could get out and take a closer look at the beauty we were beholding. Half of the picture we were admiring was a deep blue sky with a few small, white, puffy clouds that seemed to further accentuate the blueness. The bottom half of the picture featured blooming tops of trees right below us, giving way to various shades of green terrain that seemed to surround what appeared to be a lake and then continued on for miles. Those inspiring views continued for the next forty minutes until we reached the small, mountain town of Highlands.

Highlands was different than most of the Southern towns we had visited. When I commented to Linda that I felt that we were in New Hampshire, she heartily agreed. One-story buildings made of rich wood. No bricks or cheap awnings. It was as if the buildings were made to preserve the town's rich, mountain heritage. This was the type of town that a Hallmark movie could have been filmed in. I could truly see members of the community bumping into each other in town the way it is depicted on those films. Even the people looked like they could be actors and actresses. They looked healthy and wealthy.

The scene was crying for a lighted Christmas tree to be in the small town square, but Christmas in April? Even the Hallmark Channel would consider that a bit too much.

Linda and I continued for another half-mile until the GPS told us we had reached our destination. Not seeing the church from the road, we took a right on to the church property and up a steep road that eventually led us to Community Bible Church. It looked exactly like it did on the internet. What beautiful grounds! What a classy-looking church building! It looked more like a retreat center than it did a typical church. Paul had admonished us to be a Greek to the Greek and a Jew to the Jew. It seemed like Community Bible Church was being a Highlander to a Highlander. The church fit in beautifully with the neighborhood.

No one could accuse the building of being a cookie cutter church. The building seemed to be three sections of A-frames seamlessly connected together, one in the front and the other two back to back behind the first. The front A-frame section included the front doors of the church and a small A-frame covering, almost like a mud room. Going through the doors, an aisle flanked by wooden pews led the way to the front altar area. A large stained glass window stood distinctively above two slanted projector screens. Three high reaching, two-storied archways loomed majestically above, giving the church the feel of a cathedral you might see in a historic European city. As beautiful and inviting as the church building was, it paled to what we would experience the next seventy-five minutes.

It started with meeting Sandy and later her husband, Rusty. Sandy enlightened us regarding the demographics of Highlands in general and Community Bible Church in particular. As we had suspected, Highlands is a very affluent town. While there are year-round residents, many community members are seasonal, escaping the scorching summers of Florida, Georgia, and South Carolina to get away to mountain retreat homes and much milder temperatures. The church membership reflected this dynamic. Sandy and

Rusty typically spend four months in Highlands, starting on May first. Why they chose CBC became obvious to Linda and me.

The Easter service began with the song that included the following verse: "We call out to dry bones, come alive, come alive,"[53] a reference to Ezekiel 37:1-14. It seemed appropriate for this special day. The service continued with the reading of the Bible's account of the death and resurrection of Jesus. The children's choir followed with the song, "He's Alive." The final song, "In Christ Alone," continued the theme of the service.

After the time of worshipping God ended, Senior Pastor Gary Hewins took center stage. He asked us to join him in prayer for a congregation whose church building was burned down in Sri Lanka. He has been instrumental in proclaiming the Gospel in many nations among people devoted to many false gods, Sri Lanka being one of them. He spoke about what the resurrected life of the Christ-follower looks like.

I had to battle not getting distracted with my observations of the preacher. With dark hair and a booming baritone voice, the stocky and tall fifty-ish-looking leader originally from Detroit and later Atlanta (where he accepted Jesus as Lord and Savior), carried an aura of authority about him as he spoke. There was a directness and forthrightness about him that made me wonder if he were ever a lawyer. It was not an obnoxious tone, by any means—only one that gave the impression he didn't want to waste time on superfluous issues.

Regardless of his persona, it was the words that he shared that carried the most weight. He shared an interesting fact as recorded in the Scriptures. Jesus appeared to more than five hundred people over forty days following his resurrection from the dead (1 Cor. 15:6). It was not hard for the disciples to believe in the resurrected Christ because they saw Him themselves. Thomas doubted the reports that he was hearing about Jesus' being raised from the dead. When Jesus appeared to him as well, Thomas responded, "My Lord and my God" (John 20:28). Jesus responded with a truth that spoke not only to Thomas but

53   Lauren Daigle, "Come Alive (Dry Bones)," How Can It Be, Paul Mabury, 10, April 14, 2010.

also to all who would come after him: "'Because you have seen Me, have you believed? Blessed *are* they who did not see, and *yet* believed" (John 20:29).

Two important items are revealed here. First, Jesus accepted Thomas' affirmation of His deity without any objection. Second, Jesus prayed a blessing on anyone, including you and me, who would come to receive Him as Lord and Savior. That is the Good News of the Gospel.

At the conclusion of his sermon, Pastor Hewins extended an invitation to anyone at the service who did not know Jesus as Lord and Savior to invite Him into their lives at that very moment. He asked that any person who wanted to take that step of faith raise his or her hand. Three hands went up. He prayed with them to accept Jesus into their lives. Like the thief on the cross who left his best decision for last, the three young men made the best decision any human being can make. When their hands went up in response to the pastor's invitation, their hands were acknowledged by the One Who had died for them two thousand years ago. They were granted a pardon, which would allow them to live forever with the One Who was resurrected for their entry into Heaven.

Linda and I left the mountains of western North Carolina flying like eagles. We glided back through the mountain roads amazed how God had given us the opportunity to engage in the beauty of His creation, partner with such a life-giving church, and witness hearts turning to their newfound Savior. Since most food establishments were closed on this special holiday, we were more than willing to pass up a good meal for what we had experienced. Driving further on, we saw a Wendy's restaurant to our left. Their marquee by the road contained a message that made us smile contentedly: "He's alive." Yes, He is. How could we not eat there?

How could we ever top this Resurrection Sunday? A return trip to western North Carolina the next week in another picturesque small town might provide that answer.

WEEK 41

HONKY TONK CHURCH

MAGGIE VALLEY, NORTH CAROLINA

How could we ever top last week? Linda and I would never have imagined that answer would be coming so soon. We had just come home from our neighbor's graduation party that Saturday night. It was about 8:30 p.m., and Linda asked me what I thought about tomorrow's journey. I had prayed all week about Sunday's destination, but I had not heard an answer from the Lord. That didn't bother me, since most weeks, that answer came Saturday night. Not this Saturday night, however. I really wasn't sure what to do. Perhaps we were to stay local this Sunday?

I thought of a church called the Happy Trails Cowboy Church in Greenville, but we discovered that they did not have Sunday morning services, only Sunday evening. That idea was nixed. "Lord, we need to hear you," I prayed with more urgency than usual. Instantly, Maggie Valley came to my mind. Linda had always wanted to see Maggie Valley, and I had heard about it for years from my colleague at work, Barbara Brown. I did my customary Google search—"evangelical churches"—this time for Maggie Valley. A few names appeared on my screen. Truthfully, none jumped off the page at me. Knowing Linda needed to get to bed, I unenthusiastically picked one out. We agreed on a departure time of 7:00 a.m.

The drive alone to Maggie Valley was worth the trip. As the crow flies, it is a dart north toward Asheville, North Carolina, then a sudden swoop westward into Maggie Valley. Highway 19 led us to our destination. Something seemed different as we sauntered into Maggie Valley. While we had driven through the mountains many times, the roads ascended, descended, and zig-zagged throughout the journey. Highway 19 was different, however. It was a four-lane highway that was level and straight, almost like an airport runway. Restaurants, tourist traps, motels, inns, and souvenir shops adorned both sides of the highway. There were no cross streets with other businesses beyond the main junction. The mountains stood majestically behind the strip of businesses.

While driving to our destination on Highway 19, I barely noticed a church on my left that caught my attention. One second later and I would have missed it. "Wow," I exclaimed. Because we were early, I asked Linda if she would mind if we checked out that interesting church we had just passed. We made a U-turn and inched slowly to the unusual church building. It was the nicest building we had seen on this particular strip. Linda read the name, "Calvary Road Baptist Church."

Like Maggie Valley itself, the church was unique. Set back from the road, it blended beautifully with the surrounding trees and mountains as if they were together as one. We drove up the entrance to the church and parked. There was no discussion. Calvary Road Baptist was our church this Sunday. With ascending wooden stairways weaving through a kind of rock garden and water area, we passed a wooden cross that gave us confidence that we had made the right choice.

Once inside, we felt right at home. We had met friendly people and friendly churches in the course of our ten-month travels. CRBC was right up there with the friendliest. Everyone seemed to notice that we were new and went out of their way to welcome us. It must have been the reason we decided to sit three rows from the front left for a change.

I'm glad we did. The eight-hundred-seat sanctuary filled up quickly and early. There was an excitement in the air. The buzz from the collective conversation was pleasant. People seemed to really want to be where they were. When Pastor John Swanger, III, the son of a pastor, welcomed the congregants, he seemed at ease and well-connected to them. I was looking forward to hearing his sermon. Then he dropped a bomb. He announced that there would be a guest speaker that day. Quickly, I looked to the front row where Pastor Swanger had been sitting. *Him?* I thought. *He looks so young and kind of weak.* I know my thoughts don't put me in the best light when I share them with you, but I am trying to be honest with our experiences and interactions and transparent with who we are.

Boy, was I wrong! Visiting to speak at Calvary Road's three-day Bible conference, Josh Reavis is also the son of a pastor. His dad, Dr. Herb Reavis, Jr. is senior pastor at North Jacksonville Baptist Church. Josh is the associate pastor of pastoral ministries at NJBC.

Whatever his title and responsibilities, Josh has the gift of teaching. His text was Matthew 20:1-16. His sermon's title was "That's not fair." The parable of the workers reveals a lot about God, about us, and about life in general. Jesus told the story of a landowner who went out early in the morning to hire laborers for his vineyard. He hired four groups of workers at four different times of the day, agreeing with each what their pay would be. At the end of the day, he paid his workers. When the group who worked the longest saw that their pay was the same as the groups that were hired later, they grumbled at the land owner. "It's not fair," they essentially said. The landowner calmly shot back three questions:

1. "'Friend . . . did you not agree with me for a denarius?'" (v. 13);
2. "'Is it not lawful for me to do what I wish with what is my own?'" (v. 15).
3. "'Or is your eye envious because I am generous?'"

262 SUNDAYS IN THE SOUTH

Pastor Josh then explained the passage. God keeps His Word at all times. He has never broken a promise. If you have thought that God was not being fair to you, you most likely thought He made a promise that He never did. He is the Healer. But He doesn't promise to always heal. He owns the cattle on a thousand hills (Psalm 50:10). He owns everything. But He doesn't promise riches; He promises to meet our needs (Phil. 4:19). Prayer is bending our will to God's, not the other way around. We have it out of whack in our modern-day culture.

He then shared what I have noticed not only about myself but also about others. I see it in the undercurrents of many of the political discussions of today. We are wired for jealousy. It affects us more than we know. "If I had that money, I would be happy." "If I had that house, I would be content." "If I had that wife, that job, that anything." The list is unending. Perhaps the problem is not out there, Pastor Josh surmised. The problem is right in here (pointing to his heart).

When we stop and think, we can see clearly that God has been extremely gracious to us. He offered up His Son as a sacrifice for our sin. He took the punishment that was rightly ours and thrust it on His Son. He places His Spirit in all who accept Jesus as Lord and Savior. The Holy Spirit lives in those who are born again—teaching, comforting, and empowering those in whom He resides. An eternal home in the presence of God awaits those who put their trust in Him now.

God's graciousness makes our claims of "unfair" trivial. We really shouldn't be concerned about what is "fair" and what isn't. If we really were treated fairly, our sins would not have been atoned for; the righteousness that was imputed to us would remain on God's Son. Our eternal fate would be unbearable. "So the last shall be first, and the first last" (Matt. 20:16). The last know they are undeserving. The last know God's unmerited favor. The last know God's goodness in a personal, life-changing way. They know who is first.

Linda and I stood in awe at the end of the service. The Holy Spirit was present in a powerful way. We didn't want to leave His tangible presence. We spoke with Don, a soft-spoken, gentle, septuagenarian usher, who lost his wife two years before. He gave us the amazing story of Calvary Road. Twenty years ago, the church building was a honky-tonk. Big name country singers performed on the premises. With the fun and frequent flow of alcohol came many flying fists. Knives were pulled in the parking lot. One fatal gunshot closed the honky tonk for good. The building stood vacant for years.

While this was going on, the people of Calvary Road were praying for a bigger place to accommodate their growing congregation. Just as the church was about to finalize plans to build a new sanctuary, someone suggested that they take a look at the closed down honky tonk. Providentially, at the same time, a private school approached CRBC about buying the church's building. Calvary Road never looked back.

We asked Don one more important question: What restaurant would he recommend for lunch? Don didn't bat an eye. Country Vittles it was. A left out of the parking lot and a half-mile down on the left. Courtney, our waitress, shared her favorite things about Maggie Valley. She also told us that she did not attend church. We told her about a great one just a half-mile down on the right. She asked us if we planned to come back to Maggie Valley.

We hope so. We really want to. We really enjoyed our time there. One thing I am learning, though. The best place to be, greater than any town, greater than any experience, is the place where the Spirit of God leads. We didn't know what awaited us the night before. But God did. He had it all planned out for us.

How exactly do you top the best? The answer is becoming clearer each week. By being in the center of God's will. His will would prove spectacular to us again the next week but in a way that we could never have suspected.

WEEK 42
NAMELESS AND FACELESS

DAWSONVILLE, GEORGIA

What would you do if oil began to ooze from your Bible? For a humble, elderly follower of Jesus in northern Georgia named Jerry, this unlikely phenomenon became a reality. It didn't happen overnight, however. I will let a nameless voice from the website created for the oil phenomenon tell the story:

> A small group of us [in 2014)], with no agenda, gathered for weekly prayer and fellowship for a couple of years. We would get together, share a scripture, share prayer requests, pray, and worship God until He was through. After about six months these times of coming together began to intensify.

> In the fall of 2016 the Lord began to give us markers. First we believed He told us He would give us more instruction after the presidential election. When the election was over, He instructed us to live, eat, and breathe Romans 12:1-2, which says, "I beseech you therefore, brethren, by the mercies of God, that you present your bodies a living sacrifice, holy, acceptable, to God, which is your reasonable service. And do not be conformed to this world, but be transformed by the renewing of your mind, that you may prove what is the good and acceptable and perfect will of God."

From November 2016 to January 2017 our time together became more focused. The Lord again spoke to us in January and said He would show us after the inauguration what He had been preparing.

The inauguration was on January 20th. We gathered together on Monday evening the 23rd. Normally our times together would end between 8:30 pm and 9:00 pm. That night was different. Intercession and worship were very intense. Jerry was on his knees praying. Johnny and Leslie laid hands on him and began to pray. Jerry fell over on the floor and stayed there for about 45 minutes. Johnny and Leslie went over to the couch and did the same with Joyce, Jerry's wife. After praying, Joyce said the Lord had done something so deeply in her that she would never be the same. We continued worshipping until around midnight. Jerry and Joyce were so affected by what happened on Monday night that they stayed home the rest of the week reading their bibles[sic], praying, and worshipping God.

Friday morning, January 27th, Jerry's granddaughter and great granddaughter came to visit. When they left, Jerry picked up his bible[sic] to read. He had been reading in Psalms all week. His bible[sic] fell open to Psalm 39 and he noticed a wet spot on the page that had soaked through to Psalm 63. He asked Joyce if the great granddaughter had spilled something on his bible[sic]. Joyce told him the baby had not had anything to drink. Later that afternoon Jerry and Joyce took the bible[sic] over to Johnny and Leslie's home. They all agreed it was oil.

Over the next couple of weeks, the oil moved through the bible[sic] from Psalm 39 through the book of Revelation and even into the back of the bible[sic] on the maps and the concordance. The oil stopped then appeared at the front of the bible[sic] in Genesis 1. It continued to move through the Old Testament to where it started in Psalm 39. It then began to saturate the whole bible[sic]. Jerry placed the bible[sic] in a gallon size Ziploc bag. When the oil began to fill the bag, we then placed the bag in a plastic container. Once in the container, the oil began to flow even more, filling that container.

The bible is now in its fourth container. As the container fills up, Jerry takes the oil and puts it in containers until we get together and fill vials. We believe the Lord has instructed us to not advertise, to not market the oil, to not "knock" on doors, and to not try to convince people what it is. His word to us was to give the oil away so He can replenish it. He instructed us to share the story, share His word, give the oil away, and the miracles will happen "outside the building." And they have. His word was, "The church is leaving the building!" The oil has gone all over the world. We have given away over 150,000 vials. We receive testimonies every day of the miracles God is performing in the marketplace, in the hospitals, in the workplace, in the streets, in almost every country of the world.

"The church has left the building . . . "[54]

Linda and I visited Christ Church Fellowship for the second time in our weekly sojourns because we discovered that the oil was going to be present at the regular 10:30 service. We weren't necessarily seeking the manifestations of God's presence, but we desired to be where He was doing something special. Why would we not want more of God's blessings?

We were not the only ones. As soon as we pulled into the parking lot of the church, we could tell something noteworthy was happening. When we visited Christ Church back in November, there was a good size crowd. Today, we could tell it was a huge crowd! We entered the parking lot about 10:10 a.m., and the lot appeared to be completely filled. When we entered the front door of the church into the lobby area, we were surprised to see attendants checking all visitors' bags to make sure no one was bringing in any kinds of weapons.

54   "Story of the Oil," His Name is Flowing Oil.org, https://hisnameisflowingoil.org/story-of-the-oil/ (accessed May 12, 2019).

When we entered the sanctuary, most of the seats were filled. We settled for the last row toward the side. We sat next to Daniella, a regular church member who had emigrated from a small, northern town in France near the German/ Swiss border over forty years prior. Daniella told us the crowd today was much larger than most Sundays. In fact, I was told later that twenty-three hundred people were in attendance. John from New Orleans, sitting to my right, told me he came to see the oil, just as we had.

There was a buzz in the crowd. You could feel the excitement. I noticed a large group of people crowding around the front area to get a close-up picture of someone or something. I couldn't make out who it was from my seat about fifty yards away from the commotion. Phones were being held high as they pushed closer and closer. It reminded me of the time when I saw University of Florida quarterback Tim Tebow play football at Williams-Brice Stadium on the campus of the University of South Carolina. When Tebow became visible to the crowd, they stood; the noise level heightened; and people began to point toward the young celebrity. Then it occurred to me what the stir was about up front—the oil!

Christ Church Pastor, Todd Smith, greeted the crowd at the start of the service. He asked that the doors be closed, phones turned off, and God's people be attentive for the public reading of God's Word. He reminded us of how the Israelites stood for hours for the public reading of God's Word during the reign of King Josiah. Pastor Smith read Psalm 40. He then exhorted us that we had come to encounter the living God. The crowd thundered in agreement. He prayed that the shout would echo from Dawsonville to the ends of the Earth.

If the prayer didn't echo that far, then the praise from God's people just might have. The time of worshipping God through song was the most intense and liberating that we had felt in our ten months on the road in Sunday services. All twenty-three hundred in attendance seemed focused on giving God what He richly deserves—our praise and adoration. When the worship team led us through the song, "Goodness of God," it seemed like the roof could be raised. The chorus was sung with heartfelt appreciation:

"And all my life You have been faithful, ooh / And all my life You have been so, so good.

With every breath that I am able /Oh, I will sing of the goodness of God."[55]

God's goodness continued for us that Sunday. Gerry, with his completely bald head and thick, white goatee, stood up front with his pastor, Johnny Taylor. They told the story of the oil. They mentioned nothing about themselves. They said the oil was to point us to Jesus—to his healing, to His goodness, to His Lordship. God can do what He wants to do—not what He's constrained to do. What God is doing through this oil is nameless and faceless in terms of human beings. It is not about a personality. Signs and wonders must point to Jesus, or they are counterfeit, Johnny instructed us.

He used the analogy of a husband taking his wife to France. First, he brings her a brochure about France. Then, he brings home the tickets for their flight. Next, he buys her clothes for the special events that will occur in their travels. Finally, they depart for the trip of their lives.

Pastor Johnny believes an awakening is coming to our nation. Until that time, God gives us markers to encourage us as we prepare for that tremendous day. He has given Christ Church the miracles in the baptismal (see week 20). People are getting into the water and being healed of various diseases. He has given us the oil through Jerry's Bible. Many have reported healings as the oil spreads to all parts of the world. We need to be patient with God, Johnny exhorted us. To be encouraged by His sovereignty. To be about His business until He decides it's time to bring that awakening. God's timing is perfect; His love is complete.

They definitely were for Linda and me that Sunday at Christ Church. Without hesitation, we darted up front at the conclusion of the service. If I had to knock people down, I would have in order to secure a picture of Jerry's Bible

---

55   "Goodness of God," Bethel Music, 2019.

in the container of oil. With many in front of me, I took a picture with my iPad raised high above my head. I didn't think I had a chance for a good picture. So many people were crowding the container. While waiting for a clearer path, I decided to check my stored pictures. There it was—the container with the Bible and oil as if I had taken a close-up with no one else around.

Right as I was considering God's small miracle to me, I noticed Jerry allowing people to dip their hands in a different container that held the same oil. Linda and I dipped our hands, too. I put the oil on my forehead and held my hand there. I began to weep. Forcefully. I didn't care who was around. God was healing me on the inside. I felt His compassion and His love. I cried tears that were a combination of sorrow and joy. I put oil on Linda's forehead and prayed for her mind. She put oil on my umbilical hernia and prayed for my healing. Then I put the oil on my troubled right knee. I felt something. I felt more flexible.

I noticed I didn't limp when I stepped out of the car two hours later when we arrived back in Greenville. Seven days later, my knee was still pain-free. I was walking well. "And all my life You have been faithful / And all my life You have been so, so good / With every breath that I am able / Oh, I will sing of the goodness of God."[56]

And I will tell of the oil flowing from Your Word!

---

56 Ibid.

POWER

NEWBERRY, SOUTH CAROLINA

Riddle: What is small and unknown, yet heard around the world? Linda and I would find that answer in Newberry, South Carolina, a one-hour drive southeast of our home in Greenville. Most people who drive in this direction typically continue another thirty-five minutes to get to the state capital of South Carolina—Columbia.

On this overcast and rainy Mother's Day, we were glad to be visiting Glory Tabernacle in Newberry. Linda had become aware of Glory through a Facebook announcement about an upcoming Women's Aglow meeting in Greer, South Carolina. A picture of the guest speaker caught Linda's attention. The woman seemed extremely joyful. The advertisement said she attended a church called Glory Tabernacle in Newberry. Linda suggested we visit Glory Tabernacle at some point in our travels. That some point had come.

I had no preconceived notions about what GT would be like. I wasn't even sure what denomination it belonged to, if any at all. Since we arrived early, we decided to drive around the town before going to the 10:30 a.m. service. Newberry is not a town that we have heard people discuss in our fourteen years in Greenville. Myrtle Beach, Hilton Head, Charleston, Columbia, yes. Newberry, no.

Newberry County was first settled in the 1750s by the English/Welsh, Scots-Irish and Germans. That might explain the presence of Newberry College, a small Lutheran college with about one thousand students and a pretty campus a few blocks away from the downtown area of Newberry. Passing the college, we sauntered down the tree-lined College Street and caught our first glimpse of the historic section of town. It was obvious the residents of Newberry valued their rich history. The brick buildings seemed well cared for. The tree-filled town square provided much shade for those looking to sit and take in the small-town charm.

The three-story Newberry Opera House, first built in 1881, looked more like an urban school building than a place of cultural entertainment. A quick walk down the brick-laden road led to the historic-looking Hampton Inn, a building that looked like it was once a landmark place of lodging turned into a hotel. Either that or the owners went to great lengths to preserve its historic feel and fit it in nicely with the accompanying buildings in town. We were sorry to abort our self-guided tour, but the 10:30 a.m. service was calling.

The beauty of Glory Tabernacle was not in its building. Little of the building's physical appearance warranted a second look. The railroad line stood right behind the church property. However, we found out the beauty of the church was in its people and mission.

Parking in the gravel-covered lot, we were met by two umbrella-holding escorts. Because I should be voted "the least likely person to be prepared for inclement weather," the greeters settled their efforts on me. Glad that my few remaining hairs were untouched by the rain, Linda and I took our seats in the back pew.

The sanctuary included three sections of pews, ten rows deep and enough to sit about six congregants in each pew. Five windows on each side of the church lined the walls. Toward the front of the building, nine flags from foreign countries hung closest to the pews. A recessed space beyond these flags displayed an American flag on one side and the state flag of South

Carolina on the other. Behind them stood the baptismal. A cross stood to the front left with a type of red scarf draped around the cross beam.

Surveying the scene, Jesus' words came to my mind: "Go therefore and make disciples of all the nations, baptizing them in the name of the Father and the Son and the Holy Spirit, teaching them to observe all that I commanded you; and lo, I am with you always, even to the end of the age" (Matt. 28:19-20). I got the feeling that Glory Tabernacle takes Jesus' commission seriously, that it's at the core of what they are about.

The announcements supported my thoughts. Pastor Joel Mundy encouraged his members to engage in an upcoming evangelistic outreach at Mollohan Park, a joint effort with Restoration Outreach Church, also of Newberry. In addition to their local efforts, the church has a vision to impact the nations:

> Pastor Mundy and his wife, Lori, founded Nations of the Earth Ministries in 2017 after a trip to Africa where they sensed God's call to open a School of Ministry Training Center in the United States of America. The Midlands School of Ministry was established to Teach, Equip, Authorize and Release ministers of integrity into the nations for the end time harvest![57]

Pastor Mundy is also leading the Pakistan Project, a ministry where he records messages and sends them "to Pakistan and air[s] on PMI TV HD in the 10/40 window."[58]

When the announcements ended, Pastor Mundy put on his encourager's hat and reminded all in attendance who have put their faith in Jesus that they would be with Him soon in Glory. That will be a day of things unspeakable. Until that time, however, we are to "grow in the grace and knowledge of our Lord and Savior Jesus Christ" (2 Peter 3:18), to worship God "in spirt and truth"

---

57 "N.O.T.E. Ministries," GloryTabernacleSC.org, https://www.glorytabsc.org/copy-of-what-we-believe-1 (accessed May 19, 2019).
58 Ibid.

274 SUNDAYS IN THE SOUTH

(John 4:24), and to share Jesus with others. The many amens told me the audience was in agreement.

When the time of worshipping God began, I noticed that all the singers in the front were women, with the pastor's wife in the middle on piano. The sound was almost soothing and pleasant. I thought back to female Christian groups like Point of Grace and BarlowGirl. I wondered if this had anything to do with Mother's Day.

While the time of worshipping God continued, I noticed something we had not seen in our weekly sojourns. Behind the seven female singers were three male musicians. One was a drummer, and the other two were on guitar. It was the one on electric guitar that caught my eye and made me chuckle. It was Pastor Joel! *Some guys do it all*, I thought to myself.

When the time of worship ended, Pastor Joel handed the microphone to his wife, Lori. She started by stating that she was speaking to the women of the church this Mother's Day Sunday service. It was truth, however, that both genders could benefit from. Lori shared what every woman knows— that conception begins with a seed being planted.

Paul Noel Stookey of the famous folk group, Peter, Paul, and Mary, sang in his song, "There is Love": "Woman draws her life from man and gives it back again."[59] While Paul spoke of the seed being planted by the husband into his wife, a miraculous conception took place two thousand years ago that altered the course of history and brought Heaven to Earth. Matthew 1:22-23 states, "Now all this took place to fulfill what was spoken by the Lord through the prophet: 'BEHOLD, THE VIRGIN SHALL BE WITH CHILD AND SHALL BEAR A SON, AND THEY SHALL CALL HIS NAME IMMANUEL,' which translated means, 'GOD WITH US.'" Paul captured the essence of Who Jesus is: "He is the image of the invisible God, the firstborn of all creation" (Col. 1:15). He also captured the essence of Jesus' mission: "For He rescued us from the domain of darkness, and transferred

---

59   Paul Stookey, "The Wedding Song (There Is Love)," Warner Bros. Records, 1971.

us to the kingdom of His beloved Son, in whom we have redemption, the forgiveness of sins" (Col. 1:13-14).

There is another implanting of a seed that changes the course of a person's life for all eternity. This is for the person who repents of his sin and puts his faith in Jesus as Lord and Savior. The apostle Peter explains the eternal ramification of turning to Jesus for salvation: "For you have been born again not of seed which is perishable but imperishable, *that is*, through the living and enduring word of God" (1 Peter 1:23).

That enduring Word also reveals the identity of the person whose life God has entered. First, the believer has become a child of God (John 1:12). Second, the believer is now a member of Christ's Body—His Church. Third, the believer is a citizen of Heaven (Phil. 3:20). With that new identity comes promises that cannot be broken. He is accepted in the Beloved (Eph. 1:6); he is loved (Rom. 8:39); he is forgiven (Eph. 1:7); he is more than a conqueror (Rom. 8:37); he is seated with Christ in "heavenly *places*" (Eph. 2:6); he is victorious (1 Cor. 15:57); he is secure (Heb. 13:5); he is free of condemnation (Rom. 8:1); he is complete in Christ (Col. 2:9-10); he is a temple of God's Spirit (1 Cor. 3:16); he has encouragement even in failure (Phil. 1:6); and he has complete access to the throne of grace (Heb. 4:14-16).

We need to hold on to our identity in Christ. Our enemy and our flesh will try to tell us otherwise. We can take those thoughts captive and make them obedient to Christ. "No, I am not a failure. No, I am not the little boy who was not good enough. I have been bought with a price. I am a new creation in Christ. The old has passed; the new has come. I am a child of God. I am forgiven. I choose to forgive everyone, for everything, right away, every day. I choose to confess my sins to my brothers. I choose to repent of all things contrary to the will of God in my life."

Linda and I left our brothers and sisters in Christ—old, young, black, white, Hispanic—grateful that we all share the same Heavenly Father and the same purpose for living. When Linda was leaving the back of the church, a young mother who had been given a set of flowers by the church for Mother's Day approached Linda and gave her the flowers she had received. Her beaming, ear-to-ear smile told me that she was happier to give then to receive. Perhaps that explains the power of the small church in Newberry that is impacting the world for Christ. Its members have been given a new life and new identity in Christ. They now wanted to give that life away—not only to people of Newberry, the Midlands, and Pakistan, but also to two visitors who they will probably never see again until they meet once more in Heaven.

We would meet other brothers and sisters in Christ the next week as we traveled to the place that some consider to be the number one city in the United States.

THE #1 CITY IN AMERICA

CHATTANOOGA, TENNESSEE

If I were to ask you what city in the United States you thought was the most Bible-minded, what city would you choose? According to the American Bible Society's fourth annual America's Top Bible-Minded Cities study, the answer is found in the sixteenth state to be admitted to the Union back in 1796. That would be the Volunteer State—Tennessee.[60]

Now that you know the city is located in Tennessee, do you think it is Nashville? Sorry, country music fans. Memphis? No, Elvis fans. Knoxville? Wrong again. You are warmer, though. Yes, Chattanooga is the correct answer. In fact, Chattanooga has been recognized as the most Bible-minded city two of the last three times the American Bible Society has conducted its study. Birmingham, Alabama, is the other city that has captured top honors.

> To calculate each city's ranking, The Barna Group collected data by analyzing survey respondents' Bible reading habits and beliefs about the Bible. The most Bible-minded respondents said they had read the Bible in the past seven days and believe strongly in the accuracy of the Bible. Nationally, 25 percent of the population is considered Bible minded.[61]

---

60 "The Most Bible-Minded Cities in America," AmericanBible.org, https://www. americanbible.org/features/americas-most-bible-minded-cities (accessed May 26, 2019).
61 Ibid.

Visiting the city with the most Bible-minded residents was a no-brainer for Linda and me. In the city of the most Scripture readers, we settled on the church with the three highest crosses on its property. Driving on 75 North in Tennessee, it is impossible to miss the three white, commanding crosses of The Crossing Church that stand with authority to the side as if guarding a sacred ground or sacred truth. The middle cross of the three reaches 125 feet into the sky. Why the crosses? The church's website says it plainly:

> We believe Jesus is the hope of humanity, and as His church, we live to make His name known in our city and around the world. We are people of the cross. We will never get over the cross, and we will never stop telling the story – His story, our story, and the greatest story of all."[62]

The church believes so strongly in the message of the cross, that it has set up the twenty-four/seven Three Cross Plaza. It is open to the public, free of charge. In addition to the three crosses, the plaza consists of thirteen stations where visitors can learn about the events leading up to Jesus' crucifixion. The fourteenth station is an empty tomb to remind us that He did not die in vain, that death could have no victory over the Lion of Judah, that salvation would now be available to anyone who puts his or her trust in Jesus' finished work.

That completed work continues to affect lives two thousand years later. It definitely touched the life of Terry Harris, pastor of the Crossing Church. Pastor Harris was a man of authority. It is a trait to which I have always been drawn.

It started with my respect—really, fear—of my elementary school music teacher, Mr. Kemp. The fear of disappointing Mr. Kemp made me practice my trombone, something that I was not naturally inclined to do. It continued with Mr. Tobani, my junior high school basketball coach. I can still see him jumping up and down in anger in the locker room at halftime when he thought we weren't being tough enough against our rival, Westbury. No one

---

62 "Three Crosses Plaza," The Crossing Church, http://crossingchatt.com/crosses (accessed May 26, 2019).

said a word as he tore into us. We won the game! I saw it from a distance years later in Dan Reeves, head football coach of the Denver Broncos and New York Giants. When he gave interviews, he looked like he might break some teeth as he intensely described some facet of his team's play.

I saw it most of all in Bill McCartney, the former head football coach at the University of Colorado and the leader of the Christian men's organization, the Promise Keepers. Gathering with thirty-five thousand other men at Shea Stadium in New York City, Coach McCartney spoke passionately about following Jesus with all of our hearts. I turned to my good friend and former high school football teammate, Bill Lewis, and said to him, "I would have run through a wall for Bill McCartney." He nodded as if we were about to take the field one more time.

I wish I could have heard Pastor Harris' message twenty years earlier when we were first raising our three sons. He started by explaining the seriousness of the times we live in. Kids today, he explained, are targeted by the economists of today. Kids are pliable and impressionable. The marketers do not have their best interests in mind. At best, economists desire our kids' money. At worst, they know they are culture-changers. They will be carriers of the marketers' message. If they can reach these children, they can change civilization. They are not trying to influence our kids toward good goals; they are trying to use them to redefine values. They are influencing our children on issues that are life-changing. However, the greatest culture shapers should be parents, grandparents, and godly church members.

Pastor Harris was concerned about kids beyond the church's influence. It is a radically different world than the one we were raised in. Despite the very concerning shift in culture, the home and the church need to be the places where young people find direction and affirmation. The sixty-five-year-old pastor then provided a framework from which all parents need to raise their children. This framework was the one that he and his wife, Kaye, used in successfully raising their three, now adult, children.

Above all, parents need to work to instill in their children a love for God and a tender heart toward Him. That has to be the foundation from which all other goals emerge. Jesus stated, "'YOU SHALL LOVE THE LORD YOUR GOD WITH ALL YOUR HEART, WITH ALL YOUR SOUL, AND WITH ALL YOUR MIND.' This is the great and foremost commandment" (Matt. 22:37-38).

Second, parents must teach children to respect authority. The Lord is a God of order. Paul's admonition to us in his letter to the Romans provides insight on this vital area:

> Every person is to be in subjection to the governing authorities. For there is no authority except from God, and those which exist are established by God. Therefore whoever resists authority has opposed the ordinance of God; and they who have opposed will receive condemnation upon themselves (Rom. 13:1-2).

When a child has a healthy fear of those placed in authority over him, he has a much greater likelihood of functioning well in a society.

Next, a child must be encouraged to work hard. There are seven days in the week; six of them are designated for work (Exod. 34:21). When a child learns to work hard, he will be successful in whatever field he chooses. Related to working hard is the admonition to never quit. Perseverance is the greatest character-builder of all traits. A child who perseveres is a child who will be prepared to face the many challenges of life.

The child also needs to be taught to believe in himself and to believe in others. We were never meant to tackle life alone. Jesus stated the second greatest commandment: "'YOU SHALL LOVE YOUR NEIGHBOR AS YOURSELF'" (Matt. 22:39). We do not put our hope in others; we recognize their innate worth as image-bearers of God who have the potential to be great in Christ.

Pastor noted that his wife wanted their children to "dream big," "live by faith," and "be daring" (in Christ). He left us with one final truth: parents must own up to their mistakes. It is a given that parents will make those mistakes. How they respond to those errors will set a valuable example for impressionable hearts. Knowing there were parents of all ages in his audience, Pastor Harris gave some of us parents in his hearing one more promise from the Word of God: "Train up a child in the way he should go, even when he is old he will not depart from it" (Prov. 22:6). Even if a parent does everything correctly, the child still has to make his own decision to follow Jesus. If he does not, the Holy Spirit will bring conviction to the child that his life is not right with God. The prayers of the steadfast parent will be honored.

After we greeted Pastor Harris and thanked him for his message, he prayed for Linda and me. We received it with much thankfulness, grateful that God had graced us with a timely word, four hours west from our home in Greenville.

The drive home was icing on the cake. We drove on a road for miles and miles alongside a river whose rapids carried a plethora of rafters and kayakers along its choppy path. Linda's look gave me the impression she would like to jump in there with them. Moving on, we saw pasture lands with gently rolling hills. The resting cows seemed as peaceful as we were. We drove through forests, the tall trees providing protection from the westward-moving sun. We drove through Georgia, North Carolina, and finally, South Carolina, thinking about our time in the most Bible-minded city in the United States. We arrived home hoping that, like the great people of Chattanooga, Tennessee, we would become increasingly more Bible-minded, not only being hearers of the Word of God, but doers of it as well (James 1:22).

We found some courageous "doers of the Word" the following week on the largest army base in the United States.

"GIVE ME TWENTY!"

FAYETTEVILLE, NORTH CAROLINA

One of the greatest moments of my life was walking on the grounds of Fort Jackson, a United States Army installation located within the city limits of Columbia, South Carolina. This occurred three years ago when I served as a mentor to a young man in the South Carolina Youth Challenge Academy, a program housed on the army base that was founded in 1917 and named after our seventh president, Andrew Jackson. Why the excitement? I consider serving in the United States military the highest achievement a person can attain next to serving as a minister of the Gospel.

If I could turn the clock back, I would have served in the military in some capacity. Anyone who has served in the military has my immediate respect. My father, a sergeant in the army in World War II, rarely spoke of his time fighting in England and France against Hitler's advancing forces. It was only in the later years of his life that he shared stories of shooting down German planes over the English Channel in his anti-aircraft regiment. The enemy planes exploded in mid-air in the pitch dark of night and, for a few moments, lit up the historic river and its two banks. He was never proud about it, just humbly sharing what had transpired during his two years across the Atlantic. I salute his humility, his bravery, and his service to his country.

I also salute any soldier who defends the stars and stripes. I had that opportunity on this Sunday as Linda and I ventured three-and-a-half hours east to Fayetteville, North Carolina, on Memorial Day weekend. Fayetteville is home to Fort Bragg, the largest military base in the United States (in terms of population). Before we ventured to visit Fort Bragg, we had a Sunday service to attend at Veritas Church at eleven hundred hours.

Veritas gathers to worship God on the campus of Freedom Christian Academy, a biblically-based, Christ-centered, non-denominational school established in January of 2009. The school has no affiliation with the church. While the high school building that looked more like a modern manufacturing plant was not overly impressive from the outside, its inside caught our attention right away.

As we entered the building into the lobby area, two doors to our slight left invited us to enter the place where the church meets on Sundays and the students eat lunch Monday through Friday. Adorned on the huge, two-story wall that included these two doors was a painting of America's founding fathers. They were in a room together, appearing to be in the process of ratifying the U.S. Constitution. Our first president, George Washington, was standing erect, with his eyes seemingly directed above the people in the room and beyond to a place where only few men can see. The men in the picture looked authoritative, serious, and pensive at the same time. If there were a Hall of Fame of American leaders, each of them would be inducted on the first ballot.

On another wall stood a picture of the American flag draped over a wooden beam with the Liberty Bell in front of it. Above the painting were the words, "Let Freedom Ring." Next to the picture of the flag and Liberty Bell was a Scripture: "The Lord is our Judge, The Lord is our Law giver, The Lord is our King: He will save us" (Isa. 33:22). Below that Scripture was the statement, "Founding Father James Madison was responsible for the three-part (Judicial, Legislative, and Executive) government of the United States. His inspiration for that design came from Isaiah 33:22." That unique form of government gives us the best chance to keep protected from the worst of what is in a man so that the best of what is in a man has the chance to flourish. A zoo is best when the fences keep us from the animals' worst.

A phrase written on a second-story window up a staircase to our right caught our attention. It contained the words of the preamble of the U.S. Constitution:

> We the People of the United States, in Order to form a more perfect Union, establish Justice, insure domestic tranquility, provide for the common defense, promote the general Welfare, and secure the Blessings of Liberty to ourselves and our Posterity, do ordain and establish this Constitution for the United States of America.[63]

I thought to myself, what if every school in America displayed these vital words on their walls and windows? What if every student were reminded daily of the foundational genius of our country? What if every young person were taught the importance of a godly form of government as opposed to a man-centered, socialistic one that yields to the inevitable corruption of man every time? Greater yet, what if every student heeded the words of Noah Webster, our founding educator:

> The most perfect maxims and examples for regulating your social conduct and domestic economy, as well as the best rules of morality and religion, are to be found in the Bible . . . The moral principles and precepts found in the scriptures ought to form the basis of all our civil constitutions and laws. These principles and precepts have truth, immutable truth, for their foundation . . . All the evils which men suffer from vice, crime, ambition, injustice, oppression, slavery and war, proceed from their despising or neglecting the precepts contained in the Bible . . . For instruction then in social, religious and civil duties resort to the scriptures for the best precepts."[64]

---

63   Constitution of the United States of America, "Preamble."
64   Noah Webster, "Advice to the Young," in History of the United States, New Haven: Durrie & Peck, 1832, 338-340.

Grateful for what we had seen on the walls of Freedom Christian Academy, we entered the doors of Veritas Church. Leaving behind images of the wisdom of America's founding and enduring legacy, we moved on to the symbol of eternal freedom, the cross. The people of Veritas Church have full respect for the One Who went willingly to the cross for you and me. On the church's website, an unusual statement is made about the leadership of Veritas Church: "We are Jesus-ruled. Jesus is the senior pastor of our church. Elders/Pastors are men who serve under his authority and are responsible for the theological vision and spiritual vitality of the church."[65]

Speaking of Jesus, the apostle Paul stated:

> He is the image of the invisible God, the firstborn of all creation. For by Him all things were created, *both* in the heavens and on earth, visible and invisible, whether thrones or dominions or rulers or authorities—all things have been created through Him and for Him. He is before all things, and in Him all things hold together. He is also head of the body, the church (Col. 1:15-18).

With Lead Pastor John Murphy and his family away on Memorial Day weekend, second-in-command Worship Pastor Jacob Warren gave the day's message. Speaking to the youngest crowd we had seen in our weekly sojourns, the late-thirties native of the Fayetteville area continued a series on the Gospel of Luke. He explained to the congregation that Jesus was the fulfillment of the Law and the Prophets. He explained the account of Jesus walking with two of His disciples on the road to Damascus following His resurrection. Jesus said to the two disciples:

> "O foolish men and slow of heart to believe in all that the prophets have spoken! Was it not necessary for the Christ to suffer these things and to enter into His glory?" Then beginning with Moses and with all the prophets, He explained to them the things concerning Himself in all the Scriptures (Luke 24:25-27).

---

65 "Leadership," Veritas Church, http://veritasfayetteville.com/leadership (accessed June 7, 2019).

The fourth Gospel in the Bible summed it up in just three words: "It is finished" (John 19:30).

When the pastor's sermon was concluded, we thanked him for his message. Hearing about what we were doing each week, He gave us some background information about Veritas.

The church was six years old in September. It started in the living room of John Murphy with a desire to bring a "Gospel-rich" church to Fayetteville, a city of about two hundred thousand residents. In the 1970s, Fayetteville was derisively nicknamed "Fayettenam." In the 1980s, local authorities cleaned up the city, shutting down its strip joints in the process. Fayetteville is still mostly known as the home of Fort Bragg, really a town within a town. A big part of Veritas Church's mission is to reach out to the soldiers and their families. Executive Pastor Stewart Scott, who served in the army himself, told us that Fort Bragg has the most domestic violence of any military base in the world. Some of the soldiers are suffering from PTSD.

The worship team's drummer and lead guitarist are ex-military. The church's heartfelt desire is that Veritas be a haven for those who are broken and busted, a place where it is okay to come with burdens and join with others with similar kinds of weights. That message seemed to be resonating with the people of the greater Fayetteville area. The church has grown from a handful of members in 2013 to about six hundred congregants today.

The church has two Sunday services. After progressing from meeting in the pastor's living room to a CrossFit gym, then to a meeting hall and, finally, to Freedom Christian Academy, the church continued to strive to be a place whose mission is the following: To make disciples of Jesus who love God, love people, and advance the Gospel for the city, for the military, and for the fame of Jesus.

The people of Veritas Church are "laboring in prayer" for the people God brings them—people with very serious challenges and burdens. They are attempting to create an atmosphere where people can find healing and restoration. They are trying to point people to Jesus—that they may experience Him in a very real and impactful way. They are different types of soldiers in different types of battles.

The apostle Paul sums it up best:

> For our struggle is not against flesh and blood, but against the rulers, against the powers, against the world forces of this darkness, against the spiritual *forces* of wickedness in the heavenly *places*" (Eph. 6:12).

We salute the leaders and people of Veritas Church. They are fighting a noble fight.

We visited another fort the next week where other battles are being fought.

WEEK 46

THE EYES TO SEE

FORT MILL, SOUTH CAROLINA

"But blessed are your eyes, because they see; and your ears, because they hear. For truly I say to you that many prophets and righteous men desired to see what you see, and did not see *it*, and to hear what you hear, and did not hear *it*" (Matt. 13:16).

Seeing Jesus. At all times. In all circumstances. In the mundane. In the spectacular. In His Word. In the miraculous. In the quiet whisper. As the Holy Spirit teaches about Him. As His people gather together to pray and receive His direction.

Visiting MorningStar Church in Fort Mill, South Carolina, seemed to bring out a sense of expectancy in me that God was about to do something significant. This was our third time visiting MorningStar, the most we have visited any one church in our weekly sojourns. For the first time in our forty-six weeks of travel, Linda and I drove in separate cars. Linda had a head start on me for this trip to Fort Mill, a town close to Charlotte, North Carolina, and the home of the popular amusement park, Carowinds.

She departed Greenville on Friday afternoon to attend Morningstar's "Partner's Weekend Conference," a two-day event for people who support Morningstar Ministries but are not part of their regular fellowship. It is part fundraiser for MorningStar and part "equipping of the saints" for ministry for the partners (Eph. 4:12). Linda was blessed. She had heard excellent teaching by Rick Joyner, Lance Wallnau, Cindy Jacobs, and Dave Yarnes.

In the two days there, she had connected with Trina, an occupational therapist from Atlanta; Rick Joyner's wife, Julie; and Liz, who resides in a townhome just down the road from MorningStar. She had eaten gourmet food prepared by the Conference Center chef. Most of all, she had spent time alone with Jesus, spared of the noise and distractions that everyday life can bring our way.

I knew Linda was feeling good when she and I first caught up with each other early Sunday morning as I entered MorningStar's Heritage Conference Center. The twinkle in her eyes and the ear-to-ear smile told me her time alone with Jesus was rejuvenating. Because I had arrived at MorningStar well before the start of the 9:00 a.m. service, we were able to walk through the entire ministry complex for the first time since we had visited here.

Starting from the middle of the hotel where the Sunday and weekday services of MorningStar Church were held, we branched away from this central point and strolled down "Main Street," a covered replica of a typical, small town Main Street. On each side of the street were small shops, including a boutique, a book store, a pastry shop, and some ministry locations. Above the places of business were what appeared to be either condominiums or apartments. The lighted lamps in some of the windows gave me the impression that many of the units, if not all, were occupied. Above the second and third story apartments was the high, arched covering, designed, I believe, to replicate the sky above, giving the effect of being outside.

Leaving Main Street, we came to the Heritage Conference Center, a Christian facility "with the largest ballroom in South Carolina, and the largest conference center in Fort Mill."[66] This is where the speaking events were held for the weekend's partner conference.

---

66 "Heritage Conference Center," HeritageConferenceCenter.org, https://www.heritage-conferencecenter.org/meetings-events (accessed June 14, 2019).

Strolling through the expansive conference center with its many breakout rooms, we braved the ninety-plus temperature and walked over to the Bob Jones Vision Center, a facility Morningstar Ministries believes will be instrumental in equipping the body of Christ in prayer, praise, and prophecy. The facility was named for the deceased Bob Jones, "a powerful man of God who was known for his prophetic accuracy, his somewhat eccentric and humorous ways, and his spectacular encounters with God."[67]

It was a privilege to walk the grounds of MorningStar Ministries and see what God has restored to its former glory. Like the Jews who had rebuilt the walls of Jerusalem in the days of Nehemiah, Linda and I felt like we were able to see what God had once created, what man had destroyed through poor stewardship, and what God was now redeeming through the efforts of Rick Joyner and the people of MorningStar.

Taking our seats for the 9:00 a.m. service, we truly did feel more like partners in ministry than a couple from South Carolina who was just visiting for a day. That feeling deepened as the church members prayed for President Trump following the time of worshipping God. Franklin Graham, the son of the legendary evangelist and a key leader in the Body of Christ today, had called the general Body of Christ to pray for President Trump on June second. This was to be a special day of collective prayer for the president, beyond our daily mandate from the Word of God to pray for those who are in authority over us.

> I urge that entreaties *and* prayers, petitions *and* thanksgivings, be made . . . for kings and all who are in authority, so that we may lead a tranquil and quiet life in all godliness and dignity. This is good and acceptable in the sight of God our Savior" (1 Tim. 2:1-3).

The man who led the intercession for President Trump is a man whom I would like praying for me. He was authoritative and decisive, asking God to

---

67 "Bob Jones Vision Center," MorningStarMinistries.org, https://www.morning-starministries.org/bob-jones-vision-center (accessed June 14, 2019).

use the president as a tool of His righteousness and to stop the evil forces that are opposing our commander-in-chief.

With a thunderous amen, we settled in our seats to hear a message from Rick Joyner. Before he was to teach this Sunday, Pastor Joyner, or Rick as he is commonly called, prayed for all of us in attendance. The seasoned seventy-year-old prayed that everyone would have an encounter with the Lord that will overshadow any other experience. He prayed for the presence of the Lord to increase in our lives. He prayed that we would walk in God's complete salvation.

Rick Joyner, by his own admission, is not a polished orator with a charismatic personality. He sits while giving his sermons because of ailing knees. He does not make many attempts at humor. If his regular way of speaking were graded on a scale of one to ten, his sermons would probably average about a six. He is in good company, however.

Jonathan Edwards of Massachusetts, the great evangelical pastor who was used by God to spark the first Great Awakening in 1739, was similar in style. One observer of Edwards commented: "He scarcely gestured or even moved, and he made no attempt by the elegance of his style or the beauty of his pictures to gratify the taste and fascinate the imagination. Instead he convinced with overwhelming weight of argument and with such intenseness of feeling."[68]

Yet I love to hear from men like Rick. They have been through life's greatest challenges and have come out refined—better, not bitter. They have laid themselves down at the altar of self-importance and are only concerned with hearing the Holy Spirt and walking in obedience to His leading. They have died to themselves (Matt. 16:24-25) and desire nothing more than to serve Christ. They point people to Jesus, not to themselves. Don't worry; I am not exalting men like Rick Joyner. Men like him would be horrified if I did. They know their weaknesses as well as you and I know our own. But I do honor

---

68 "Jonathan Edwards: America's Greatest Theologian," ChristianityToday.com, https://www.christianitytoday.com/history/people/theologians/jonathan-edwards.html (accessed June 14, 2019).

men like Rick. And I listen carefully to their words, to what God is saying through them.

I heard the Holy Spirit speak a lot to me as Rick taught today. Above the many things that were poignant, one in particular stood out for me. The Bible is clear that Jesus paid a heavy price to purchase my salvation. His body was bruised for my iniquities. His blood was shed for my transgressions. He gave His life as a ransom for mine. He invested His very life into mine. As the recipient of His grace and in response to His incredible sacrifice, I am expected to make a return on that investment.

It has been estimated that two-thirds to one-half of the teachings in Scripture on righteousness have to do with stewardship. The parable of the talents is one of those verses. Regardless of whether we have been given five talents, three talents, or just one, we are expected to make a return on those talents for the Kingdom of God. If I were hired into a family business, I would be expected to make contributions, to work hard, to add to the overall prosperity of the business. Working in the Kingdom of God is no different. Yet our efforts are not our own. Paul, the apostle, knew this very well. "But by the grace of God I am what I am, and His grace toward me did not prove vain; but I labored even more than all of them, yet not I, but the grace of God with me" (1 Cor. 15:10). Later, Paul said to the Colossians, "For this purpose also I labor, striving according to His power, which mightily works within me" (Col. 1:29).

Paradoxically, even our work in response to His call is governed by His grace. We ask the Holy Spirit within us to empower us. We actively yield to Him. We make Him our priority. We worship Him in spirit and truth. We spend time each day studying His Word. We spend time alone with Him, listening carefully to His instructions and His leading. We invite Him into every situation, asking Him for His perspective before we speak or act. We gather with other believers, encouraging each other to keep our eyes fixed "on Jesus, the author and perfecter of our faith" (Heb. 12:2). We abide in Christ daily (John 15:4).

I agree with Rick Joyner. Being "in Christ" is the most earnest life, the most fulfilling, the most fruitful life a person can live. Peter, the apostle states, "And though you have not seen Him, you love Him, and though you do not see Him now, but believe in Him, you greatly rejoice with joy inexpressible and full of glory, obtaining as the outcome of your faith the salvation of your souls" (1 Peter 1:8). Jesus said to doubting Thomas after His resurrection, "'Because you have seen Me, have you believed? Blessed *are* they who did not see, and *yet* believed" (John 20:29). Blessed, too, are people today who have not seen God but believe in Him, trust Him, and yield to His leading.

We left MorningStar with gratitude in our hearts—thankful that God allowed us to be a part of their Sunday gathering and a part of the Partners Weekend. Most of all, we were grateful that we have the spiritual eyes to see and the spiritual ears to hear. We say that humbly, knowing full well that our spiritual vision and hearing are gifts from God.

We would need those spiritual eyes and ears the following week as we faced our greatest challenge yet.

SEEING GOD

TAYLORS, SOUTH CAROLINA

It did not look good. "Lord! Please! Take it away! I don't know if I can take this anymore! This is torture!" Twelve a.m., 1:00 a.m., 2:00 a.m., 3:00 a.m., 4:00 a.m., 5:00 a.m., 6:00 a.m., 7:00 a.m.—still no sleep. The more I scratched, the more I itched.

I staggered toward Linda, walking like a bull-legged cowboy who had ridden his last horse. "Linda, I am sorry, I think I have to cancel this week. It is unbearable!"

It didn't seem right. Forty-seven weeks of getting up each Sunday morning and driving to the place where God had called us was something Linda and I did together—alone and without distractions. It was special. Each week was revelatory and fresh. There was always something new to be discovered, something new that God was showing us. Could one week off really hurt?

I wobbled back to Linda. "Let's go," I uttered. "I don't want the devil determining what we do."

I have read the Scripture for years. "[God] *disciplines* us for *our* good" (Heb. 12:10). It's God's Word. I believe it; I trust it; I have come to a place in my life that I know all of God's Word is good for us, even the verses we don't want to hear. But I have always left out the last part of that verse that seemed so new,

295

so revelatory to me that day: "[God] *disciplines us* for *our* good, **so that we may share in His holiness**" (emphasis mine).

Why hadn't I seen that before? I mean, really seen it? There is a purpose to everything God does. For years, I have prayed that God would deliver me from my idolatry of eating. Many times, I have felt His grace to say no to the temptation of the food that was staring right back at me. Each time, I gave in, however, I believed the lie that I couldn't go on without the food that had given me so much false comfort through the years.

I often wondered what was going to happen to me as a result. The Lord answers all prayer—I know that. He works "for good to those who love God, to those who are called according to *His* purpose" (Rom. 8:28). So, what would happen to me if I did not allow Him to work in this area of my life? A heart attack? A stroke? He is going to deliver me from my idolatry of food, somehow, some way! Which way would it be? How would it look?

In hindsight, I can see now that the torture I had lived with, the horrible rash that I had experienced for four weeks the previous Christmas and the one I was experiencing six months later were gifts from God. Satan wanted to rob us of the next leg of our tour. God wanted to deliver me from the prison I had put myself in.

I couldn't see it that way Sunday morning, however, as we walked into the doors of Calvary Christian Fellowship. Why Calvary Christian Fellowship in Taylors, South Carolina? Our youngest son, Joe, is a student at Greenville Technical College in the Personal Trainer program on the Benson campus in Taylors. Until he gets his driver's license, Linda is his chauffeur to classes. Each Tuesday and Thursday morning, the two of them made the twenty-five-minute trek to school. In the beginning of the spring semester, Linda would drop Joe off and head back home. Lately, on Tuesdays, however, that had not been the case.

After dropping Joe off at GTC for his first day of classes of the new session, Linda saw a message on Calvary Christian Fellowship's marquee that stands on the side of the road: "Cereal needed for food pantry." Linda has rarely turned down a plea for help. She drove to the nearest Ingles supermarket and purchased six boxes of cereal for the pantry. With her sack of grain in hand, she knocked on the doors of the church. A pleasant, smiling, elderly woman named Charlene opened the door for Linda. After Linda explained to Charlene why she was in the area, the septuagenarian accepted Linda's gift and invited her back to Calvary the following Tuesday for a 10:00 a.m. prayer meeting.

Linda and Charlene weren't the only two present the following Tuesday when Linda returned. Ann, another septuagenarian, joined them in the church's sanctuary. Anne and Charlene aren't buying into the idea of retirement. Anne runs the church's food pantry. The church serves an average of seventy to one hundred people each Saturday morning. While not a requirement to receive food, Calvary offers a 9:30 a.m. to 10:00 a.m. devotional time for anyone who is interested. Typically, an average of twenty-five people attend the devotional. Some have come to a saving knowledge of Jesus during this devotional time. In addition, a significant number of people who have come for the food are now volunteering at the pantry. This group of elderly people have formed a type of community where they share their lives together. The church then opens the doors from 10:00 a.m. to 11:30 a.m. to distribute the food. Workers arrive at 7:00 a.m. to prepare for the day.

In addition, Reggie Garrett, the pastor at the oldest black church in the Upstate of South Carolina, Jubilee Baptist Church (established in 1864), occasionally speaks at the Saturday morning devotional. Calvary and Jubilee partner together for the cause of the Gospel. One week, Jubilee and four other area churches held an old-time outdoor tent revival meeting on Calvary's fourteen-acre campus. Jubilee Baptist, a community-minded church like Calvary, offers a free fish fry every Friday evening for community members during the summer months.

Ann's work is not limited to the food pantry. She has also been a prominent voice in the pro-life movement in South Carolina. When the state government of South Carolina was awkwardly silent on the abortion issue in 1998, she worked tirelessly for the dignity of the unborn. It spurred her to write the book, *The Awakening: The Pro-life Movement in South Carolina—Learning from the Past to Shape the Future*. Ann was also horrified to hear that Greenville, South Carolina, in the heart of the Bible belt, was home to three abortion clinics at the time. Today, through her work and countless others, that number has dwindled to one. One too many, I would add.

Ann, Charlene, and Linda prayed with all their hearts. They prayed for the Body of Christ—for the church to have the eyes to see and the ears to hear. They prayed for the church family at Calvary Christian Fellowship. They prayed that the darkness we see in this world would be pushed back and that hearts would be softened to issues like the ending of innocent lives in the womb. They prayed that an increasingly boundary-less culture would realize that sex is not a consumer product but is meant to be a blessing between a man and a woman in a covenant relationship (marriage). They prayed for their families, especially for those who are not walking with God, that they would repent and turn to the plan that God has for their lives.

I met Anne and Charlene our first Sunday at Calvary. I also met Charles, the worship leader of the church. He had a similar testimony to mine. He was raised in a Roman Catholic family in Southern Florida. I was raised in a Roman Catholic family in Long Island, New York. He came to Christ through the influence of his born-again cousin. I came to Christ through the influence of my born-again brother. On this Sunday, our lives intersected at a kind of halfway point between the Empire State and the Sunshine State. We spoke like long-lost brothers, which we are in Christ.

Charles led the group of thirty-five who were present this Sunday. He started with the song, "Celebrate Jesus, Celebrate." It brought me back to the early 1990s. In my mind's eye, I could hear my brother singing the verse, "He is risen He is risen / and He lives forevermore! / . . . Come on and celebrate / The resurrection of our Lord."[69] I was singing with an earthly choir; Bill is now singing with the heavenly one!

When the singing concluded, Pastor Phil Long stepped up to the mike. With his six-foot, three-inch frame and his big bones, I said to myself that he had to have been a football player. When the service ended, he confirmed my suspicion. In fact, he had played offensive tackle at Travelers Rest High School. When I asked him if he had played with Joe's high school football coach, Greg Styles, he excitedly told me that Greg had played right tackle at the not-so-impressive weight of 170 pounds as a senior in high school. He did say Greg was tough, though. Knowing Greg like I do, I believe it.

Pastor Phil asked the congregation if anyone had any prayer needs. Linda shot up her hand. She needed prayer for clogged arteries (sixty percent). She added that I needed prayer for my skin problems. The teddy-bear-like pastor asked us to come forward. He and the elders of the church prayed for us. After anointing us with oil, he thundered a prayer for our healing. There was no doubt in his voice. No doubt in his words. If Jesus is the same yesterday, today, and forever, then His healing is the same. I had experienced that healing in my knee instantaneously a few months prior in Dawsonville, Georgia. I am experiencing that healing gradually as He is delivering me from my addiction to food.

It really didn't look good that morning—until we spent a few hours with a group of committed Christians in a small church in a non-descript town. We left that small group of people feeling so powerfully touched. We left encouraged that elderly followers of Christ were maximizing the years that they have left before they go to their eternal home. They were not just about their grandchildren, but about the serious business of the Kingdom of God, even in their twilight years. We felt encouraged that a mighty God used a food pantry request to connect us so powerfully to people only a stone's throw from our son's college.

---

69   Gary Oliver, "Celebrate Jesus, Celebrate," Hope Publishing Co.

It really ended well that morning. It ended far greater than we could ever have imagined. Little did we know that another great surprise awaited us as we prayed about the next week's journey.

TO THE BEACH

MYRTLE BEACH, SOUTH CAROLINA

My heart was heavy. I could sense more than just by looking at the calendar that our adventure was coming to an end. I could sense it in my spirit, too. In fact, I was wondering if it was over at that moment.

I am at the point in my life that if I sense the Holy Spirit is telling us to shut something down right away, we will shut it down. No questions asked. Or very few, anyway. But we sensed something different, something we had not experienced in the forty-eight weeks since we started. Linda and I have a large map of the southeastern states in our living room. Each week after we returned back home, we placed a push pin on the city or town that we had just visited. It was a good visual to show us where were had been and, more importantly, to remind us of what God had been doing in our midst.

This time when we prayed, we sensed very clearly that the Holy Spirit was revealing the final steps of our tour. The final five weeks of our journeying would involve the following five cities: Myrtle Beach (South Carolina), Jacksonville (Florida), Meridian (Mississippi), Lexington (Kentucky), and our final stop, Lynchburg (Virginia). We looked at the map again with squinted eyes. Going clockwise, the five cities formed a kind of trapezoid/circle around the locations we had visited over the past year. While not exactly a victory lap, it would be a chance to pray for the Southeast, for the Bible Belt, for the churches we had visited and the ones we had passed, for the many people we had encountered along the way. We would pray for another Great Awakening. Somehow, I feel that the hope of America lies in the hearts and souls of the followers of Christ in the Southeast.

This would not be easy on Linda, I thought. The shortest of the five trips would be four hours away, and the longest would be six-and-a-half. While I have tried to make the "Big Guy" (my nickname for our 2003 Honda Odyssey) as comfortable as possible for Linda, the mattress in the back of the car was not a bed at the Holiday Inn. Like Linda, the Big Guy had been a trooper. He had taken us to ten states, four stops at the Atlantic Ocean, and a trip to the highest point east of the Mississippi River, Mount Mitchell. He had braved the stifling, hot, Southern summer temperatures, borne the brunt of winding mountain turns, and guided us through an unlikely winter snowstorm.

He had not done it alone, however. Gladys P. Smith, or GPS as we have lovingly come to know her, had been a steady rock for all of our wanderings. Although she often blurted out instructions while Linda and I were in deep conversations, especially when Linda was talking, we could not have made this journey without her. She had consistently offered great advice throughout our entire journey, even providing alternative directions when unforeseen traffic lay ahead. The Big Guy and Gladys were friends for life. Their contributions will never be forgotten.

At 4:15 a.m., the four of us, with eyes at half-mast, started the first leg of the final stretch of our destination, Myrtle Beach, South Carolina, a popular vacation getaway for families and golfers. Our target was not the beach or the fairway, however. We had a double-header planned for the day. The first stop would be NewSpring Church, right off George Bishop Parkway. The second would be Seacoast Vineyard, right in the middle of downtown Myrtle Beach, in walking distance of the historic Patricia Grande Resort. Since Seacoast is a stone's throw from the ocean, we planned on attending the 9:15 a.m. service at NewSpring and then making the eleven-minute journey to catch Seacoast Vineyard's 11:00 a.m. service. A walk to the beach afterward would be the cherry on the sundae.

Linda and I are not strangers to Myrtle Beach. When we first relocated to Greenville, we received numerous phone calls from telemarketers inviting us to Myrtle Beach for three days and two nights—for free! I don't like to mislead people. When I told the persistent callers that I wasn't interested, they didn't throw in the towel. They offered us an additional night for free. They even threw in free dinner coupons if we accepted their offer. With a young family of five and a limited budget, the offers were too good to pass up. Linda packed the bathing suits; I wedged the tiny, portable television between the two front seats of the car; and the children watched *Veggie Tales* for the next four hours in the back seat. The free hotels, the lazy river tubing, the walks on the beach, and even sitting through the required three-hour timeshare sales pitch (the kids had their introduction to buffets—all-you-can-eat popcorn and chocolate chip cookies while playing video games in a side room while Linda and I were being serenaded) made our trips to Myrtle Beach memorable. This happened for five years, despite my being forthright about our not being likely to buy a timeshare. After five years of free trips to Myrtle Beach, we have not heard from the timeshare companies again. I fear we have been blacklisted.

Our return trip to Myrtle Beach felt like a homecoming. The unobstructed views of the horizon welcomed us as we approached the city. The raised highways escaped the marshy waters below. The palm trees lined Ocean Boulevard. The piercing smell of the ocean was as potent as the smell of freshly brewed coffee in the waking hours of the morning.

We saw another familiar sight, similar to the one we had seen four hours away in the city of Anderson six months previously. Like the McDonald's arch that was legendary to my generation, I could recognize the white "N" and the green circular backdrop that has become recognizable to another generation in South Carolina. We could see it perched high on the vertical wood column of the church building as soon as we exited George Bishop Highway: NewSpring Church. This Myrtle Beach campus is one of the fourteen NewSpring campuses throughout the Palmetto State. This location stood at the edge of a big shopping mall. Across the highway sat the massive Riverwalk Inn & Suites Conference Center.

The contemporary feel of the outside continued as we stepped inside the walls of the church. It seemed like a long journey as we strolled along the level floor to the front area. Five sections of seats covered the sanctuary. Each section consisted of roughly fifteen seats across and eighteen rows deep. If my math is correct, the seating capacity was approximately 1,350. Not many of those seats appeared to be empty by the conclusion of the service.

After a time of worship and a moving baptism of a young boy by his father, Clayton King appeared on the three screens of the church. Feeling like we were sitting at the main campus of NewSpring in Anderson, Clayton delivered a passionate message on this Father's Day. Interestingly, on this day seventeen years previously, Clayton presided at his dad's funeral. This was his adoptive dad, the one who had raised him and taught him the ways of God. Clayton had also discovered recently that his biological dad had died three years earlier. They had never met. But his newly found uncle, Clayton's biological dad's brother, told Clayton that he had watched Clayton preach online and was amazed at the similarity between Clayton and his biological father. Even the way Clayton's upper lip raised when he was talking reminded the uncle of his deceased brother. Both shared a six-foot, three-inch, 230-pound frame.

Clayton has a Heavenly Father, however, Who lives on. So do we if we have accepted Jesus as Lord and Savior.

> See how great a love the Father has bestowed on us, that we would be called children of God; and *such* we are. For this reason the world does not know us, because it did not know Him.

Beloved, now we are children of God, and it has not appeared as yet what we will be. We know that when He appears, we will be like Him, because we will see Him just as He is. And everyone who has this hope *fixed* on Him purifies himself, just as He is pure (1 John 3:1-3).

Clayton explained that the Father longs to bless His children, to work for their good, to give them a liberty that brings true freedom. Like our earthly father, we have our Heavenly Father's DNA, Clayton added. It comes from Him when we receive the Holy Spirit the moment we are born again. We, too, have the desire to bless our own children and to work for their good. But as we saw firsthand last week, we have an adversary whose job is to "steal and kill and destroy" what God has done (John 10:10). He is a counterfeit father. All lies come from him because he is "the father of lies" (John 8:44). He reminds us of our past, trying to derail us from our forward movement in Christ. We are not to get smart with the devil, but we need to remind him that we have authority over him because of Jesus' redemptive work and our right standing with God. When Satan provokes us with our past, we need to remind him that God has "cast all [our] sins Into the depths of the sea" (Micah 7:19).

At times, we need to stand firm and resolute against the evil one. Like the earthly father who puts his foot down and sternly puts an end to his children's bad behavior, we need to put our foot down and sternly rebuke the devil for his harassment of our family. The presence of God in our lives gives us fathers the authority to be both tender and tough. We are to love our wives as Christ loves the church (Eph. 5:25) and to bring up our children in the discipline and instruction of the Lord without provoking them to anger in any way (Eph. 6:4).

As men of God, we carry a heavy weight. We grind at our jobs and work hard to provide for our families. We carry the burden of caring for our families financially and emotionally. We can never fulfill our mandates on an island. We need to be engaged with the family of God. Like a proud father himself, Clayton reported that God has been working powerfully among the men at NewSpring. So far in 2019, eighty-eight men have been saved through their efforts. Seven hundred fifty have completed "connect classes." Twenty-eight have been baptized. Two thousand six hundred twenty now serve as volunteers. Four thousand seven hundred eight-nine give regularly to the church. One thousand men are mentoring other men or young boys. God is working powerfully in Clayton King's life and in the lives of the men of NewSpring. He is working powerfully in a group of believers in Christ who call NewSpring Myrtle Beach their home.

We were just visiting that Sunday, but we, too, felt like we belonged. It was where our Heavenly Father had called us. We left the sand and waves of Myrtle Beach as refreshed as anyone who has vacationed there for two weeks. Furthermore, we had completed twenty percent of the final leg of our journey. The sadness had lifted. The excitement of God's Spirit living in us propelled us forward to complete the remaining eighty percent. We continued our journey the next week—also at the beach. This time it was further south in the Sunshine State, in northern Florida.

We would see a father-son duo like no other.

FATHER AND SON

JACKSONVILLE, FLORIDA

How many father-son duos can you name quickly? Don't check your phone. Think. Quickly!

Okay, let me help. In the political realm, how about two of our founding fathers, John Adams and his son, John Quincy Adams? Or more currently, George H.W. Bush and George W. Bush? In sports, how about Archie Manning and his record-setting quarterback son of television commercial fame, Peyton? On the diamond, how about sluggers Ken Griffey, Sr., and Ken Griffey, Jr. Or the entertainment industry (not my favorite), which has produced the Downeys, both Robert, Sr., and his Iron Man son, Robert Downey, Jr. Or Carl Reiner and Archie Bunker's favorite son-in-law, Michael Stivik—I mean, Rob Reiner?

Not bad, but I have *my* favorite father-son duo. They hail from the state that produces the most oranges and grapefruits in the United States. Linda and I were first introduced to the younger half of the duo, Josh Reavis, a few months earlier when we visited Calvary Road Baptist Church in Maggie Valley, North Carolina. He was the guest speaker at the church the day Linda and I ventured to the westernmost point of North Carolina. On this particular Sunday, we were introduced to the elderly half of the duo, Herb Reavis, Jr., in Jacksonville, Florida, our southernmost destination in our year-long sojourn.

Jacksonville was not what we expected. Because the journey from Greenville to Jacksonville is about five-and-a-half hours long, we decided to take our first overnighter. We approached the outskirts of the city named for our seventh president, Andrew Jackson, on Saturday night when the sun had long lost its normal effect. Jacksonville is a surprising city. It is the most populous city in Florida, the most populous city in the southeastern United States, and the largest city by area in the contiguous United States. In other words, it is really spread out. You feel like you have room to breathe—more so than in Atlanta and Charlotte, two of the other big cities that we encountered this year.

Harbor improvements since the late nineteenth century have made Jacksonville a major naval and civilian deep-water port. All roads, it seems, lead to some kind of bridge—over rivers, creeks, and canals. St. John's River is its most noteworthy body of water. I hear the real estate cliché thrown around a lot these days in regards to Jacksonville—"a major metropolitan city with a small-town feel." In Jacksonville's case, it is no cliché.

Linda and I wanted to see more of Florida's "First Coast" before attending North Jacksonville Baptist Church's 10:30 a.m. service. Waking before the roosters were able to make their first announcement, we headed for the town of Atlantic Beach, a part of the Jacksonville Beaches community. I drove quickly through the well-lit and noticeably level streets, not wanting the sun to get there before we did. It was worth the sacrifice of sleep. Like only He can, the Lord led us to a parking spot in a residential condominium community a few steps from the beach.

We walked through the gracious, but firm, sand and waited patiently for the sun to arrive. With a gradually brightening sky to the east, a long strip of orange appeared over the ocean and below the incremental clouds. It gave the appearance of a fire, as if Europe were burning on the other side of the pond and we were watching helplessly from a distance. Only the occasional pelicans and terns joined us as we watched in awe-inspired silence. It was like we were watching the Artist do the work that only He can do. The heavens truly do declare the glory of God (Psalm 19:1). Somehow, it seemed easier to "be still and know [He is] God (Psalm 46:1—NIV) when we were alone with Him in His open-air studio. It made me think that somehow, some way, even the most committed of atheists has to sense that something can't come from nothing, that behind every book is an author, that behind every piece of art work is an artist, behind every creation is a Creator (Rom. 1:20).

We left one piece of artistry for another. The North Jacksonville Baptist Church campus was a thing of beauty. The crape myrtle trees and cypress trees draped with Spanish moss seemed to cover most of the forty-acre campus that the parking lot and church building did not. The church edifice, though on Main Street, seemed isolated from other buildings and hidden behind the beauty of the campus terrain. It was as if the crape myrtles were guarding the church grounds from the noise and bustle of the four-lane traffic in front.

Once parked, we stepped out of our car and entered into what felt like an arboretum. We weaved in and out of the Spanish moss that hung from the cypress trees. We saw the bright, reddish-pink blossoms of the crape myrtles up close and personal. Approaching the church building, we encountered a very tall, silver, ornamental frame with a cross perched high on top. The message seemed clear: This was a church that was serious about the cross of Jesus and all that it encompasses.

The twenty-eight hundred-seat capacity sanctuary was about as nice as we had seen in our forty-nine weeks on the road. The huge organ pipes on the front of the sanctuary were as prominent as the crape myrtle and weeping willow trees outside. They stood upright and proud like the Queens Guard at Buckingham Palace. High up between the two sets of organ pipes was a baptismal, its position of prominence sending the message that the church's priority was to bring people to a saving knowledge of Jesus. Below the baptismal and the organ pipes were four rows of ascending chairs for the choir. The men stood front and center while the women split into two groups, to the right and left of the men. Below them were the twenty-member orchestra/band. In front of the orchestra members stood the six vocalists lined across the stage. In front of them was the pastor's wooden pulpit in the shape of a cross.

The setting exuded a sense of reverence for God, a sentiment noticeably missing in our increasingly boundary-less culture. The band started with the background music to the chorus of "O Praise the Name." While the music played, Psalm 23:6 was displayed on both screens. After a few announcements and an opening prayer by Josh Reavis, Worship Pastor Tim Rigdon led us in a time of worshipping God. The style of music reminded me of the Gaither Vocal Band, a Southern Gospel group started by the ageless Bill Gaither and his wife, Gloria. Coincidentally, or providentially, the last song sung during the time of worship was one of the Gaithers' all-time hits written in the early 1970s, "Because He Lives." The sound of the chorus, the band, and the singing of the congregants was heavenly.

When the worship time ended, a missionary from Africa led us in a prayer for the offering. He explained who he was and where he lived. He and his family of five serve in a country that is ninety-five percent Muslim. I am purposely leaving out their names and the country where they live for security reasons. He shared excitedly about a well that his missions group had just dug for the Muslim people. The grateful recipients recognized that the "Jesus-followers" were the ones who provided them the much-needed access to fresh water. The missionary group had also built a Christian radio station that will broadcast the Good News of Jesus to places where people are forbidden to proclaim it. Through much red tape, they finally secured governmental approval for a frequency and put the antenna together that made them go live by the end of the summer.

After the encouraging and challenging word from our brother from Africa, Pastor Herb Reavis, Jr. stepped up to deliver his sermon. While we are told in Scripture to only worship God (Exod. 20:3-5), we are also told to hold in high regard those who teach and preach the full Gospel of Jesus. Paul told his son in the faith, Timothy, "The elders who rule well are to be considered worthy of double honor, especially those who work hard at preaching and teaching" (1 Tim. 5:17). My impression of Pastor Reavis was that he works hard at what he does. He has the rare gift of being humorous and authoritative at the same time. The Gospel is the most exciting endeavor to which a human being can devote his or her life. The presentation of it should be exciting as well.

Pastor Reavis used Psalm 23 as his text that day—what he calls the "Psalm of Psalms." He said the Word of God provides no greater picture of the relationship of God and His people than through this inspired piece of literature. Psalm 23 starts with the foundational truth of this relationship: "The LORD is my shepherd" (v. 1).

Pastor Reavis then took us forward in the Bible to Jesus being revealed as the "good shepherd" in John 10:11, as the "great Shepherd" in Hebrews 13:20, and the "Chief Shepherd" in 1 Peter 5:4. He becomes our Shepherd when we put our faith in Him and follow His leading. Like a shepherd's relationship with his sheep, Pastor Reavis described the type of relationship that Jesus, the Good Shepherd, has with His people.

First, it is a personal relationship. "The Lord is my Shepherd," not *a* shepherd. Second, it is a calming relationship. Human beings are extremely fearful, more than we can probably see. The Shepherd's presence calms us automatically. Third, it is a forgiving relationship. He restores the souls of His people for His name's sake. Fourth, it is a comforting relationship. In a life filled with valleys, He will walk through them with His people, never leaving them or abandoning them (Heb. 13:5). Fifth, it is a supernatural relationship. He will change His people in the midst of their circumstances. He leads His people by His Spirit, which He has implanted in them (Rom. 8:14). Sixth, it is a lasting relationship. "Surely goodness and lovingkindness will follow me all the days of my life. And I will dwell in the house of the LORD forever" (v. 6).

312 SUNDAYS IN THE SOUTH

When Pastor Reavis finished his sermon, he asked the audience if anyone needed to surrender to the Good Shepherd, Jesus—to surrender to His rule and to His leadership. A young man and a young woman of about high school age responded to the invitation and came forward. The Word of God says that all of Heaven rejoices when one sinner repents (Luke 15:7). Today, in Jacksonville, all of Heaven had two reasons to rejoice.

Linda and I also had reasons to rejoice. We witnessed two salvations. We witnessed a church that is committed to Jesus, to the cross, and to the full counsel of God (Acts 20:27). We witnessed a father-son duo who are worthy of honor—more praiseworthy than any famous athlete or entertainer could ever be. We continue to witness a God who is comforting us, teaching us and guiding us for His name's sake.

He would continue that leading the next week in the heart of Dixie, right in the Magnolia State.

WHEN A DOOR CLOSES

MERIDIAN, MISSISSIPPI

I had my heart set on seeing Birmingham, Alabama. To a young boy growing up in New York, Alabama seemed like a world away. For all I was concerned, there was Africa, England, and Alabama. Bear Bryant in his fedora, the one he would not wear inside a dome stadium because his mama told him to never wear a hat indoors. Johnny Musso with the cut-off jersey, running off tackle on first down. And second down. And third down. I can still hear Keith Jackson welcoming the nationwide television audience to the college football game of the week, "Live from Tuscaloosa, Alabama! We got a dandy here tonight." Life couldn't be any better for a wide-eyed youth who would have a hard time choosing Christmas over a brisk, clear, autumn afternoon if he were given the choice.

I could feel the excitement churning in me as we headed west on Interstate 70 through the countryside of northern Alabama. Our plan was to stop off in Birmingham to see 16th Street Baptist Church, the site of the tragic bombing and murder of four young girls in the teeth of the Civil Rights movement of the 1960s. We would then continue on to our destination for this Sunday, hoping to reach Meridian, Mississippi, before nightfall.

Then Linda dropped a bomb.

Her unsettled voice told me something was wrong. With a sense of urgency and a tightness in her speech, she informed me that hot air was blowing forcefully through the air vent above the rear passenger tire. The hot air was making the mattress in the back dangerously hot. We pulled off the road and settled in a parking spot at the Circle K gas station in a remote part of Alabama. The gas station seemed like the only place of business for miles. It is not good when your wife knows more about cars than you do—especially when you are facing a major car problem. It is even worse when you are having a major automobile crisis on a Saturday night.

My mind began to race. I remembered being told that I should have our catalytic converter replaced. If not, the car could catch on fire, the mechanic had warned me. Is this what was happening? Was our car about to catch on fire? I approached an elderly man in a pickup truck. I asked him if he knew anything about cars. With eyes half-closed with suspicion, he seemed to look at me with one eye while glancing over at Linda standing by the Odyssey with the other.

"A little," he responded hesitantly.

After a few minutes of interacting, I could tell he was raised in a family like mine—very good manners but little-to-no knowledge of car repair. Regardless of whom I asked, no one could come up with a solution. With shoulders drooping and a voice barely above a whisper, I told Linda we had to turn around and go home. I hated to abort a mission right in the middle of it, but we couldn't take a risk going on.

Just as we were about to drive away, I spotted a young man and his wife pulling into a gas terminal in their minivan. With one final attempt at salvaging our trip, I asked him if he knew what might be causing the hot air problem. He came over and checked. Politely, he informed me he had no idea and returned back to his minivan. Not having a clue what I was looking for, I got down on the ground on my stomach and looked under the car one last time.

I am not sure if a sense of pity set in on the young man or not, but he came back and checked our situation again. He asked us if our air conditioning knob had been taken off recently. It had. He then instructed us to take it off and put it back on, making sure the arrows were aligned. We started the car. Cold air! No fire! Just a misplaced AC knob.

With renewed vigor, we continued west. The darkened sky only told us we would now have to bypass Birmingham and head straight to Meridian. I silently wondered if I had misheard God's leading to go to Birmingham at all. Either way, I was happy that our car was not about to catch fire! We continued west with my foot on the pedal a little heavier—hoping to make up for lost time.

My foot had to pull back, however. The brake lights ahead and the many orange signs delivered more bad news. A major section of 70 West was closed due to construction. We would have to follow the detour signs. With the lights of downtown Birmingham off the highway to the left, we began to follow the cars heading on the alternative route. I wasn't sure how much time this was going to cost us. It seemed like we were getting a closer glimpse of Birmingham with each turn. Twenty-second Street, Twentieth Street—wait a minute! Eighteenth Street.

"Linda, there it is!" I exclaimed, like a sailor who had spotted land. "Sixteenth Street Baptist Church," I said slowly, as if we were approaching discovered gold. I am not sure why but I was surprised by what I read, but my mouth dropped open slightly: "16th Street Baptist Church—Where Jesus is the Main Attraction." *Wow*, I thought. I stared at the sign for ten seconds and then stared again for another ten.

Thoughts and images flashed through my mind. The hosing of men who were peacefully protesting. Dr. Martin Luther King's speech at the Washington Mall. Four families losing their little girls. Words seemed so insignificant as I stood there. Injustice, tragedy, unspeakable pain. Yet so much was spoken through that one phrase. Forgiveness, mercy, perseverance. Overcoming evil with good. Pointing people to Jesus, the only real Answer to the sin that was in the killer's heart. To the sin that is in my heart. And, as the people of 16th Avenue Baptist Church seem to know so well, to the sin that is in their hearts. The sinless Savior truly is the main attraction. Even though nightfall had invaded, I took two pictures of the church before we left. We continued on, arriving at our hotel room around midnight, tired but grateful that God had given me the desire of my heart (Psalm 37:4).

I got the sense that not much had changed in downtown Meridian since I was that starry-eyed youth back in the 1970s. I wonder if the phrase "as quiet as a Sunday morning" originated in this sleepy town of about thirty-eight thousand residents. Cars and people were nowhere to be found. The old Union Hotel with its "Rates Reasonable" sign attached to the outer wall remained from days gone by. The old railroad depot with its many tired railroad cars stood by idly, waiting patiently to be called into action. The monument of the Confederate soldier raised high into the sky, seemingly unfazed by the Union victory led by General Sherman in the Battle of Meridian in the War Between the States. The pretty, purple myrtle trees lining the middle section of the streets seemed to be inviting us to delve further into this charming old town. The nostalgic-looking clock in the village green accentuated the quaintness of this section of the downtown area. I didn't mind that it insisted that it was 7:15 a.m. when, in reality, it was an hour later. This was how a Sabbath Sunday must have been like in the Old South. We left the past of Meridian to encounter much of what was new.

That new was Life Church. Situated on Frontage Road, Life Church's building was a converted movie theater standing next to the Dirt Cheap store on its left. The converted movie theater might explain the rich sound system inside. It would also explain the three sections of bucket seats, four seats across and eleven rows deep in the two outer sections and eleven seats across and eight rows deep in the middle section.

Roughly sixty people filled the seats of the first of two services as many members, including Pastor Gary Morris, were away on vacation. Interestingly, Ronnie Anderson, one of the leaders, stepped in to give the message. The leader of the prayer team, Mr. Anderson calmly exhorted us to search through the Scriptures to get to know its Author. He reminded us that the Holy Spirit teaches us as we read, revealing to us what we need to know and growing us in the process. He brought us through the redemptive work of God, starting with Adam's original sin and climaxing to Jesus' atoning work on the cross for that sin. He told us how that redemptive act continues to touch lives, even two thousand years later.

Mr. Anderson shared the moving story of his son's drug use, the subsequent loss of his job and house, and the many prayers offered by his friends for the salvation of his son. Today, Mr. Anderson's son runs a home for addicts in San Antonio, offering the same comfort to those in need that he himself received from God.

After the service, I thanked Mr. Anderson for his transparency and his encouraging message. His eyes reinforced the words that he had just shared. The pain had been great, but the redemption had been sweeter.

I thought of 16th Street Baptist Church and its version of redemption. Instead of letting evil imprison them, they chose to point others to the One Who comforts and heals. I thought of our car situation, amazed that we had been one minute away from missing the riches that God had prepared for us in two states that seemed out of our grasp.

We left the Magnolia State, slicing effortlessly through Alabama and Georgia before settling in our temporary home in Greenville, South Carolina. That is not our primary residence. That place awaits us and is more glorious than anything we have seen in our weeks of travel and the decades we have lived. We only experienced a small sampling of what is to come. In the meantime, we look for God's hand at work in our lives and in the lives of those who have put their trust in His Name alone. In the lives of two former

New Yorkers, in the lives of the members of 16th Street Baptist Church, and in the lives of the congregants at Life Church in Meridian, Mississippi.

We saw it again the following week on a very large boat that once saved eight men and women in the greatest flood ever recorded in human history.

BIG AND BIGGER

LEXINGTON AND WILLIAMSTOWN, KENTUCKY

Question: How do you combine old Southern sayings with the Hebrew Scriptures? Answer: You go to the Blue Grass State, of course. Known as the state that is home to the Kentucky Derby, it is also famous for Colonel Sanders and his KFC restaurants, the Louisville Slugger baseball bat, Kentucky Wildcat basketball, and Bill Monroe—the Father of Bluegrass Music. More importantly, it is becoming increasingly known as the home of Southland Church in Lexington and the Ark Encounter in Williamston. These two destinations provided insight to the riddle above.

When Linda and I departed our home in Greenville early Saturday afternoon, our plan was to take the six-and-a-half hour drive to the Ark Encounter in Williamstown, rest for the night in a hotel in Lexington, and then attend the Sunday service of Southland Church the following morning. Driving in areas we had passed through earlier that year, we merged on to Highway 76 near Knoxville, Tennessee. The trek that took us 208 miles north to Williamstown, Kentucky, proved to be a combination of scenic, rolling hills and pasture lands, intermittent downfalls, and traffic jams. Many traffic jams! So much that I began to fear we would not make it to the Ark Encounter before its 9:00 p.m. closing time.

Just as were about to get off Highway 76 for the Ark Encounter exit, we looked up and smiled broadly. Was it really what we thought it was? Yes, it definitely was! A rainbow! The rainbow had great significance for God's people roughly forty-three hundred years earlier. It has the same significance for humankind today. The Scriptures give us an account:

> Then the LORD saw that the wickedness of man was great on the earth, and that every intent of the thoughts of his heart was only evil continually. The LORD was sorry that He had made man on the earth, and He was grieved in His heart. The LORD said, "I will blot out man whom I have created from the face of the land, from man to animals to creeping things and to birds of the sky; for I am sorry that I have made them (Gen. 6:5-7).

"But Noah found favor in the eyes of the LORD . . . Noah was a righteous man, blameless in his time; Noah walked with God" (v. 8-9 emphasis mine).

The result was dramatic. God spared Noah and his family. God gave Noah his marching orders with detailed instructions on how to construct the ark. After the worldwide flood, God established a convent with Noah and his sons, saying to them:

> "This is the sign of the covenant which I am making between Me and you and every living creature that is with you, for all successive generations; I set My bow in the cloud, and it shall be for a sign of a covenant between Me and the earth. It shall come about, when I bring a cloud over the earth, that the bow will be seen in the cloud, and I will remember My covenant, which is between Me and you and every living creature of all flesh; and never again shall the water become a flood to destroy all flesh" (Gen. 9:12-15).

The sign of the rainbow was not only a general reminder to the world that God will not flood the Earth again, but also a specific sign to me in that moment that God was in control. Despite the rain and heavy traffic, He made sure we would experience the Ark Encounter just as we had hoped.

I had expected to see the Ark Encounter from the highway. After all, it is the most authentic, full-sized replica of Noah's Ark in the world. The grounds were so large, however, that we did not see the Ark until a bus took us from the ticket office in the front of the park to its location in the rear. The wait was worth it. There it was! Five hundred ten feet long, eighty-five feet wide, and fifty-one feet high. Let's try those dimensions another way. Roughly a football field and three-quarters of another field long, almost a football-field wide and half a football field high. Wow! Answers in Genesis estimates it took Noah and his sons fifty-five to seventy-five years to build the ark. In contrast, it took a little over six years to build the Ark Encounter from contract to completion. Both constructions are incredible feats.

While not ideal, arriving an hour and a half before closing had its advantages. No long ticket lines and no crowds of people competing for views. Just Linda, me, and three stories of exhibits. The biggest decision was to decide between quantity or quality. Due to lack of time, we chose the former. We had no time to enjoy the gardens, the Ararat Zoo, or the zip lines soaring across some valleys. Instead, we focused all our remaining minutes on the exhibits, moving quickly from station to station, taking in the real-to-life exhibits that captured what life must have been like on the ark during the flood. Noah's sons' living quarters, scores of animals being fed, waste being disposed of . . . No detail was left uncovered. Genesis 5-10 came alive to us right before our eyes. The cleanliness and professionalism of the museum were noteworthy.

It was also different. We felt like we were on holy ground. There was a reverence that was tangible, noticeably present in an increasingly flippant world. The God depicted in this setting mirrored the God of the Bible—the true and living God Who is unchanging. Not the twenty-first century, feminized deity who is compassionate but impotent, blind, and tolerant of all behaviors. The one who does not hold men accountable for their actions. The one who has been reduced to the image of man.

We left the Ark Encounter thankful that God had moved on the hearts of men such as Ken Ham to build such an exhibit. In an entertainment-crazed society, it is an oasis in the desert. We drove the forty-seven minutes to our hotel in Lexington not realizing that we would experience another move of God the following morning.

A few years ago, there were three malls in Lexington, Kentucky. Today, there is only one. One of those former malls has become one of the four campuses of Southland Church, a unique church with a simple, yet powerful, vision. The leaders of Southland Church desired to restore the church to its original biblical foundation found in Acts 1. As part of the restoration movement worldwide, the "'creed' (from the Latin 'credo,' meaning 'I believe')" of Southland is the following: "We believe in Jesus Christ the Son of God, as Lord and as Savior. Our book of doctrine, or list of beliefs, is simply the Word of God. Thus, as one man has expressed it, 'We have no creed but Christ, no book but the Bible, no name but the name Christian.'"[70]

The message of Southland seemed to be resonating. When we commented to Vi, the greeter who enthusiastically introduced herself to us, how huge the Lexington campus was, she commented that the main campus in Nicholasville was actually quite bigger. Despite the size of the building, the people made the setting feel quite intimate. Lead Teaching Pastor and Elder Scott Nickell connected well with his audience. His title for the sermon was "Southern Sayin's." Here are a few that he shared: "Too big for your britches"; "Bless your heart"; "Y'all come back now"; "There ain't no 'taters where you're diggin"; and "That dog won't hunt." Even I understood that one.

After a few laughs, Pastor Scott reminded us of three blunt questions Jesus asked His disciples. The first was, "'Who do people say that the Son of Man is?' And they said, 'Some *say* John the Baptist; and others, Elijah; but

70 Robert Mallett, "What Do You Mean, Restoration Movement?," TheChristianRestorationAssociation.org, https://www.thecra.org/home/what-is-the-restoration-movement (accessed July 21, 2019).

still others, Jeremiah, or one of the prophets" (Matt. 16:13-14). Today, forty-four percent of Americans would respond, "A religious leader like others."

The second blunt question was, "'But who do you say I am?'" (Matt. 16:15). Pastor Scott said that an unschooled, redneck fisherman responded, "'You are the Christ, the Son of the living God" (Matt. 15:16). "And Jesus said to him, 'Blessed are you, Simon Barjona, because flesh and blood did not reveal *this* to you, but My Father who is in heaven" (Matt. 15:17). The final blunt question is one that every person needs to reflect on: "'For what will it profit a man if he gains the whole world and forfeits his soul?'" (Matt. 16:26).

Jesus asked questions to invoke responses, not answers. Our pop culture has fostered a false image of Jesus as a pushover, One Who caters to our demands. Yet, He is the polar opposite. He challenges us to "take up [our] cross[es] and follow [Him] For whoever wishes to save his life will lose it; but whoever loses his life for My sake will find it" (Matt. 16:24-25).

Comfort is our enemy. Self-help is little help apart from God. Self-sacrifice is the key to a fruitful life in Christ. The biblical worldview tells us to care for ourselves so we are able and ready to serve others. Pastor Scott shared that a healthy response to Jesus is two-fold: First, Jesus is the Messiah. He is the King of everything, or He is the King of nothing. We cannot compartmentalize and pick and choose what we will let Him be Lord of. Second, Jesus' agenda is better than mine. Am I willing to let Jesus lead, or am I attempting to make Him follow me?

After Pastor Scott finished his challenging message, the worship team led the congregants in a song by country singer Cody Johnson, "I Can't Even Walk (Without Holding Your Hand)":

> I thought number one
> Would surely be me
> I thought I could be

What I wanted to be
I thought I could build
on life's sinking sand
but now I can't even walk
without you holding my hand

I thought I could do a lot on my own
I thought I could make it all day long
I thought of myself as a mighty big man
but Lord I can't even walk without you holding my hand

Oh Lord, I can't even walk
without you holding my hand
the mountains too high
and the valleys too wide
down on my knees
that's where I learned to stand
Oh Lord I can't even walk
without you holding my hand

I think I'll make Jesus my all and all
and if I'm in trouble
on his name I'll call,
if I didn't trust him
I'd be less of a man
cause Lord I can't even walk
without you holding my hand.[71]

71 Cody Johnson, "I Can't Even Walk (Without You Holding My Hand)," Self-Released, https://www.azlyrics.com/lyrics/codyjohnson/icantevenwalkwithoutyouholding-myhand.html, 2016.

Like Jesus, the people of Southland Church seemed to be forthright and hard-hitting. Also like Jesus, they seemed to be humble and compassionate, not willing that any should perish. They were committed to the simple, yet profound, message of the Gospel. They reminded me of the people who founded the Ark Encounter and the Creation Museum just forty-five minutes from it. They were willing to go against the tide of culture—not for the sake of being contrarian, but to point others to the Creator and Redeemer, the One Who has power over our eternal state. That is true for all of us, whether we hail from the Commonwealth of Kentucky or are just a husband and wife team visiting the Bluegrass State for a weekend.

It is also true for the people in the town of the largest evangelical university in the nation, the site of the final act in our Southeastern journey.

NEVER QUIT

LYNCHBURG, VIRGINIA

"You do not determine a man's greatness by his talent or wealth, as the world does, but rather by what it takes to discourage him" (Jerry Falwell).

This was it. Our final trip. It was fitting, in many ways, that our yearlong adventure would end in Lynchburg, Virginia, a town of little renown in the world but of great importance to the Kingdom of God and for me. Like most great things, that importance took years to unfold.

On June 17, 1956, thirty-five adults and their children gathered in the Mountain View Elementary School in Lynchburg, Virginia for the church's first Sunday worship service. That week, leaders of the church and a particularly aggressive young man named Jerry Falwell, the church's founding pastor, searched for a place to house their new church. They located a building which was formerly used by the Donald Duck Bottling Company.

In a matter of weeks, the church had started its radio ministry. Six months later it began to videotape the Old Time Gospel Hour in a local studio and aired the program on a local television station. By 1958, the church had moved into a new sanctuary to accommodate the ever-growing church attendance. The following year, Elim Home was established for alcoholic men on a 165-acre farm just outside of Lynchburg.

In 1964, the congregation moved into its third auditorium on Thomas Road which seated 1,000 people. The following year, the two-story Spurgeon Building was completed, offering temporary relief for the overcrowded Sunday School.

By 1968, average attendance passed the 2,000 level, and the Carter Building was constructed to hold some of the overflowing Sunday School crowd. The following year, ground was broken for two educational buildings and for a new 3,000-seat sanctuary.

With the goal of training Champions for Christ to go into all walks of life, Thomas Road Baptist Church founded Lynchburg Christian Academy in 1967 and Liberty University in 1971.[72]

Countless persons have been impacted by the ongoing work of Thomas Road Baptist Church and Liberty University. As a young man searching for my place in this world, I enjoyed Dr. Falwell's talks with me as I sat on our living room couch, and he spoke to me from our television set. I never thought at the time that I would one day be earning a degree (at that time, a correspondence program with on-site summer courses) from his college, Liberty University. I never thought that my niece, Kerri, would graduate from Liberty's law school, eventually serving as the top spokesperson for the Department of Justice in the Trump Administration. I never thought my oldest son, Austin, would earn his bachelor's degree in psychology from LU. I never thought my deceased brother's wife, Gail, would move from Long Island to live near and be a part of what I consider to be the finest university in the country.

Linda, my sons, and I had journeyed to Lynchburg a few times since we moved to South Carolina. This time, we did not take the scenic, five-hour trek via 77 North and 81 East as we had so many times previously. This time, only

---

72 "History," ThomasRoadBaptistChurch.org, https://trbc.org/history (accessed July 28, 2019).

the husband and wife team departed, taking the straightest path possible in order to spend some time with Gail, our sister in Christ and sister-in-law.

Seeing Gail was also connecting to our past. She, too, has had an exciting walk with God, coming to know Christ personally in her twenties, only a short time ahead of my oldest brother, Bill. They were married for forty-three years until the Lord called Bill home six years ago. Linda, Gail, and I shared memories of the past and challenges of the present. While it was great to see Gail, it was still odd not to see Bill. There is a significant part of me that is still grieving his loss. How do you replace a brother, a best friend, a wise counselor, and an exhorter in the faith all rolled into one? I am learning the hard way. He is daily on my mind.

Liberty University was also on my mind as I woke up early that Sunday morning. With Linda still asleep in our guest room and Gail seemingly on the kip upstairs, I ventured the twenty-minute drive to the home of the Flames and parked my car on the sleepy campus. The entire complex was all mine for a short time. Accompanied only by a few intermittent sprinklers, I strolled to Jerry Falwell's resting place. He and his wife, Marcel, were buried on the grounds of Liberty. Five quotes from Dr. Falwell adorned the wall of his memorial. The most profound, yet simplest, was "Never quit." He never did. He worked tirelessly for the cause of Christ.

From the gravesite, I explored the newly renovated campus. According to the college website, the renovation plan was to organize the many previously fractured aspects of campus life into a cogent assembly of quads, academic facilities, and student amenities, all connected by a new 1.5-mile-long accessible campus walk. Mission accomplished. The thick, dark green fescue grass and the stately looking brick buildings were evidence of Liberty's promising future. The adjoining Vines Center (basketball arena) was a testament to Liberty's rich past. All in all, it remains a place that I would recommend strongly for any young Christian high school student (or adult) who is in the process of investigating colleges. Like saying goodbye to an old friend I hadn't seen in years, I departed the campus grateful for the opportunity to reconnect and excited about the Sunday service that lay ahead at Thomas Road.

How do you replace a legend? How do you follow Johnny Carson? Vince Lombardi? Bear Bryant? Mickey Mantle? Billy Graham? How do you replace the senior pastor of a large church, who also happens to be the founder of the largest evangelical college in the United States? The short answer is you prepare for it. You prepare many years in advance.

Waiting in the wings of the iconic figure were two very capable leaders. Both happened to have the same last name of Falwell. Jerry Falwell, Jr. attended Liberty University as an undergraduate and graduated from the University of Virginia School of Law, where he obtained a Juris Doctor degree in 1987. He took over as college president of Liberty University upon Jerry, Sr.'s death in 2007. Jonathan Falwell earned his Bachelor of Science degree from Liberty University in 1987, his Master of Arts degree in Religion from the Liberty Baptist Theological Seminary in 1996, and a Juris Doctor degree in 2005 from the Taft Law School in Santa Ana, California.

According to author Michael Winters, during a 1974 family discussion about abortion as the "national sin" of America, Jonathan asked his father why he didn't do something about it. The question spurred the elder Falwell into action, leading the evangelical church into the thick of the abortion battle. Jonathan's greatest claim to fame is that he was a classmate of mine for one course while we were both students for a summer course at Liberty University. His second greatest claim to fame is that he is the senior pastor of Thomas Road Baptist Church. Jonathan does not look like his father or even sound like him. He doesn't need to. Jerry, Sr. had his own unique set of giftings that impacted not only central Virginia but also the entire country as well.

Jonathan, too, has unique gifts and talents that he is using "for the equipping of the saints for the work of service, to the building up of the body of Christ" (Eph. 4:12). On this day, it was evident that he was being true to his

God and true to himself. He was not trying to duplicate his father. There has never been another George Whitfield. There has never been a carbon copy of Corrie ten Boom. Jonathan needs to be Jonathan—a son of God, a husband, a father, and a big part of the Body of Christ. He seems comfortable in his own skin. He appears to have a heart for God that is admirable and contagious. How do you replace a legend? Be yourself.

I don't think Jonathan would like all this talk about him. He would rather share the truth of God's Word as he did so effectively this Sunday at TRBC's 10:00 a.m. service. Speaking to roughly twenty-six hundred people in the audience, including eighty from Liberty University's summer ice hockey camp, Jonathan spoke of "Good News for Hard Times."

Using 1 Peter as his text, Jonathan said that the great hope that we have is found in the promises of the Word of God. In the darkest of times, we will be challenged to allow Christ to be our God. We will be challenged to rejoice in the midst of our suffering. Why is it important to trust God in the midst of our anguish? Those moments are the times of great testing. They expose our true allegiances. They show us the condition of our hearts. Our reaction to them determines our growth. Job, after his exorbitant amount of suffering, cried out, "Though He slay me, I will hope in Him" (Job 13:15).

Jonathan then quoted from 1 Peter 2:20: "But if when you do what is right and suffer *for it* you patiently endure it, this finds favor with God." God is pleased with us when conscious of His will, we patiently endure unjust treatment. We treat others right even when they have treated us wrong. Jesus never defended Himself. He was only concerned with doing His Father's will. Our attitude should be the same. Our actions are not determined by the actions of others. Our self-worth is not dependent on others' opinions of us. Our goal is to please God, allowing the Word of God to lead us, not our emotions or any desire to get even.

Whether we realize it or not, we represent Christ in our home, in our job, and in our community. Paul said we are read by others: "You are our letter, written in our hearts, known and read by all men; being manifested that you are a letter of Christ, cared for by us, written not with ink but with the Spirit of the living God, not on tablets of stone but on tablets of human hearts (2 Cor. 3:2-3). We are also watched by God, when no one else is looking. He sees all things. He knows all things. He will empower us as we seek to do His will. That is where our focus needs to be. That is the only place that we are guaranteed to be successful.

Jerry Falwell, Sr. was correct. You do measure a man's greatness by what it takes to discourage him. Jonathan Falwell is right as well. There is no greater place to be than in the will of God. It is there that the promises of God manifest. It is there that we realize that the Kingdom of God is at hand. "For we are His workmanship, created in Christ Jesus for good works, which God prepared beforehand so that we would walk in them" (Eph. 2:10).

God has been doing a great work in Lynchburg, Virginia, for many years. It began in the life of Jerry Falwell, Sr. and Thomas Road Baptist Church. It continues in the lives of his two sons, Jerry, Jr. and Jonathan. It echoes in the lives of TRBC members and in thousands of Liberty University graduates spread throughout the world. It was fitting that Linda and I ended our journey here. This was our final resting place for an adventure started fifty-two weeks ago. Yes, Dr. Falwell, by God's grace, we never quit.

CONCLUSION

A year before I finished this book, Linda and I thought we were embarking on a one-day road trip, taking a two-and-a-half-hour drive to Moravian Falls, North Carolina, one unsuspecting Sunday morning. We initially departed thinking we were going to discover what had happened to John Huss' descendants in Moravian Falls, North Carolina. We had no idea at the time that it would lead to a year-long adventure, one in which we could have never planned ourselves.

For fifty-two Sundays, we set out to some part of the Southeastern United States, driving to wherever we sensed God was leading us to go. We tried to be obedient to His wishes. We visited megachurches and tiny churches. Historic churches and new ones. Churches in large cities and churches in the most remote parts of this incredible country. We met old and young alike, black and white, rich and poor. We experienced history, covering our fight to be independent of England to our struggle to stay as one, to our quest to be treated equally. We saw battlefields, cotton fields, and even solar panel fields. We glimpsed many American flags, a small number of Confederate ones, and many with orange and crimson, especially in the fall. We felt the ocean breeze and breathed in all of the mountain's splendor. We experienced the uniqueness of each season.

In the totality of it, we saw God's glory. We sensed His sovereignty. We marveled at the leading of His Spirit. Like the driver who is skeptical of the GPS command to turn left when he thinks he should turn right, we sometimes ventured cautiously, even trepidly, when God's leading seemed contrary to what we were thinking. Slowly, however, our confidence began to increase as His leading proved fruitful over and over again, far beyond anything we could have hoped or imagined (Eph. 3:20).

If Linda and I had to point to the single most exhilarating aspect of our year-long journey, that would be it: Seeing the Creator of the Universe—the One who took on human flesh, the One who died for the sin of the world, the One who rose from the dead, the One who ascended into Heaven and is seated back on His glorious throne—reach out to two very imperfect human beings and lead them on an adventure of a lifetime. In the process, He showed us many aspects of His character—His faithfulness, His love, His mercy, and His grace. He revealed His Word to us, teaching us, comforting us, correcting us, and challenging us. He showed us how simple it is for a person to know Him, to grow in Him, and to walk with Him. He showed us that He is no Respecter of persons, that He will accept anyone who comes to Him with a sincere and humble heart, one who is willing to align his or her life with Him and allow Him to lead the way.

I can hear Jesus saying to us, "Do not be afraid, little flock, for your Father has chosen gladly to give you the kingdom" (Luke 12:32). For very fortunate persons like Linda and me, Heaven has its beginnings on this Earth. Yet we only see in part in this life, but the part seems to expand more and more as we follow Him and seek Him for Who He is.

For fifty-two weeks, the Lord showed us the splendor of His Church, the greatest thing on the face of this Earth, even with its many deficiencies and imperfections. He showed us that unity does not require uniformity. Anyone who calls on the name of Jesus will be saved (Rom. 10:13). Any church that proclaims Jesus as Lord and upholds His Word as the authority on which they believe and live is part of the Body of Christ.

I was amazed how different evangelical churches can be. Spontaneous, liturgical, Baptist, charismatic—we experienced the diversity of His people throughout the South. Yet far above the many surface issues, Jesus was proclaimed as Lord in each of the Bible-believing churches we encountered. No human can claim the title of leader of the church; Jesus is truly the Head of His Body. Paradoxically, I am amazed how similar the evangelical church is. There truly is "one Lord, one faith, one baptism, one God and Father of all, who is over all and through all and in all" (Eph. 4:5-6).

We ended up finding what we had set out to discover. We found the descendants of Reformer John Huss. They only looked different than what we had expected. We found them in Florida and Mississippi. We saw them in North Carolina and West Virginia. We heard them preach in Alabama and Kentucky. We saw their churches in Tennessee and South Carolina. We conversed with them in Georgia and Virginia. They are the ones who have accepted Jesus as Lord and Savior. They are the ones who are filled with the Holy Spirit. They are not perfect; they are a work in progress, slowly becoming more Christ-like day by day, year by year, many times two steps forward and one step back. When they breathe their last, they will keep on living. They will be with God for all eternity.

What about you, fellow sojourner? Where do you stand in relation to the Savior of the world? God has done His part. Jesus' last words on the cross were "It is finished" (John 19:30). The atonement of sin was completed. It is available to anyone who responds by faith in Jesus' finished work alone. "For God so loved the world, that He gave His only begotten Son, that whoever believes in Him shall not perish, but have eternal life'" (John 3:16). Are you ready to repent from your sins and turn to the Savior? He is awaiting your response.

This is a prayer you can pray to accept Jesus as your Lord and Savior to receive the gift of salvation. Pray it from your heart, and God will hear it:

> Father, I confess that I am a sinner who has fallen short of Your glory. I believe You sent Jesus to die for my sins. I repent of my sins and ask You, Jesus, to come into my life and be my Lord and

Savior. Thank You for forgiving me of all my sin. From this day forward, I will choose to follow You. I pray this in Jesus' Name. I thank You for my new life. Amen.

If you prayed that prayer from your heart, *congratulations*! All of Heaven is rejoicing over your decision to put your faith in Christ. Remember this day. Write it down so you can see it. When your adversary tries to come in to discourage you, you can always point to the day that you accepted Jesus as Lord and Savior. The greater truth is that God has made a commitment to you as you asked Him into your life. It is a covenant relationship that cannot be broken. I would encourage you to seek out a Bible-believing church to help you grow as a new follower of Christ. A new plant needs sun and water to flourish. Reading the Word of God—I would encourage you to start in the New Testament—and walking with other believers are ways that we protect and enhance our walk with God. God bless you.

BIBLIOGRAPHY

"About Us." NewSpring Church online. https://newspring.cc/about (accessed November 18, 2018).

American Bible Society. "The Most Bible-Minded Cities in America." AmericanBible.org. https://www.americanbible.org/features/americas-most-bible-minded-cities (accessed May 26, 2019)

Ballotpedia.org. "Bethlehem, Georgia." https://ballotpedia.org/Bethlehem,_Georgia (accessed April 7, 2019).

Bethlehem Church. "Our Team." BethlehemChurch.us. https://bethlehemchurch.us/staff (accessed April 7, 2019).

Bible Study.com. "Meaning of Numbers in the Bible: The Number 7." https://www.biblestudy.org/bibleref/meaning-of-numbers-in-bible/7.html (accessed February 26, 2019).

Billy Graham Evangelistic Association. "Billy Graham Trivia: What Is Life's Greatest Surprise." https://billygraham.org/story/billy-graham-trivia-lifes-greatest-surprise (accessed August 12, 2018).

Boling, Kevin. "1st Peter." Sermon, Mountain Bridge Bible Fellowship, Travelers Rest, SC (September 2, 2018).

Christianity Today. "Jonathan Edwards: America's Greatest Theologian," ChristianityToday.com. https://www.christianitytoday.com/history/people/theologians/jonathan-edwards.html (accessed June 14, 2019).

Citadel, The. "At a Glance," Citadel.edu. http://www.citadel.edu/root/at-a-glance (accessed December 23, 2018).

Citadel, The. "Core Values," Citadel.edu. http://www.citadel.edu/root/core-values (accessed December 23, 2018).

Citadel, The. "Welcome to the Citadel!," Citadel.edu, http://www.citadel.edu/root/info (accessed December 23, 2018).

Copeland, Larry. "Life Expectancy in the U.S. Hits a Record High." USA Today.com. https://www.usatoday.com/story/news/nation/2014/10/08/us-life-expectancy-hits-record-high/16874039 (accessed August 12, 2018).

Crossing Church, The. "Three Crosses Plaza." http://crossingchatt.com/crosses (accessed May 26, 2019).

DiscoverSouthCarolina.com. "Church of the Holy Apostles: Thoroughbred Country." https://discoversouthcarolina.com/products/1540 (accessed January 13, 2019).

Dunn, Andrew. "The 16 Largest Charlotte Churches by Membership and Attendance." CharlotteAgenda.com. https://www.charlotteagenda.com/20052/the-12-largest-charlotte-churches-by-membership-and-attendance (accessed October 14, 2018).

Flynn, Jean Martin. *A History of North Greenville College.* Greer: North Greenville Junior College, 1953.

Funk, Tim. "Fallen PTL preacher Jim Bakker is back with a new message about the Apocalypse." CharlotteObserver.com. https://www.charlotteobserver.com/living/religion/article200297074.html (accessed August 26, 2018).

Funk, Tim. "Jim Bakker's theme park was like a Christian Disneyland. Here's what happened to it." CharlotteObserver.com. https://www.charlotteobserver.com/living/religion/article205362719.html (accessed August 26, 2018).

Gugliotta, Guy. "New Estimate Raises Civil War Death Toll." NYTimes.com. https://www.nytimes.com/2012/04/03/science/civil-war-toll-up-by-20-percent-in-new-estimate.html (accessed March 3, 2019).

"Heritage Conference Center," HeritageConferenceCenter.org, https://www.heritageconferencecenter.org/meetings-events (accessed June 14, 2019).

His Name is Flowing Oil. "Story of the Oil." His Name is Flowing Oil.org. https://hisnameisflowingoil.org/story-of-the-oil (accessed May 12, 2019).

"History." DCFClemson.org. https://www.dcfclemson.org/our-origin-story (accessed April 14, 2019).

"History." ThomasRoadBaptistChurch.org. https://trbc.org/history (accessed July 28, 2019).

"History of Greenville, SC, A: The Textile Capital of the World," https://upstatesouthcarolinanews.wordpress.com/tag/poe-mill (accessed March 24, 2019).

Jesus Film Project. "55 Old Testament Prophecies About Jesus." JesusFilm.org, https://www.jesusfilm.org/blog-and-stories/old-testament-prophecies.html (accessed December 23, 2018).

Jesus Warehouse, The. https://www.facebook.com/groups/JesusWarehouse/about (April 21, 2019).

"Leadership." Vertias Church. http://veritasfayetteville.com/leadership (accessed June 7, 2019).

Mallett, Robert. "What Do You Mean, Restoration Movement?" TheChristianRestorationAssociation.org. https://www.thecra.org/home/what-is-the-restoration-movement (accessed July 21, 2019).

Marshall, Peter and Manuel, David. *The Light and the Glory.* Grand Rapids: Fleming H. Revell Company, 1973.

Merriam-Webster Dictionary, s.v. "commission," https://www.merriam-webster.com/dictionary/commission (accessed August 5, 2018).

Merriam Webster, s.v. "different," https://www.merriam-webster.com/dictionary/different (accessed December 16, 2018).

"Michael Youssef: Founding Rector." The Church of the Apostles. https://apostles.org/leadership/ (accessed August 12, 2018).

"Moravian Falls: A Brief History of the Moravians." MoravianFalls.org. http://www.moravianfalls.org/aboutmoravianfalls.html (accessed June 24, 2018).

MorningStar Ministries, "Bob Jones Vision Center," MorningStarMinistries.org, https://www.morningstarministries.org/bob-jones-vision-center (accessed June 14, 2019).

Mosaic Church, Lead Pastor, Naeem Fazal," MosaicChurch.tv, http://mosaicchurch.tv/lead-pastor-naeem-fazal/ (accessed Feb. 17, 2019).

Niebuhr, Reinhold. "Prayer for Serenity." CelebrateRecovery.com. https://www.celebraterecovery.com/resources/cr-tools/serenityprayer (accessed September 16, 2018).

"N.O.T.E. Ministries." GloryTabernacleSC.org. https://www.glorytabsc.org/copy-of-what-we-believe-1 (accessed May 19, 2019).

"Our Facility." Apostles.org. https://apostles.org/about (accessed August 12, 2018).

"Our Story: Sharing the Gospel of Jesus Christ," Northstar, https://northstarknox.com/our-story (accessed November 11, 2018).

Schaff, Philip. *History of the Christian Church,* Vol. 7. 2nd edition. New York: Charles Schribner's Sons, 1910.

Schecter, Maayan and Eric Conner. "Greenville named fourth fastest-growing U.S. city." Greenvilleonline.com. https://www.greenvilleonline.com/story/news/2017/05/25/greenville-named-fourth-fastest-growing-u-s-city/344009001/ (accessed March 24, 2019).

Schmucker, Leslie. "The Uncomfortable Subject Jesus Addressed More Than Anyone Else," The Gospel Coalition, Inc., https://www.thegospelcoalition.org/article/the-uncomfortable-subject-jesus-addressed-more-than-anyone-else (accessed August 12, 2018).

"SC City Nicknames Guide." SCIWAY.net. https://www.sciway.net/ccr/sc-city-nicknames.html (accessed December 23, 2018).

SC Picture Project. Williamston Mineral Spring Park—Williamston, South Carolina." https://www.scpictureproject.org/anderson-county/williamston-mineral-spring-park.html (accessed November 18, 2018).

"UNC-Asheville: Women, Gender, and Sexuality Studies." UNC-Asheville. https://www.unca.edu/programs/women-gender-and-sexualitystudies (accessed July 29, 2018).

Warren Wilson College. https://www.warren-wilson.edu. The comment has since been taken off the website (accessed July 29, 2018).

Webster, Noah. "Advice to the Young." In *History of the United States*. New Haven: Durrie & Peck, 1832.

DISCOGRAPHY

Bethel Music. "Goodness of God," 2019.

Cash, Johnny R. "Were You There (When They Crucified My Lord)." Kobalt Music Publishing, 1960.

Church of the Highlands. Highlands Worship. *Jesus You Alone*. 12. March 1, 2019, Compact Disc.

Daigle, Lauren. "Come Alive (Dry Bones)." *How Can It Be*. Paul Mabury. 10. April 14, 2010.

Denver, John. "Take Me Home Country Roads." *The Essential John Denver*. 3. Sony Legacy, 2007. Compact Disc.

Emmett, Daniel D. "Dixie Land." 1859. Public Domain.

Gray, Jason. "Good to Be Alive." *A Way to See in the Dark*. Centricity Music. 4. 2011.

Johnson, Cody. "I Can't Even Walk (Without You Holding My Hand)." Self-Released. https://www.azlyrics.com/lyrics/codyjohnson/icantevenwalkwithoutyouholdingmyhand.html, 2016.

Lemmel, Helen. "Turn Your Eyes Upon Jesus." Public Domain.

Oliver, Gary. "Celebrate Jesus, Celebrate." Hope Publishing Co.

Springer, Rita. "Defender." *Battles*. Gateway Publishing, 2017.

Stanfill, Kristian. "Jesus Paid It All (with Passion)." Sparrow Records, 2006.

Stookey, Paul. "The Wedding Song (There Is Love)." Warner Bros. Records, 1971.

Vertical Church Band. "The Rock Won't Move." Essential Worship, 2013.

For more information about

Tom Kupec
and
Sundays in the South
please visit:

www.tomkupec.com

MORE FROM AMBASSADOR INTERNATIONAL

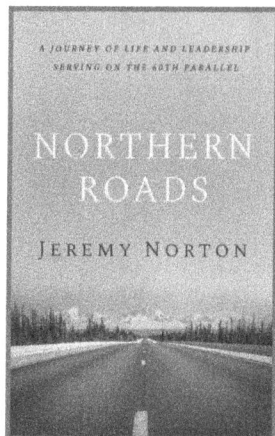

The small-town, isolated Alaskan territory is the perfect place for one to stretch himself and to learn to love your neighbor in the local coffee shop. So, grab your own cup of coffee and take a trip down memory lane with Jeremy Norton on the Northern Roads as he reflects back on his early days as a pastor when he still had a lot to learn about loving people and be challenged to grow in your own walk with Christ.

Through vignettes of fresh water springs and fly fishing analogies, *Theology From the Spring* provides the reader with eyes for seeing how God's creation—the natural world—can provide answers to the oldest divine mystery and make sense of the beauty and chaos we see within the created order.

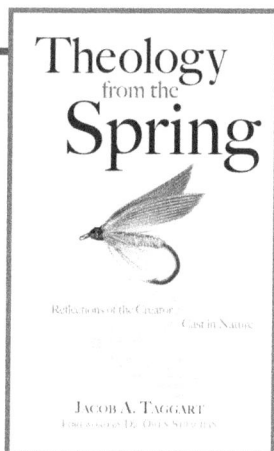

Martin's weekly devotionals found in *A Whisper in the Woods* take the reader out of the noise that often accompanies living in this world and into the quiet escapades of wooded areas where the voice of God is more clearly heard. As you walk with Martin through the mountain valleys and over the high summits, you too will hear God whisper words of comfort to you.

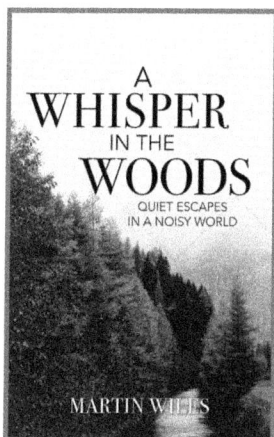

www.ingramcontent.com/pod-product-compliance
Lightning Source LLC
Chambersburg PA
CBHW062148080426
42734CB00010B/1604